Jonathan Marty...

STUD
YEARBOC
CAREER
DIRECTORY

Physics

'96 - Q10
'90 - Q9
'92 - Q9
'95 - Q9
'92 - Q12

PART 2

2000 EDITION

EDITORS

Joseph Duddy and Richard Keane

Exam No: 122835

PUBLISHED BY:
Student Yearbook Ltd.,
"Shancroft" O'Hanlons Lane,
Malahide,
Co. Dublin.
Fax 01-845 4759

Le Millénaire

ISBN 0-9533081-3-8

DESIGNED & PRINTED BY FUTURE PRINT LTD., DUBLIN

C o n

e n t s

Many of the photographs used in this publication were taken in Heywood Community School, Laois.
Student Yearbook would like to thank the staff, pupils and photographer Fred Tuite.

Personal Organiser

PERSONAL NOTES

Name _Jonathan Harty_

Address _Lurofin, Cummer_

Tuam, Co. Galway

Rep. of Ireland

Phone _093 - 41448_

School/College _St. Jarlath's College, Tuam_

Parents' Work Phone _093 - 41649_

Examination No. _____

CAO No. _____

Department of Education Pupil No. _____

STUDENT YEARBOOK & CAREER DIRECTORY

2000 Edition
This is the Nineteenth edition of **Student Yearbook and Career Directory**. Since its initial launch by the Minister for Education it has established itself as the biggest selling and most successful career publication in Ireland.

Editors
Joseph Duddy & Richard Keane

Contributors
Fiona Galligan, Eileen Lucey, Cathy Milner, Sarah Murphy, Laura Slattery & Fred Tuite.

Every effort has been made to ensure information, especially dates, is accurate. No responsibility, however, can be accepted for omissions or errors that may have occurred.

Whatever your choice of career or lifestyle STUDENT YEARBOOK AND CAREER DIRECTORY can help you plan and organise it.

It is designed to provide ready access to a wide range of information quickly and easily.

Look again at the table of contents. Note that the Yearbook is divided into five sections.

1. ➤ **Planning:** setting overall goals and objectives.

2. ➤ **Careers Research:** getting down to the specifics of careers information.

3. ➤ **Subject Matters & Examinations:** An outline of all the Leaving Cert. options. For a more effective organisation of your study and social time, keep a record with our special week-to-view Diary.

4. ➤ **Time Off:** A guide to leisure activities and healthy living.

5. ➤ **Third Level Education & Training:** Pass and Honours students are catered for in the Yearbook's comprehensive coverage of the **CAO** , up-to-date analysis of point schemes, post-Leaving Cert. courses and apprenticeships.

Don't hope for the best . . .
. . . Plan for the best

Millennium Mission...
...Mission Accomplished

The New Millennium is just around the corner.

Does September 2000 seem far away? By then your career should be taking off. Whether you are hoping to set off for work, study or training you could get left behind if you don't plan. Your guidance counsellor can help only when YOU have done some career exploration. If you do, your career mission will be accomplished.

Career exploration check list

In the following pages, a Career Exploration Checklist is presented. You can use this to assess your level of involvement in the guidance process.

Before you visit your guidance counsellor check that you have undertaken the following activities. Place a tick next to each completed item.

1. Careers project. Do not wait to be given such a project. Do one yourself using the following headings:

- Career category or an individual career ☐
- Training/3rd Level ☐
- Career interview/profile ☐
- Company profile (Write to Public Relations Dept.) ☐

2. Work Experience ☑

3. Aptitude Test ☐

Assessment tests will help you understand how aptitudes and interests play an important role in career choice.

5

4. Interest Test ☐

5. Curriculum Vitae ☑

6. Exams completed or preparing for:
- Junior Certificate ☑
- Leaving Certificate/LCA/LCVP ☑

7. Transition Year ☐

8. Extra Qualifications/Training/Courses ☑
(e.g. computers, driving lessons)
Provisional License, ...

9. Careers exhibitions visited e.g. FÁS National Exhibition or Higher Options. ☑
...*IEI Engineering Careers Day* ....

10. Career publications consulted (specify) ☑
...*CAO Handbook, my thing* ....
....

11. Career videos/software consulted (specify) ☐
....
....

12. Prospectuses consulted/received? ☑
...*Galway, Limerick* ....
....

13. Open Days attended (Specify, e.g. Universities/Post Leaving Cert.) ☑
...*NUIG* ....
....

14. Projected costs. Have you done your sums if leaving home is an option next year? ☐
What will it cost you per week to live away from home next year (if appropriate)?
....

15. Competitions/Awards Schemes (e.g. Gaisce/ESAT Young Scientist and Technologist) ☐
....
....

16. **Membership of organisations (e.g. Scouts, Order of Malta, Social Work, FCA)** ☑

17. **Talents/Skills/Special Interests (e.g. Music, Sports)** ☑

18. **Portfolio (Artistic/Media/Architecture, etc.)** ❑

19. **Applied to:**
   - CAO ☑
   - UCAS ❑
   - PLC ❑
   - Others ❑

20. **Jobs applied for:** ❑
   ....NONE..
   ....

21. **Applied to:**
   - FÁS ❑
   - CERT ❑
   - TEAGASC ❑
   - Other (please specify) ❑
   ....

22. **Three hours per day, five days a week for Study/Homework** ☑

   Total Score on Career Exploration Checklist 13
   (Give yourself one mark for every X)

Student's Signature: ....*Jonathan Hurley*..............................

Parent's Signature: ....*George Hurley*....................

Date: ...00\00\00...

Scoring: Assessment of your scores on the Career Exploration Checklist.

SCORES

0-10 You should be too embarrassed to visit the guidance counsellor.

11-20 If they are in generous mood your guidance counsellor may give you an encouraging smile. Chalk up a few more credits.

21 + A big improvement. You deserve a pat on the back and extra pocket money. You can now begin to look your guidance counsellor straight in the eye.

STUDENT YEARBOOK APPLICATION RECORD

Summarise your applications to courses and jobs below. Note that each of these records are repeated in detail in the relevant section of this yearbook.

CAO Degree List			CAO Cert/Diploma List		
Code	Course Title	'99 Points	Code	Course Title	'99 Points

Applications to Other Colleges/Training Agencies
(e.g. UCAS Colleges, Private Colleges, PLC Colleges, CERT, FÁS, TEAGASC etc.)

College/Agency	Course Title	Date Sent

Portfolios (e.g. artistic, media, architecture, etc.)

College/Agency	Course Title	Date Sent

Intended Job/Apprenticeship Applications (e.g. private firms, civil service, semi-state bodies,

Employers Name	Job Description	Date Sent

Student's Name _____

Class _____ Date _____

JOB SEARCH

5 easy stages

Whatever your level of education or experience, when job hunting, you will generally have to succeed with each of the following:

1. **Job File**
2. **Networks**
3. **Application**
4. **Interview**
5. **Medical.**

1. Job File

Collect personal documentation (birth certs, exam certs, references, etc. with several copies). Keep record of advertisements, application, etc. A supply of notepaper, envelopes and stamps

Visit careers exhibitions, observe people at work – all part of the job hunt.

2. Networks

Contacts … contacts … contact relatives, friends, your local FÁS office, etc.

3. Application

Letters, forms, CVs; presentation is all-important. Avoid that bin.

4. Interview

Don't waste this chance – prepare with care. Know about the job, the company. Know what you want to tell them about YOU.

5. Medical

The final stage – even million pound footballers have come a cropper at this stage.

Need more help?

. . . Read on

JOB SEARCH JOB FILE

With our economy really picking up speed there should be plenty of jobs on offer for school leavers – especially if you have a Leaving Certificate. However, if you want a job in a particular career area and want it soon you will need to get a job file organised well before you sit the Leaving Certificate.

It should include the following:

- Birth Certificate & copies
- Certified copies of educational certificates
- References and photocopies
- Job advertisements
- Copy of letters/forms sent

- Curriculum Vitae
- Record of job applications
- Passport sized photographs
- Stamps for a speedy reply

JOB SEARCH TOP TEN

Surveys in Ireland have shown that about one third of people get jobs through personal contacts. Your relations, neighbours, teachers, classmates, your fellow members in clubs, football teams etc. are all potential contacts. Using such contacts to gather information about jobs and vacancies is called 'networking'.

The following checklist of sources and agencies may help you to gather more useful information:

(1) PEOPLE ALREADY AT WORK

As well as your relatives and friends, be prepared to talk to other adults and young people already at work. Apart from providing some realistic advice they may, if aware of your ambitions, know of some opportunities in the pipeline.

(2) DIRECT APPROACH

Most vacancies are not suddenly created, they are known about in advance, e.g. someone leaving, being promoted, a new office or factory opening, so why wait until jobs are advertised. Many employers, especially with vacancies for schoolleavers, no longer advertise, knowing that the more determined and enthusiastic will apply "on spec". The Telephone Directory, in particular the "GOLDEN PAGES" are invaluable resources for the serious job seeker. Watch out for "Business and Finance" annual companies list.

Many libraries have set up information services such as the EMPLOYMENT OPPORTUNITIES COLLECTION initiated by Dublin Corporation. This comprehensive "One Stop" resource pack, containing information produced by statutory bodies, semi-state bodies, local authorities – and voluntary organisations active in all areas of employment promotion. It includes:

Opportunities – information on starting your own business, setting up co-operatives, training for the unemployed, people with disabilities, etc.

Help with Job Seeking – design a C.V., interview techniques and much more. The pack is now available in every Dublin Public Library service.

(3) FÁS

The principal services provided by FÁS are in training, employment community and enterprise development. FÁS provides a free job placement service to all jobseekers. You should register with your local FÁS Employment Services Office after you have received your Leaving Certificate results. Each FÁS Employment Services Office has a range of job vacancies on display which can be checked on a daily basis for new ones. A selection of current job vacancies is also advertised on AERTEL Jobfinder as well as information on other FÁS services. Each day on Jobfinder a selection of vacancies is displayed from a different FÁS region. Should you fail to find employment, it may be recommended that you improve your skills by undergoing a FÁS training course or temporary employment scheme.

(4) MEDIA
National (*especially Thursdays – Irish Independent, Fridays – Irish Times and Sundays – all*). Though less popular advertising medium for jobs, both the radio and television may give you the lead you need. Regardless of how jobs are advertised, most will require the minimum of delay in replying, particularly if a telephone number is provided and a closing date not specified.

(5) RECRUITMENT AGENCIES
There are numerous recruitment agencies throughout the country, and their services are usually free to the job hunter. However, as many tend to specialise in particular types of work e.g. clerical, nursing, accountancy etc., they may be more relevant to those with further training. Check the Golden Pages for lists.

(6) SCHOOLS
Local employers often contact guidance counsellors to help them fill vacancies, so do complete and return any questionnaire your school may send you about your current status, especially if you are looking for a job. Even if the school does not contact you, call in to see your guidance counsellor and let them know that you are available.

(7) OTHER RELEVANT BODIES
   (a) CERT – the national body responsible for coordinating the education, recruitment and training of personnel for the hotel, catering and tourism industry.

   (b) IDA Ireland - is the body responsible for industrial development, providing grants for new and existing manufacturing and technical service industries.

   (c) NRB – the National Rehabilitation Board provides vocational and guidance services for the disabled and operates a national rehabilitation and placement service.

   (d) UDARAS NA GAELTACHTA – the Gaeltacht Development Authority establishes and develops job-creating industries and services in the Gaeltacht regions. The Authority's Management Development Programme for Gaeltacht graduates provides training and career opportunities for third level graduates in the engineering, accounting, production and marketing fields. The Apprenticeship Scheme gives young Gaeltacht school leavers the opportunity to develop various skills, for example electrical and joinery skills. For further information on training and employment opportunities within the Gaeltacht contact: The Training Services Division, Udaras na Gaeltachta, Na Forbacha, Gaillimh. Tel: 091 592 0011.

(8) CAREER PUBLICATIONS
Check the publications section of this Directory for lists of helpful career publications now available. Many should be available in your school's careers library, or from your local public one.

**(9) YOUTH INFORMATION
CENTRES/CITIZEN ADVICE CENTRES**
Located throughout the country, these provide free information on a wide range of topics including careers, education, employment and training.

(10) INTERNET
The internet is a very rich source of information on jobs. There are now many websites dedicated to job searching, like http://www.jobfinder.ie/

member of the global JobUniverse network

Ireland's No. I jobs website

Luck is where preparation meets opportunity. This means that the more prepared you are and the harder you try the luckier you become. Remember this as you set about getting that job and be prepared!

Your first contact with an employer will usually be

a telephone call • a curriculum vitae with a covering letter • an application form

Preparation and attention to detail at this stage could help you get that vital interview.

DIAL A JOB

Often an advertisement asks you to telephone for an appointment or application form, but before you call be prepared and...

- Have the advertisement and your CV. with you.
- Have plenty of change or a spare call card if using a public phone. Find one in a quiet place.
- Know the name of the person you wish to speak to.
- Know when you will be available for interview.

During the call

- Speak slowly and clearly, giving your name and reason for calling.
- Ask to speak to the person you want.
- Refer to your CV. to answer questions. Keep answers short and concise.
- Ask for directions if needed.

WRITTEN APPLICATIONS

Written applications are either by CURRICULUM VITAE (CV) or by application form. A short covering letter usually accompanies a CV.

CURRICULUM VITAE (C.V.)

Curriculum vitae is simply a description of your education, accomplishments, work experience and personal skills. Its content therefore is similar to that of a form. However, unlike the form, you have the opportunity to design what is basically an advertisement for yourself.

It is important that the presentation be of a high standard, typed, preferably by a competent typist on an electric typewriter or word processor.

The information can be presented on a single page but can extend to a 2—3 page document. Your application is the first contact with a prospective employer and you know what they say about first impressions, and you don't get a second chance to make a first impression!

There is no right or wrong way of presenting the information; this is entirely up to you and your typist. However, apart from Personal Details and Education/Qualifications, which can simply be listed, the following may help you in compiling your own C.V.

YOUR INTERESTS & ACHIEVEMENTS

Rather than providing a list, write a brief paragraph about your extra curricular activities and achievements. Include any positions of responsibility in school or clubs you are involved in.

EXPERIENCE/OTHER SKILLS

This is a very important section and often underestimated by students. Describe briefly any summer or part-time jobs, or voluntary activities you have been involved in; perhaps you have mastered certain other skills, e.g. driving, computers, artistic or practical. It is not enough to say you worked in the local creamery for the summer — spell out the kind of tasks you had to do. It is this section that makes you stand out from the other applicants.

ACTION WORDS

In composing these sections, action words that show your involvement in voluntary work, your responsibilities in school, sports, clubs etc. are far more effective than statements about your personal qualities.

ambitious	designed	implemented	prepared
analytical	developed	improved	produced
achieved	directed	managed	promoted
attained	established	organised	represented
coordinated	expanded	planned	researched

See if you can demonstrate by your actions that you possess some if not all of these qualities:

articulate	dependable	persistent
competent	efficient	resourceful
conscientious	industrious	versatile

APPLICATION FORMS

If possible, make a photocopy of any forms you have to complete and do a rough draft first. Read any instructions on/with the form, e.g. BLACK INK, BLOCK CAPITALS, but remember that some forms require certain sections in you own hand-writing.

Much of the information which you have prepared for your C.V. will be required so keep a copy at hand for guidance.

Forms come in a variety of styles and sizes, some may be merely one page while others stretch to more than six.

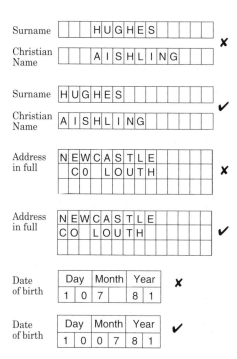

Quite a number of forms are badly designed and fail to give sufficient room for some details. In these cases use your own judgement and make the most of it — everyone else will have the same problem, but if necessary it is normally acceptable to add an extra sheet of paper. The computer input document type form is becoming increasingly popular, in particular with organisations dealing with large numbers of applicants e.g. CAO. In many ways the design removes the concern for layout but can lead to other problems, such as not starting in the first box or leaving more than one space between words. A combination of both types is also quite common.

WORDS ON FORMS

The following words can cause problems and are often misunderstood.

Spouse: Wife or husband as the case may be.

Next of Kin: nearest relative i.e. mother, father, husband, wife.

Title: Miss, Ms, Mr, Mrs, Dr, Sr, etc. (Ms is a more recent development and is used instead of either Miss or Mrs and like Mr it carries no indication of marital status — married, single, widowed etc.)

Place of Birth: Town or city in which you were born and not THE COOMBE or the local maternity hospital.

Date of Birth: Sure! We all know what that means. Then how come so many people claim to be born the year they are applying!

Siblings: Number of brothers and or sisters.

If a particular section does not apply to you, write in "not applicable" or N/A.

WHY DO YOU WANT THIS JOB?

The most difficult section on any form is that which asks "Why do you want this Job?" "Why do you consider yourself suitable?" and "How do you see your future with this company?" Only you know the answers and you do have them but they need to be thought out carefully and put down on paper. Go back to your C.V., in particular to the sections on interests and work experience. Read some of the references which past employers and teachers have written about you. Study careers literature for descriptions of the kind of person suited to the work. However, the most important task, is to read the advertisement to establish not only those requirements which are stated but those which are hidden or unspecified.

REFERENCES

Two referees should be named along with their position, address and telephone number. Their permission should be sought beforehand and keep them informed as to what position you are applying for. School Leavers should have one referee from school and the other a past employer or any responsible adult who will stand by your character. You do not have to use the same referee all the time; select those most appropriate, e.g. if applying for a place on a Physical Education course then ask your P.E. teacher or the coach at your local sports club.

A typical CV will contain a handy presentation of essential information about you. It should be typed or word processed, and don't forget to photocopy it to send to the various positions you are applying for.

CURRICULUM VITAE (CV)

NAME: MARIAN WALSH

ADDRESS: Tralee Rd., Castleisland, Co. Kerry

Date of Birth: 14/6/1982

Post-Primary School:
Castleisland Community College, Castleisland, Co. Kerry from September 1994 to June 2000

QUALIFCATIONS

JUNIOR CERTIFICATE 1997		
Subject	Level	Grade
English	H	D
Irish	H	C
Mathematics	H	B
Geography	H	C
History	H.	D
Science	H.	B
Home Economics	H.	C
French	O	D
Business Studies	O	D

LEAVING CERTIFICATE 1999		
Subject	Level	Grade
English	O	
Irish	O	
Mathematics	O	
Economics	O	
French	O	
History	O	
Physics	H	
N.B. Results available in August 2000.		

Dept. of Education Transition Year Certificate (1998).

INTERESTS AND ACHIEVEMENTS

Foroige: October 1995 to present. I have been involved in public speaking and outdoor pursuits. I have been a leader organising activities for the 12-15 year olds since 1997.

Gaisce Award: In Transition Year I achieved the Bronze Award- my activities included community service and training for a lifesaving certificate.

Sport: Basketball, Member of the school Senior team. Runner up in the County Championship.

Football: Member of school team and Castleisland Desmonds Ladies Football Club.

WORK EXPERIENCE AND OTHER SKILLS

Kennelly's Newsagents (1997-2000) serving customers, stacking shelves and stock control.

Dept. of Education Elementary Typing Certificate.

Provisional driving licence.

REFERENCES

Ms. A. O'Rourke,
Principal,
Castleisland Community School,
Castleisland,
Co. Kerry.

Mr. Brendan Kennelly,
Kennelly's Newsagent,
Main Street,
Castleisland,
Co. Kerry.

Signature: .... Date: ....

ABOVE IS A SAMPLE CURRICULUM VITAE; CHANGE THE FORMAT TO SUIT YOURSELF.

CVs CAN BE SUBDIVIDED INTO FIVE SECTIONS

(1) PERSONAL DETAILS

Name, Address, Date of Birth, Telephone No. (can be neighbour's).

(2) QUALIFICATIONS

Post-Primary School attended and dates, Junior and Leaving Certificate Results, School based qualifications, e.g. Transition.

(3) INTERESTS & ACHIEVEMENTS

This includes how you like best to spend your leisure time. Employers like to know how you busy yourself and what kind of games you play and past-times you have. It is better to describe briefly your main interests and achievements.

(4) EXPERIENCE/ OTHER SKILLS

This is a very important section and often underestimated by students. Describe briefly any summer or part-time jobs, or voluntary activities you have been involved in; perhaps you have mastered certain other skills e.g. driving, computers, artistic or practical. It's not enough to say you worked in the local creamery for the summer – spell out the kind of tasks you had to do. It is this section that makes you stand out from the other applicants.

(5) REFERENCES

Locate and inform some responsible person who knows you well and is prepared to go to the bother of standing by your character. Perhaps the manager of a place you had a summer job or anywhere you have helped/worked voluntarily. Indeed don't exclude a good neighbour. Most employers of first-time job applicants will demand a school reference.

NOW TURN OVERLEAF AND FILL OUT YOUR OWN C.V.

CURRICULUM VITAE (CV)

NAME ...... *Jonathan Hearty*

ADDRESS ...... *Some where over the rainbow (coeofin)*

Date of Birth ...... — ...... Telephone ......

Post-Primary School: *SIC Tipan*

QUALIFICATIONS

JUNIOR CERTIFICATE 19...

Subject	Level	Grade
English	EO	E
Irish	O	D
Mathematics	F	DEC
Geography	EO	EC
History		DEE
Science	FO	EE
French	O	E
Business Studies	O	
Technical Studies		

LEAVING CERTIFICATE 19...

Subject	Level	Grade
English		
Irish		
Mathematics		

INTERESTS AND ACHIEVEMENTS

Getting lost in Corofin, doing Mathematical Questions, getting drunk on molasses and Ivomec + other such substances

EXPERIENCE AND OTHER SKILLS

I once got lost in Corofin for 3 weeks, until I found a sign just to say I was in West-Clare.

REFERENCES

Name ... Mr. Sufilupocas

Address ... Scasem:C Street

America

Telephone ... —

Name ... Elmo

Address ... Scasmie Street

America

Telephone ... —

Signature: ... Jonathan HARLY

Your Street Name and Number
Town/City
County
Today's date

Give Ref. No. here if given one in ad. and underline

Person's Name
Position,
Organisation,
Address.

→ *Ref: Job Title / Vacancy / Reference Number*

Dear persons name,
Your opening paragraph should state why you are writing i.e. applying for a particular position and state when and where you saw it advertised.

2cm Margin

Your middle paragraph should arouse interest in you, make your enthusiasm and interest for this particular job pretty obvious and create a desire on the part of the reader to interview you. Give details of your background that will show why you should be considered, referring to general qualifications, work experience or interests related to the position.

2cm Margin

In your closing paragraph refer to some aspects of your enclosed c.v. Indicate that further details will be supplied if requested.

Yours sincerely,

Your Signature
Your Name Printed

Paragraphs to start one under each other about 1cm in from the margin

Start just right of centre page

LETTERS

Letter writing tends to be governed by certain conventions rather than strict rules. However, certain guidelines are best adhered to and one should start by choosing WHITE, UNLINED, A4 SIZED PAPER. Letters should be written in dark ink, though some employers prefer them typed — check the advertisement — it may state handwritten.

Application letters should be business-like but avoid phrases like "re your exciting advertisement of 29th July" or "I beg to remain". Simply use familiar words, keeping your sentences short and to the point. Although the content is important, careful selection of words can set the tone of your letter and help to create a positive impression of you, your skills, strengths, abilities and work habits. Choose action words such as those discussed under compiling a C.V.

Your letter should be no longer than one page if possible. Phrases such as "During the summer . . .", "For the past two years . . .", "Last year . . .", sound better to start sentences with than "I . . ." The conventional endings are "Yours faithfully," if the letter is addressed to a position i.e. Personnel Officer, Sir/Madam, and "Yours sincerely", if it is to a named individual.

THE PURPOSE OF INTERVIEWS

(a) To enable employers to better acquaint themselves with you and your suitability for the job.

(b) To allow you to find out more about your potential employer and the job you have applied for.

Naturally you will feel a little nervous coming up to the interview. Rather like an examination, the better prepared you are the more successful you will be. You must research and practice thoroughly for the interview so that you can give a satisfactory account of yourself on the day.

PREPARATION CHECKLIST

*   Get information on the company (annual reports, sales brochures, etc.)
*   Getting your hands on the job description will do wonders to your answers.
*   Acquire all necessary documentation well in advance, i.e. references, birth certificates, and examination results.
*   Try talking to somebody who is already doing the type of work you are applying for. This should inform you more on the nature of the job and its daily routine.
*   Be alert to current affairs by reading newspapers regularly.
*   Prepare some intelligent, but relevant, questions concerning the firm, or job you are applying for; but not things like the quality of food in the canteen or facilities in the social club.
*   Review what you actually wrote on your application form — hobbies, pastimes, reasons for applying, etc., as much of what you have written here will form the basis of your interview.

DON'T SPOIL YOUR CHANCES!

*   Be well rested (go to bed reasonably early the night before).
*   Dress appropriately, be neat and well groomed.
*   Do not be late for your interview — check your route in advance and plan to arrive about ten minutes early.
*   Don't forget your references, curriculum vitae, examination results, etc.

Remember that the interviewer is primarily concerned with your suitability for the job and will be endeavouring to assess your speech, manner, enthusiasm, sense of responsibility, confidence and your overall career intentions.

THE INTERVIEW ITSELF

*   Act naturally, don't put on any phoney accents or adopt strange mannerisms.
*   Don't smoke unless invited.

You may undergo many interviews before success comes your way but you must keep on trying. More often than not there is nothing wrong with the standard of interview but rather a question of too many applicants for too few jobs.

*   Be enthusiastic and display your willingness to learn and work hard with others.
*   Interviewers do not like "yes" and "no" answers so be ready to expand your ideas when given the leads.
*   Show you have the knowledge of the job and prove you are suitably qualified for this work.
*   The end of an interview is not the time to jump up and disappear — don't forget those questions you had prepared!

INTERVIEWERS ARE HUMAN TOO!

As in most human situations, interviewers can and do make mistakes; the wrong candidate can be chosen.

INTERVIEW ASSESSMENT CHART
(This is often the assessment method adopted by interviewers)
(A tick ✓ is placed in the appropriate box)

	Excellent	Good	Average	Poor	Very Poor
	5	4	3	2	1
Application form/letter					
Knowledge of job					
Knowledge of company					
Intelligence					
Special Aptitudes					
Health					
Appearance					
Hobbies/Pastimes					
General Knowledge					
Enthusiasm					
Overall Impression					

- When going on holidays ask somebody to look after your correspondence. Provide them with a **forwarding address** so you can attend appointments for aptitude tests, interviews or confirmation of places on a training course.

- Please allow some time for preparation and typing of a reference. Do not leave it until the day before the interview.

INTERVIEW QUESTIONS

There are many questions you may be asked at interview; employers put different emphasis on these but there is no great mystery here. Common questions would centre on the following.

I N T E R V I E W S		
	Interest	Why are you interested in this work?
	Neatness	Your neatness grooming and presentation manner will be noticed
	Training	What training is involved?
	Education	Education record - Junior/Leaving/ other certificates/skills, etc.
	Research	Have you done your homework on the job and company?
	Vision	Where do you see yourself in five years time?
	Income	Your expectation of wages/perks/conditions of work etc.
	Enthusiasm	Evidence of your enthusiasm for the job.
	Workers	How will you fit in with the other workforce?
	S!	Sigh of relief at an interview well done!

APTITUDE TESTING

APTITUDE TESTING as a selection procedure for third level places is more the exception than the rule. However, large organisations such as the Banks, Aer Lingus and the ESB make regular use of them as a means of shortlisting the most suitable candidates for interview.

If you have never taken such tests then don't worry, as most of the learning and knowledge they seek is the kind one picks up from life rather than schooling. Most consist of problems or puzzles to be solved, many are multiple choice and all require you to follow directions carefully! Some test verbal skills and may look like this:

BIRD is to CAGE as DOG is to _____

(a) *Stable*; (b) *Tank*; (c) *Kennel*; (d) *None of these*

Numerical tests ask you to make a number of calculations — multiplication, addition, subtraction, division. Brush up on how to add in fractions etc. especially how to calculate square roots and cubed roots.

EMPLOYMENT & TRADE UNIONS

Feeling a bit nervous on your first day of work is not unusual. For most of us, entering the workplace signals the beginning of independent living and as such can be a big upheaval in our lives. The days are now longer, the holidays fewer and the responsibility greater. It may even be a time when you decide to move out and get your own accommodation.

Like every new situation though – it is just a matter of time. Having confidence in yourself and your abilities is the key to feeling at ease. Know your role and what you can give to the job. Don't underestimate the part you play. Fortunately however a lot of organisations now put their staff through 'induction programmes' to familiarise new staff with the work environment and the job itself. This is the best time to ask any questions you might have. Don't be shy!

- What is my job specification?
- What are my holiday entitlements?
- Is there a canteen?
- Do I have bonuses or benefits?

TRADE UNIONS

A trade union is a group of workers who join together to protect their interests and the interests of fellow workers.

Since the Industrial Revolution at the turn of the century the trade union organisation has been one of the driving forces in improving the conditions in the workplace. Trade Unions provide many services for their members, such as:

- Explaining basic rights to an employee

- Negotiating on behalf of it's members for wage increases, better working conditions or greater promotional prospects.

- Acting as 'go-between' between employee and management should a grievance (problem) arise

The role of the trade union has grown to include 'outside' work issues too, such as health-care, housing and social welfare benefits. The union is divided up into sub units at each branch. An employee at the branch is elected as the 'shop steward', the person who can be contacted to join or for general member information.

Larger organisations may have a variety of unions open to the employee but smaller organisations just have the one. Types of Unions include:

General Unions
These unions serve employees of every type of industry or service; skilled, semi-skilled or unskilled. One of the largest is SIPTU (Services Industrial Professional Technical Union) which has over 200,000 members.

Craft Unions
Craft Unions are the oldest type of unions. Their members are skilled workers and must serve an apprenticeship in a trade before they can become full union members.

White Collar Unions
Members of the 'White Collar' unions are professional, technical and clerical workers. An example would be the different unions present within the Civil Service who represent the different grades of workers i.e. CPSU (Civil Public Service Union) who represent the clerical grades and PSEU (Public Service and Executive Union) who represent the Executive Officers upwards.

Most Trade Unions are affiliated to the ICTU, Irish Congress of Trade Unions. This is the central organising body which co-ordinates the Trade Union movement in Ireland, including Northern Ireland. Further information can be obtained from:
I.C.T.U., 19 Raglan Road, Dublin 4
Tel: (01) 6680641

Legislation
Finally, it is important to realise that Human Resource department and Trade Unions aside, employment legislation does exist to protect the rights of workers. For more information on the legislation passed and for some useful publications contact:
I he Dept. of Enterprise, Trade & Employment, Kildare Street, Dublin 2. Tel: (01) 6614444.

WAGES, TAX & BENEFITS

If you are a student who was previously used to claiming back your 'emergency tax' at the end of summer you may get a big fright when it comes to holding down your first full-time permanent job. TAX is now going to be a part of your life you could previously avoid. Unfortunately, now the pay you take home will be at a much reduced rate after you pay your taxes, PRSI and sometimes union and persion subscriptions

ALLOWANCES
Just in case you are fearful that all your hard earned cash is going to be taken away don't fret! Each individual is given an allowance of money they can earn before they get taxed (as per P2 form below). These allowances tend to vary from year to year and come under review during the annual budget.

DEDUCTIONS
PAYE (Pay as you earn) is a tax which is non-negotiable, it is deducted straight from your gross earnings by your employer. The amount of PAYE you pay depends mainly on your income but is variable based on individual circumstances. If you are entering a new job or have recently been given a pay rise it is advisable to contact the Revenue Commission and make them aware of your change in circumstances. They will provide you with an *Application for Certificate of Tax Free Allowances and Social Registration Form (F12A)*. On receipt of your completed form your tax inspector will send you and your employer a *Notice of Determination of Tax Free Allowances (P2)* and your *Revenue and Social Insurance Number (RSI)*.

PRSI & LEVIES
PRSI (Pay Related Social Insurance) is a contribution made by the employee and the employer to cover many social welfare benefits they may look to in the future, including unemployment, maternity, disability, optical and pension benefits. The normal rate of contributions is referred to as 'Class A'.

Income	Employer	Employee
up to £24,200	12%	6.75%

Employees can earn up to £100 per week before they are liable to pay PRSI. PRSI rates vary according to the type of work you do. In addition to your contribution, your employer pays a further percentage of your income to RSI.

TAX FORMS

The whole world of tax can be very confusing so most of us just limit ourselves to the basics. A P45 and a P60 are the two tax forms that we will all ocme across in our working career.

- P45 is a certificate which our employer issues when we leave the job – it states the employee's total income, tax and insurance deductions from the start of the curent tax year.

- P60 is issued to each employee at the end of the financial year, April 5th. This form lists your earnings, tax and insurance paid for the tax year just ended. If you are making a claim for a tax rebate or for social welfare benefits it is essential you have this form, so keep it handy.

UNEMPLOYMENT BENEFIT AND ASSISTANCE

If you are unfortunate enough to become unemployed, you may be entitled to unemployment benefits. This is provided you have 39 weeks of PRSI contributions (as explained above) paid. In addition to this basic benefit, you may be entitled to Pay Related Benefit, calculated on a sliding scale as a percentage of your earnings.

If you are over 18 and not entitled to unemployment 'benefit' you may just qualify for unemployment 'assistance'. However this is means tested.

SOCIAL WELFARE ALLOWANCES

For those individuals whose means are not enough to meet their needs and those of their dependants, supplementary welfare allowances are provided (e.g. for rent, mortgages etc.). This scheme is administered by the Health Boards and as such your local board can supply you with the full details.

Employers' PRSI Exemption Scheme

SW 73

There are many useful brochures provided by the Department of Social, Community and Family Affairs (information service), Áras Mhic Dhiarmada, Dublin 1. Tel: 01-8748444.

A Guide to Unemployed People (SW64) is an invaluable new publication available from the Dept. of Social Welfare. Its 44 pages of advice and information is essential reading for those out of work.

Full details of your entitlements are available in two very useful publications: *Guide to Social Welfare Services (SW4)* and *Social Welfare Rates of Payment (SW19)*. Both are updated regularly and are available, free of charge, from the Information Service, Department of Social Welfare, Áras Mhic Dhiarmada, Dublin 1 (01-8748444).

'*Everything you need to know . . . to get a Supplementary Welfare Payment*' is a guide book launched by the Irish National Organisation ot the

Unemployed (INOU). Its aim is to highlight the payments available to people under the Supplementary Welfare Allowance Scheme and to enable people to use this scheme more effectively. In addition, INOU publishes a more comprehensive book - Working for Work. Both publications are available, free of charge, from local centres for the unemployed, local Citizens Information Centres, local libraries or directly from the INOU, 6, Gardiner Row, Dublin 1(please include an A5, self-addressed envelope with a 48p stamp).

For further information contact your local **Citizens Information Centre.** There are over 80 of these voluntary centres established by the **National Social Service Board** to provide information on taxation, social welfare and many other statutory services, Contact the NSSB at Hume House, Dublin 4 (01-6059000).

23

SAVINGS

If you suddenly find yourself in an improving financial situation, maybe it's time to review how much you are spending and see if you could manage to put away a few pounds. The reality is that whether you are working full or part time it is not a good idea to blow all your money on pay-day.

Budgeting
One of the best ways to save is to prepare a budget for yourself. Putting pen to paper and keeping a record can be a great way to control your money. As per our sample budget, you basically list your total income for the week/month and then subtract your total deductions for this period. Make your budget out for the same period as you get paid asking yourself a few questions along the way:

- What do I spend money on every week?
- Will I need new clothes this week/month?
- Is Christmas/John's birthday coming up soon?
- Should I start putting money away for my holidays?

SAVING INSTITUTIONS

Hopefully after all your brilliant budgeting you may have a few pounds left over to save. So where's the best place to put your money? There are several different places to save:

- Banks provide a variety of services and accounts to their customers. The student and current accounts are probably the most applicable and have limited charges.
- Building Societies are good for longer term saving. In the future they can be relied upon to lend out large sums of money for the likes of mortgages etc.
- Credit Unions are co-operative institutions run and founded by local communities. All savings are pooled and members can apply for loans from this shared money.
- Post Office: many people start their saving career with a post office account. Members are issued with a savings book and receive interest on a yearly basis. It is a handy way to save considering there are so many post offices throughout the country.

SAMPLE BUDGET

INCOME:

Wages _____

Tax & other deductions _____

Total nett income: _____

REGULAR SPENDING:

Rent/Contribution at home _____

Transport _____

Food _____

Entertainment _____

Other expenses _____

Total regular spending: _____

PERIODIC SPENDING:

(divide yearly bills by 12)

Electricity & heating _____

Phone _____

Hire purchase/Loans _____

Medical expenses _____

Clothes _____

Holidays _____

Presents _____

Other expenses _____

Total periodic spending _____

Nett Income _____

Regular payments _____

Periodic payments _____

TOTAL SAVINGS _____

CAREER CATEGORIES

The most comprehensive list of careers available in Ireland is produced in the Student Yearbook and Career Directory; literally hundreds upon hundreds of careers are identified.

All of the careers are grouped into nineteen categories, i.e. placing within a category types of jobs which have something in common with each other. The Garda Síochána and Army have peacekeeping in common so they are classified together in the security section.

AGRICULTURE/HORTICULTURE/ FORESTRY/ANIMALS

CAREERS IN THIS CATEGORY
Many of the careers listed below are outlined on the FÁS Gairm Database

Agricultural Contractor; Agricultural Engineer; Agricultural Mechanic; Agricultural Machinery Operator; Agricultural Product Salesperson; Agricultural Officer; Agricultural Economist; Animal Nursing Auxiliary; Animal Welfare Society Worker; Assistant Agricultural Inspector; Butter and Cheesemaker; Co-op. Worker; Creamery Manager; Farmer; Beekeeper; Farm Manager; Farm Worker; Farrier; Forest; Forestry Graduate; Aquaculturist; Greengrocer; Greyhound Breeder and Trainer; Groundsman; Hatchery Worker; Horse Transporter; Horse Trainer; Horticulturist; Inspector of Agriculture; Inspector in Farm Home Management; Inspector in Horticulture and Beekeeping; Kennel Assistant; Land Drainage Worker; Landscaper; Market Gardener; Park Attendant; Petshop Assistant; Poultry Technician; Riding School Personnel; Saddler; Seed Analyst; Serological Assistant; Shepherd; Stable Groom; Stockperson — Pigs, Cattle, Sheep, etc.; Stud Farm Employee; Timber Merchant; Veterinary Surgeon; Wild Life Ranger; Zookeeper; Zoologist; Bog Cultivation — Machinery Operator, Apprentices; Drivers, Fruit Picker; Jockey; Artificial Inseminator; Milkman; Pest Controller; Jam Maker; Instructor in Farm Home Management; Garden Centre Worker; Cattle Breeder.

Farm incomes reduced

In October last year the streets of Dublin crawled to a halt for several hours as 40,000 farmers marched to protest what the IFA called "Government and EU inaction on collapsing farm incomes, disastrous cattle, pig and sheep prices". A warning that 50,000 jobs will be lost in agriculture within five years as a result of the collapse in farm incomes was given by the IFA president, Mr. Tom Parlon, at the march.

Over the past year, many farmers, especially those in the beef and sheep sectors, have seen their incomes reduced. in addition, they face a future without the same level of EU supports and

subsidies, worth an estimated £1.5 billion last year. The implementation of CAP reforms as part of Agenda 2000 will lead to a drop of 20% in farm incomes by 2007 according to a Teagasc economist.

It is clearly a difficult time for a sector once seen as the most important in the economy. The figures speak for themselves: in 1960, around 390,000 people were employed in agriculture; last year the figure was 134,000 and that number is set to decline further. In the same period agriculture's share of total employment has fallen from 37% to 10%.

On the positive side to Irish farming the value of Irish farms is estimated at £40 billion. Ireland produces only 5% of total EU food and , with an EU population of 360 mullion, a small increase in market share would provide enormous opportunities.

Food exports from Ireland are worth £5 billion and 2,000 jobs have been created annually in the industry since 1994. Food production employs 40,000 and remains one of the country's largest industries. Of the top 100 companies in Ireland 20 are food and drink manufacturers.

Most training in agriculture, horticulture and forestry is run by Teagasc.

The Farmer: Courses are run in conjunction with Teagasc at eleven agricultural colleges as well as Teagasc centres around the country. The certificate in farming is awarded after one-year full time or two years part-time training. Students can then progress to the Diploma in Agriculture and specialise in dairying, farm machinery, pig management or poultry management. The Farm Apprenticeship Board, Foroige and Macra na Feirme run courses. Also keep in mind British colleges such as Sparsholt College in Hampshire.

Dairying: Following the certificate students spend a year at agricultural colleges in Clonakilty or Multyfarnham followed by 1 months work experience to get the diploma in dairying.

Farm Machinery: There is a residential nine month course on operation, care and maintenance of farm machinery at Pallaskenry, County Limerick. Check out the new "Agricultural Engineering" course in Heywood College, Laois (Tel: 0502-33333).

There are good employment prospects with graduates getting jobs as agricultural contractors, fabricators, mechanical and sales demonstrators in agri-business.

There is also a two-year certificate course in agricultural engineering in Tralee IT.

Pig Management: The two-year diploma in pig management in Mellowes College, Co. Galway is

Vivian Doyle
Horticultural Student

Vivian Doyle received a diploma in horticulture from Warrenstown College in Dunshaughlin, County Meath. As a mature student at the age of 27, she found it difficult to begin the routine of studying again, but wanted to follow up on her active interest in horticulture.

Before the diploma course, she had completed a one-year introductory course to horticultural studies through FÁS. Working in garden centres and reading books on the subject, she became interested in pursuing further qualifications. Warrenstown College is a commercial agricultural college, and the emphasis was placed on the production of vegetables and plants for commercial use and not on ornamental nurseries. The course lasted two and a half years and was quite intensive, offering a good deal of practical information and experience.

"There are a lot of different opportunities working in the industry...There wasn't any problem getting a job," Vivian says. After graduation, she worked full-time for two years with people with learning difficulties in the gardens at St. John of God Hospital.

She then started her own garden maintenance business, arranging hanging baskets and providing other gardening services to clients: "I was careful not to take on anything I couldn't do on my own, (for example), any huge landscaping projects," she says.

Being self-employed meant working in "a completely different environment", she admits. The pay was not always very good and demand for work can be seasonal. But Vivian plans to continue her horticultural work in the future and hopes to find a suitable site outside the Dublin area, where she can produce organic vegetables and herbs.

open to students who have completed the certificate in agriculture and have three months work experience in a pig unit.

Poultry Production: Similar to the other area students complete the 1-year certificate in agriculture followed by 9 months in Mellowes college and a year's work experience. There is a shortage of skilled people to work in the poultry industry so graduates currently have good employment prospects.

Agriculture and Food Engineering: Concerned with the application of engineering technology to food production, agribusiness, food processing and biotechnology. Graduates are employed in organisations such as food processors and manufacturers, equipment manufacturers and suppliers, co-operatives and agribusinesses, computer companies, and engineering and management consultants.

This course is available as an option in the common entry degree course in engineering in UCD.

UCD has a four-year degree in food processing engineering.

Food Science: UCC has a food science department and UL has a food technology degree course. Dundalk, Sligo and Letterkenny IT's have courses available in food science. Some common entry science courses as well as the agricultural science degree in UCD offer food science as an option.

Agribusiness: 50,000 people are employed in supplying farmers and marketing their produce. A two year certificate course is run jointly by the Franciscan Brothers' agricultural College, Mountbellew, Co. Galway and Galway IT. Graduates can go on to the diploma course at Tralee IT.

Butter and Cheesemaker: As well as the major dairies and Co-ops, there are now some 40 farmhouse cheesemakers – of which about fifteen are commercial. There is a part-time (4 week) course at UCC usually for people with associated work experience.

Environmental Science: Sligo IT has a diploma

and follow on degree in environmental science and pollution control. UL has a four-year degree in Environmental Science, which includes environmental protection, clean technology and environmental impact assessment. There is a three-year diploma course in environmental resource management in DIT. Certificate courses are on offer in Limerick and Dundalk ITs.

Agricultural Science: The four-year common entry course in UCD offers degrees in commercial horticulture, landscape horticulture, forestry, animal and crop production, animal science, agribusiness and rural development, food science, agriculture and environmental science, engineering technology.

Alternative Farming: Activities regarded as hobbies some years ago are now "big business", creating jobs and keeping people in rural Ireland. Teagasc is setting up some 50 Enterprise Establishment training courses to cater for a range of family-based enterprises, including food, rural tourism, free-range poultry, amenity horticulture, mushrooms and deer.

Commercial Horticulture is the production of food crops, flowers, trees and shrubs.

The horticulture industry is very labour intensive, providing thousands of jobs in production, distribution and retailing and is seen as having the potential to provide more. Although mushrooms are one of the areas of fastest growth, cultivation of other food crops is also on the increase.

One of the fastest growing production areas of horticulture is the nursery stock industry, producing trees and shrubs for sale to landscapers and through garden centres around the country. This has developed over recent years to the stage where we now export nursery stock to other EC countries. In addition Ireland has become more environmentally conscious and home owners are using more plants in their gardens, while the network of new roads under construction has soaked up hundreds of thousands of plants and tress in landscaping schemes. At present job prospects for graduates and trainees are excellent with an excess of job opportunities.

Amenity or Landscape Horticulture is concerned with the design, management and development of the landscape. This is an area where opportunities appear to be on the increase, with job opportunities available with local authorities in maintenance of public parks and gardens, with landscape companies in design and construction, and in nurseries and garden centres along with commercial horticulture graduates.

Courses: both the commercial and landscape horticultural options can be explored and developed through UCD's Bachelor of Agricultural Science degree, the only course of its kind in Ireland. Diploma and Certificate courses in Horticulture are available at College of Horticulture, An Grianan, Termonfeckin, Co. Louth; Kildalton College, Pilltown, Co. Kilkenny; Warrenstown College, Drumree, Co. Meath; and National Botanic Gardens, Glasnevin, Dublin 9. The modular nature of courses at these 4 colleges allows the trainee to select their subject area, and to choose a commercial or amenity orientated programme. A basic Horticultural skills program is offered by the Franciscan Agricultural College, Multyfarnham, Co. Westmeath, and PLC courses in horticulture are provided by some VEC's e.g. Killester, Ringsend, Pearse College, Dundrum College.

Greenkeeping: There are now about 400 golf courses, 300 pitch and putt clubs as well as driving ranges dotted around the country – all good news for anyone considering a career in greenkeeping.

School leavers who want to be greenkeepers can either do a full time course, or apply to a golf course for employment, and from there apply for a place on the GUI/Teagasc block release course leading to the NCVA Certificate in Greenkeeping. Students take turfgrass science and maintenance, golf course maintenance and construction, and learn about the machinery necessary to do the job, as well as budget management. It is estimated that over the next twenty-five years, direct and indirect employment in the sector should increase by 11,000 to 27,000.

Courses: A full time Diploma in Horticulture –

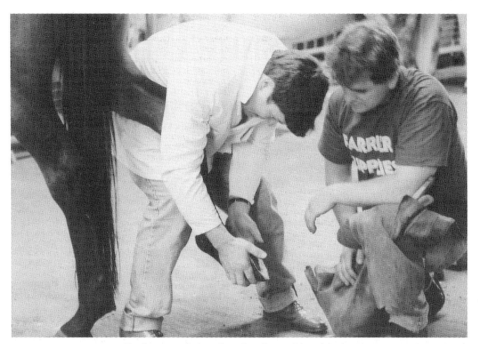

Farrier at work, keeping alive the traditional trades.

Sportsturf Management is offered by the College of Horticulture, An Grianan. The GUI/Teagasc course is provided by both the College of Horticulture, An Grianan, and by the National Botanic Gardens

PLC Courses are available at Scoil Stiofan Naofa, Cork and Kilkenny City Vocational School.

Florist: Two year day release course at DIT Mountjoy Square. Also PLC at Crumlin College of Business and Technical Studies. Some private schools run courses. Teagasc and FÁS have run them in the past, and the Irish Flowers Council is looking at starting one as well. Most people tend to approach a florist's shop directly upon leaving school.

Forestry: In 1996, the Minister predicted that forestry could be worth more than the beef industry by 2016, becoming a £2 billion sector. The National Forestry Programme, announced that one million acres would be brought into production. Last year, however, there were 13,500 hectares of forest planted in Ireland, just over half the predicted level, and actual plantings this year are expected to be equally low. Forestry and its associated activities, planting, harvesting, transport and processing, currently employ 12,000 people directly, with perhaps twice as many indirectly employed. the Government forestry strategy planned an expansion of output by over £1 billion by the year 1015 with 11,000 extra jobs.

This strategy was based on annual new planting levels of 25,000 hectares a year until 2015, but there has been a sharp decline in planting and there is little sign of recovery. Coillte, the state owned forestry company made net profits of £14.2 million last year.

Graduates from the Degree in Agricultural Science (Forestry) at UCD become forestry inspectors or foresters. This is a four year course. Course graduates are employed to assess land for planting, oversee planting and maintenance and also in the saw mill – buying timber.

Two new diplomas are now available in the forestry area, at Waterford Institute of Technology, and Galway Institute of Technology. At IT Tralee the national certificate in agricultural engineering programme will allow students to specialise in forestry for the first time.

Ballyhaise College and Coillte Teo run a Certificate in Agri-forestry programme, incorporating a placement. Teagasc also runs special short training courses.

Animals: Ireland is a major player on the world sage in the bloodstock industry with centres like the Coolmore Stud enjoying an intenarional reputation.

Irish racing is now entering a golden era with top businessmen like Michael Smurfit, Dermot Desmond and JP McManus giving badly needed financial backing to the industry.

The training facilities operated by top Irish trainers like Aidan O'Brien, John Oxx and Dermot Weld are among the finest in the world and this has encouraged leading breeders like the Maktoum brothers and the Aga Khan to locate here.

REASEHEATH

C O L L E G E

HOME FROM HOME FOR IRISH STUDENTS

Reaseheath College, within easy access for the whole of Ireland, offers courses to Irish students that are "the best in Europe"

The most popular courses for Irish students are:

- Agricultural Engineering
- Specialist Dairy and Farm Management
- Golf Course Design and Management

Over 700 Irish Students in the last 10 years

Although some Irish students are accepted through direct entry, the majority are encouraged to complete a Certificate in Agriculture at one of the many excellent Irish Agricultural Colleges.

• Reaseheath has very close links with all of the Irish Agricultural Colleges •

The **NEW** PLC Agricultural Engineering Course at Heywood College, Laois, has been designed to allow progression to Reaseheath

The **NEW** Machinery Diploma Course at Kildalton College, Pilltown, has taken advice from Reaseheath and also encourages progression to Reaseheath

Probably the best facilities and hands-on training of any college in Europe

For further information, contact:

Reaseheath College   **Tel: 00 44 1270 625131**
Nantwich, Cheshire   **Email: rheath1@reaseheath.ac.uk**
England CW5 6DF   **Web Site: www.reaseheath.ac.uk**

Links with Major Employers in the U.S.A.

Irish jockeys like Michael Kinnane, Charlie Swan ant Tony McCoy regularly capture the big race headlines on racing courses as far afield as Melbourne and Dubai as well as at Punchestown, Cheltenham, Ascot, Fairyhouse and the Curragh and their success has been another factor in attracting increased investment in Irish horses.

Veterinary Medicine: five year degree course at U.C.D.; 61 places, and 70 per cent of graduates find employment in Ireland.

Six British Universities also train vets – The Royal Veterinary College of London, as well as Bristol, Cambridge, Edinburgh, Glasgow and Liverpool universities.

There is virtually 100% job placement at the moment.

Veterinary Nurse: Two-year on-the-job training course. Training takes place in eight centres throughout the country and specialises in small animals. Unfortunately there are not many job opportunities when qualified. Over 200 people are training at present and there are approximately 300 working in this field. Further information from Irish Animal Nursing Association, Veterinary College, Pembroke Road, Dublin 4.

Horse Production/Stud Farming: B.Sc. in Equine Science at the University of Limerick – leads to opportunities in teaching, research, breeding, training, racecourse management, insurance and equine tourism.

One year post-graduate diploma in Equine Studies, Faculty of Agriculture, UCD. Courses at Kildalton College, the National Stud, Tully, Co. Kildare and Thomastown Vocational School, Kilkenny. Portlaoise Equestrian Centre also runs a full-time post-leaving cert course in Equestrian Studies. Contact Vocational School, Naas for details of equestrian PLC course.

Jockey: The Racing Apprentice Centre of Education in Kildare takes on about 26 pupils annually. Only a few make it as full-time jockeys, but the centre has a 100% record in placing students.

SUGGESTIONS

Join local branch of Foroige and carry out different agricultural projects . . . Visit local agriculture-based factories and co-ops in your area. Visit ENFO (Environmental Information Service . . . join conservation volunteers and get involved in environmental projects

Agriculture: Study Agricultural Science, Biology and Chemistry . . . rear your own stock . . . cultivate your own crops.

Horticulture: Take an interest in gardening/house plants . . . visit public gardens: Japanese Gardens, Kildare town, or Botanic Gardens, Dublin or National Garden Exhibition Centre, Kilquade, Co. Wicklow.

Forestry: Visit the National Forests and Parks . . . Cultivate an interest in wild life and your natural environment.

Animals, etc.: Attend local horse shows . . . go horse racing . . . attend dog shows, cat shows, etc. . . . join an animal welfare society.

FURTHER INFORMATION

TRAINING CENTRES

AGRICULTURE
Agricultural College, Ballyhaise, Co. Cavan. (049-38108)
Agricultural College, Darrara, Clonakilty, Co. Cork. (023-33302)
Franciscan Brothers Agricultural College, Mountbellew, Co. Galway (0905-79205)
Franciscan Agricultural College, Multyfarnham, Co. Westmeath. (044-71137)
Gurteen Agricultural College, Ballingarry, Roscrea, Co. Tipperary. (067) 21282
Kildalton Agricultural College, Piltown, Co. Kilkenny. (051-643105)
Mellowes Agricultural College, Athenry, Co. Galway. (091-845200)
Rockwell Agricultural College, Cashel, Co. Tipperary. (062-61436)
St. Patricks Agricultural College, Monaghan (047-81102)
Salesian Agricultural College, Pallaskenry, Co. Limerick. (061-393100)
Salesian College of Agriculture, Warrenstown, Drumree, Co. Meath. (01-8259342)

HORTICULTURE
An Grianan Horticultural College, Termonfechin, Drogheda, Co. Louth. (041-22158)
College of Amenity Horticulture, National Botanic Gardens, Glasnevin, Dublin 9. (01-8374388)
Kildalton Horticultural College, Piltown, Co. Kilkenny. (051) 643105
Salesian College of Horticulture, Warrenstown, Drumree, Co. Meath. (01-8259392)

OTHER ADDRESSES
Conservation Volunteers, Ballsbridge, Dublin 4. (01-6681844
Department of Agriculture, Kildare St., Dublin 2. (01-6072000).
ENFO (Environmental Information Service), 17 St. Andrews St., Dublin 2 (01-6793144).
Farm Apprenticeship Board, Irish Farm Centre, Bluebell, Dublin 12. (01-4501166).
Forestry Service, Leeson Lane, Dublin 2. (01-6199200).
Foroige, Irish Farm Centre, Bluebell, Dublin 12. (01-4501166).
Irish Animal Nursing Association, Veterinary College, Pembroke Rd., Dublin 4 (01-6687988).
Irish Creamery Milk Suppliers Association, 15 Upper Mallow St., Limerick (061-314677).
Irish Farmers Association, Irish Farm Centre, Bluebell, Dublin 12 (01-4500266).
Irish National Stud, Tully, Co. Kildare (045-521251).
Macra na Feirme, Irish Farm Centre, Bluebell, Dublin 12. (01-4508000).
Society of Irish Foresters, c/o Dept. of Forestry, 2 Lr. Kilmacud Road, Stillorgan. (01-2781874).
Teagasc, 19 Sandymount Avenue, Dublin 4. (01-6688188)
The Director, R.A.C.E., Curragh House, Kildare, Co. Kildare (045-521678).
Your local Teagasc office has information on grants, scholarships and training courses.

READ/VIEW
Video – Growing with Forests – Dept. of Agriculture
Irish Farmers Journal, Farming Independent, Irish Farmers Monthly, Irish Veterinary News, Pony Ireland, The Irish Garden.
Teagasc advisory leaflets available on all aspects of agriculture (free). ENFO leaflets on all aspects of environment (free), farming gardening, wildlife series on radio and TV.

ART/DESIGN/CRAFTS

Crafty collectors invest wisely

These are good times for new and emerging artists. The buoyant economy means that private collectors and corporate interests have more to spend on art, and indeed, given the low rates of interest available on savings at present, many are doing so not just for pleasure, but also for investment purposes.

But, while art dealing is a cyclical business which reflects the state of the economy, Irish artists are no longer dependent upon the Celtic Tiger. Irish art is increasingly being recognised internationally, and is no longer the poor relation of its European cousins. One recent, trusted barometer of the international art market put Irish 20th century painting up more than sixty per cent in value.

A scheme introduced by the Government three years ago has been especially beneficial for artists and sculptors. Under the scheme, one per cent of the construction budget for new and renovated public buildings and infrastructure can be used to purchase paintings, prints, sculpture and other specially commissioned art pieces.

Although the scheme has a ceiling of £50,000 on art per project, it has meant a huge boost for the emerging artistic community, galleries and associated businesses such as framers and artists' suppliers.

There's good news on the crafts front as well, with the current all time high demand for Irish pottery and craftware in Europe and America. Younger customers are looking for something distinctively Irish, but not the cliched shamrock and harp crafts their parents might have bought. Even some of Irish companies with a more traditional and loyal clientele are tapping this market now. John Rocha has designed bowls, glasses, vases and lamps for Waterford Crystal, while Paul Costello lent his talents to a range of glassware, and some very stylish and contemporary cutlery for Newbridge.

Irish pottery is especially popular abroad and at home, and has become an important industry for this country. Potters such as Louis Mulcahy, Nicholas Mosse, and Judy Green in Galway have expanded and established thriving export markets – banishing the image of pottery as the preserve of the hippy.

Crafts: Designing and making artifacts in ceramics, glass or metal. Courses in pottery, weaving and other crafts are available at College of Art and ITs around the country, also some post-leaving cert courses. The Crafts Council of Ireland runs courses in Design and Business Skills, which aim to make craftspeople more commercially aware.

Industrial Design: This is concerned with the design of manufactured goods – mass produced rather than crafted. There are two divisions – goods manufactured for industrial use and goods manufactured for consumer use. The industrial designer must ensure that the products he/she designs are easy to use, safe and good to look at.

Art colleges and ITs offer courses. At Letterfrack in Galway there's a unique two year diploma in fine woodwork and the making and design of furniture. It's run by Connemara West, a community-owned and management development organisation, with Galway-Mayo IT. Minimum entry requirement is a grade D in five Leaving Cert. subjects, including Maths and English or Irish. There is also a follow-on degree programme.

Animation: Animation is an element of some art college and IT courses. Studios often run in-house training for new employees. At the moment, it tends to be restricted to smaller companies, and there's more work in games than in film animation.

Don't forget to get working on your portfolio if you have an art college course in mind.

JOB SPEC

Arts Administrator

The expanding role of the Arts in Ireland has led to an increase in employment for Arts Administrators. These are employed in Arts Centres, County Councils, theatres, art galleries, festivals and community groups.

The work involves promoting artistic, musical or theatrical events, activities and festivals. This can vary from booking events and acts, to marketing, fund raising and publicising activities. The activities can include devising and organising programmes of events and exhibitions, arranging tours and dealing with accounts and reports.

For this job you would need to have good administrative skills for running your office and centre. You would need to be a good negotiator to arrange tours, artists, locations and publicity. You would need to be good at speaking in public and at promoting the arts and the events that you are organising. There may also be an educational aspect to your role in terms of promoting, interpreting or supporting the events in the centre.

Along with the capacity to administer and do the "housekeeping" of the centre, you must also have a deep and abiding interest in the arts. You must be passionate and enthusiastic about art and its capacity to inform, impress and communicate. So, a background in some of the arts would be very useful along with a qualification in some of the Arts Administration Diplomas and Degrees (UCD, NUIG, Dundalk etc.). This career offers you an opportunity to share your love and appreciation of the arts with a wider public and to promote greater participation and personal development.

Interior Designer: A lot of this work would involve deciding on decor and furnishing for show-houses and apartments, corporate offices etc. Also employed in some of the major stoes, as well as working on individual customers' homes. Must keep up with ever changing trends in furniture, fabrics and paint. A number of courses available in private colleges.

History of Art: Specialist degree courses at UCD and TCD. Art history is also an element of most art related courses. Opportunities in teaching, museum and gallery work.

Artist: Wide selection of art courses available at ITs and Vocational schools around the country, e.g. as well as the National College of Art and Design in Dublin, Dun Laoghaire IT, the Crawford Municipal School of Art in Cork, and Limerick IT. Most include drawing, sketching, painting, mixed media, print making, sculpture and photography in the first year and students later specialise. The NCAD DIT has a B.A. degree course in fine art. Most art colleges provide one-year foundation courses in art and design, or visual communications for students aspiring to a career in this field. Entry levels vary but a good portfolio is essential.

Photography: Two full-time courses available: a three year diploma course in Kevin Street College of Technology and a two-year course in the Dun Laoghaire IT. There is also a one year course in

33

Marino College, Dublin 3. (01-8339342) with City & Guilds and NCVA Certification. Photography is also an element of the Communications courses at DCU and DIT Aungier Street and of many art courses.

Arts Administration: The business of arts management has mushroomed in the last ten years. Previously, arts managers were often volunteers, but now there are 300 professional arts managers in the country. UCD offers a one year diploma course – applicants should have a degree and/or relevant work experience. UCG is also offering a one year Diploma in Arts Administration.

Perhaps one of our more famous arts administrators today is Dubliner Brian Kennedy, formerly Assistant Director of the National Gallery of Ireland and now Director of the National Gallery of Australia in Canberra.

Antiques: In somewhere like the United States, antiques advisors need their qualifications. Here, there's no certification system – it's mainly about contacts. The Institute of Professional Auctioneers and Valuers run a one year Diploma in Fine and Decorative Arts. UCC also has a Diploma in Irish Heritage Management for graduates in Irish History and Irish Studies.

SUGGESTIONS

Students interested in art should visit some of the following: Museums, Art Galleries (not forgetting the many private galleries), Shops, especially those specialising in antiques or crafts, e.g. Kilkenny Design or the Kilworth Craft Centre in Cork . . . Courtyards in Strokestown, Co. Roscommon; Roundstone near Connemara and Marley Park, Rathfarnham, Co. Dublin . . . Try to attend any local art exhibitions . . . there is an annual antique show in the Mansion House, Dublin, which is worth a visit . . . a craft exhibition is also held to coincide with the Horse Show in Dublin's R.D.S. . . . craft shows are frequently a feature of local agriculture shows.

Aspiring artists should also enter some of the many art competitions, e.g. Texaco Art Competition . . . borrow a picture from your local library . . . Visit community Arts Centres . . . Attend part-time and short-term courses available at VECs and ITs, as well as NCAD. These include Photography and Advertising Graphics, Interior Design, Display, Furniture Restoration, Lace Making, Crafts, Printmaking and Etching, Tailoring, Woodcarving, Pottery, Leathering, Enamelling and Weaving.

FURTHER INFORMATION

Art Teachers Association, Blackrock Teachers' Centre, Carysfort Ave., Carysfort, Blackrock, Co. Dublin.

Artists Association in Ireland, Arthouse House, Temple Bar, Dublin 2 (01-8740529).

Crafts Council of Ireland, 12 East Essex St., Dublin 2 (01-6778467).

Grafton Academy of Dress Designing, 6 Herbert Place, Dublin 2 (01-6767940).

Grennan Millcraft School, Millstreet, Thomastown, Co. Kilkenny (056-24514).

Forbairt Enterprise Centre, Pearse Street, Dublin 2 (01-6775655).

Institute of Advertising Practitioners in Ireland, 8 Upr. Fitzwilliam Street, Dublin 2 (01-6765991).

Irish Countrywomen's Association, 58 Merrion Road, Dublin (01-6684052). The Association has provided some courses.

Kilworth Craft Centre, Kilworth, Co. Cork.

Marley Park Craft Courtyard, Grange Road, Dublin 14.

Society of Designers in Ireland, 67A Upper Georges St., D'Laoire (01-2841477).

The Arts Council, 70 Merrion Square, Dublin 2 (01-6180200).

Tiernan Design School, G.C.D., Dublin 8. (01-4545599).

READ/VIEW

A Guide to Art Galleries in Ireland by Patricia Butler (Gill & Macmillan).

Career in Design — Society of Designers in Ireland.

CDCTV video on art portfolio preparation.

Directory NCEA approved courses in Higher Education (NCEA).

Essential reading is the *Writers and Artists Yearbook*.

Irish Arts Review, Amateur Photographer, Antique Collector, Art and Craft, Art Journal, Artforum, Craft Review, Design, Practical Photography.

Setting up and Running your own Craft Workshop (Craft Council of Ireland).

CIVIL SERVICE/LOCAL GOVERNMENT/SEMI STATE

Dramatic Drop in Application Numbers

CAREERS IN THIS CATEGORY

Many of the careers listed below are outlined on the FÁS Gairm Database

Administrative Officer; Arts and Science Graduates; Clerical Officer; Clerical Assistant; Coroner; Executive Officer; Assistant Officer of Customs and Excise; Higher Officer of Customs and Excise; Higher Tax Officer; District Court Clerk; Junior Clerk in the Offices of the Supreme Court and High Court; Court Stenographer; Inspector of Taxes; Third Secretary in Foreign Affairs; Social Welfare Officer; Cartographical Trainee; An Post Clerk; Post Person; Telephonist; Local Government Clerical Officer; Clerk Typist; Clerical Officer in Dublin Corporation; General Worker in Dublin Corporation; Firefighter; Town Clerk; Agricultural Officer; Industrial Inspector; Air Traffic Control Assistant; Architectural Technician; Draughtsman; Forester; Forestry Graduate; Forensic Scientist; Laboratory Technician; Civil Engineer in Civil Service; Assistant Agricultural Inspector; Driver Tester; Inspector of Taxes; Assistant Meteorological Officer; Statistician; Meteorologist; Press Officer; Typist and Shorthand Typist; Trainee Installer; Trainee Technician; Night Telephonist; Health Inspector; Library Assistant; Porter; Paper Keeper; Refuse Collector.

Jobs in the civil service were once highly sought after by school leavers and graduates. This was particularly true during the bad employment years of the eighties. Although there was little civil service recruitment, such jobs represented security at a time when employment prospects were grim.

But the booming economy has had an impact even upon the civil service, with a dramatic fall now in the number of people applying for such jobs. This suggests that the increasing demand for workers from the private sector, which has affected areas like recruitment to nursing, is extending across the public service.

At the time of writing, the Civil Service Commission, which had just compiled its first panel in four years, was expected to have to start another recruitment programme to have enough clerical staff. Last year 10,000 people applied to the civil service for interview, compared with 27,000 four years ago. Only 16,000 turned up for interview, compared with 19,000.

Yet, the civil service does retain some if its attractions. Although the wages for clerical grades aren't high, there are promotion prospects, and opportunities to work outside Dublin for those who seek them.

Under the Government's programme of decentralisation, which is nearing completion, almost half of the civil service now operates outside the capital. The size of the public service in Dublin has remained the same for almost twenty years, while an increase of over two thirds in the number of local authority staff, together with large scale civil service decentralisation, has doubled the number of public servants in many counties around Ireland.

The Government has put in place a retraining programme for civil servants, parts of which have yet to be implemented. Known as the Strategic Management Initiative, it aims to encourage greater responsibility and accountability, and bring in a system of merit pay, to award high performing civil servants at every level.

The Civil Service can be divided into three broad categories:

1. The general service grade, so called because all or most of them are found in all departments, e.g. clerical officers, executive officers and administrative officers. Open recruitment is available to school leavers at clerical assistant and executive officer level, although increasingly, the latter will be degree holders. Recruitment then to positions such as clerical officer and higher executive officer is by internal promotion. Administrative officers would be selected at graduate level . . . some would even be qualified as barristers or solicitors.

2. Grades specialising in work peculiar to one department, e.g. Inspector of Taxes at the

Office of the Revenue Commissioners, or Third Secretary at the Department of Foreign Affairs – again these would be graduates.

3. Professional/technical grades. These would range from driver tester or prison officer to agricultural officer or trainee auditor.

Recruitment to all positions is through the Civil Service Commission, and advertisements are placed in the national newspapers. The selection process for the general grades usually involves written tests and interview – it can be complex and time consuming, as taking on new people involves a significant investment by the State.

Local Government: In all there are 117 local authorities, made up of county councils, county boroughs, borough corporations, urban district councils, and boards of town commissioners. Local Government decisions are largely made by the country's 1600 elected councillors, and are then implemented by administrators and a range of employees in a wide variety of departments such as housing, traffic, planning, engineering and general service.

Recruitment has been steady in recent years. Clerical vacancies particularly can often be filled at some time later from a panel of applicants selected from competition, so it's important to go forward for jobs as they arise.

Apprenticeships: Recruitment in a variety of trades such as bricklayer, plumber, plasterer and fitter.

Librarian: Diploma course at UCD. Students are either graduates or have worked as library assistants.

Arts Officer: UCD arts administration qualification and/or relevant experience.

Fire Fighter: The vast majority of local authorities have their own fire brigades. The biggest is Dublin Corporation, where 740 fire fighters respond to 75,000 calls a year – many of which are emergency ambulance calls.

Applicants must be male, aged between 20 and 25 and over 5'6" tall, with an Inter/Junior Cert. and full driving licence. A knowledge of mechanics and building techniques is also an advantage.

Fire Prevention Officer: Local authorities take on both male and female architects or engineers for this job.

Meteorological Service: 325 people are employed to look after the collection, processing and supply of weather information in Ireland. People involved in weather-sensitive pursuits have a special interest in the weather and sea forecasts. They include aircraft crews, oil explorers, fishermen and crews of fishery patrol vessels.

Assistant Meteorological Officer: Makes weather observations, examines climatological records and handles the processing of meteorological data.

Meteorological Officer: Compiles statistics, analyses weather conditions and plans weather reports.

Semi-State: Under EU competition law, the State companies can no longer have a monopoly on the services they provide. Over the next few years, customers will increasingly be able to choose which phone company they subscribe to, where they buy their electricity etc. Indeed much of this is already in place in the telecommunications sector, with companies like ESAT competing with Telecom for the mobile phone market, and, more recently, business and domestic landline accounts.

Many of the semi-states, like Telecom, the ESB and Bord Gais, have been shedding jobs rather than taking people on, as they trim down their operations in preparation for the open market. EU membership has had its impact in other ways too, particularly upon Aer Rianta, which is under pressure because of the abolition of duty free sales within Europe.

SUGGESTIONS

Get involved with local community activities — Have you considered joining a working committee to tidy your locality or organise summer projects? Watch current affairs programmes . . . Use your local library more effectively thus familiarising yourself with a job like librarian — some libraries now provide cassettes, records, paintings and they may even be able to offer a photocopying service . . . Students should visit their local youth information centre . . . Specialist jobs like meteorologist will mean paying particular attention to physics, geography and also to radio and T.V. weather reports . . . For administrative positions typing and computer skills would help . . . Arrange to sit in on corporation or council meetings.

FURTHER INFORMATION

Addresses of Local Authorities and Boroughs are listed in this directory (see Index).

Government Information Services, Upper Merrion Square, Dublin 2 (01-6624422).

Government Publications Office, Sun Alliance Building, Molesworth St., Dublin 2 (01-6613111).

Institute of Pubic Administration, 49 Lansdowne Road, Dublin 4. (01-6059530). (Training body for the Civil Service and Local Government).

The Secretary, Civil Service Commission, 1 Lower Grand Canal St., Dublin 2 (01-6615611). (Recruits all Civil Servants).

READ/VIEW

A Key to the Services of Dublin Corporation
Annual Reports of semi-state bodies.
Specialised magazines, e.g. *CARA* produced by Aer Lingus.
The Institute of Public Administration have publications which are essential reading for those interested in the Public Service – *Administration magazines, Administration Yearbook and Diary.*

COMPUTERS & INFORMATION TECHNOLOGY

CAREERS IN THIS CATEGORY

Many of the careers listed below are outlined on the FÁS Gairm Database

Non-Management:
Programmer/Software Developer/Software Engineer; Programmer/Analyst; Systems Designer; Database Designer; Systems Engineer; Systems Programmer; Systems Analyst; Business Analyst; Data Modeller; Network Administrator; Database Administrator; Technical Writer; Researcher; Software/Product Tester; Technical Support Consultant; Sales Support Consultant; Software Trainer; Consultant; Sales Engineer.

Management:
Team Leader; Project Leader; Data Processing Manager; Information Technology Manager; Information Systems Manager; Product Manager; Project Manager; Director of Information Technology; Marketing Manager; Sales Manager.

Software boom in Ireland

Ireland boasts one of the most high-tech economies in Europe. After the US, Ireland exports more software than any other country in the world. Over 40% of all PC packaged software sold in Europe is produced in Ireland.

According to the Expert Group on Future Skills, Ireland is going to need 2,400 computer science graduates and 2,100 computer science technicians each year up to 2003. Opportunity Ireland aims to encourage 5,000 skilled software and electronics professionals to Ireland in the next three years. This shortage is not just confined to Ireland or even Europe; the US for example is said to need an extra 100,000 software professionals. Because of this shortage computer science graduates can command starting salaries up to and in some cases more than £15,000.

The IT industry is a very competitive one. Lower grade assembly work in the hardware part of industry has been affected in Ireland this year with the loss of 450 jobs in Apple Computers in Cork.

Computer courses generally have both hardware and software units, as well as other options such as business studies and languages, which could be useful in some of the areas detailed below. Also, maths, science and engineering courses often allow for specialisation in computing.

For instance, a computer systems degree will tend to be suitable for students who see themselves working as computer programmers, systems analysts, consultants or researchers. Students who take languages and computing may end up in software localisation and technical writing.

A huge variety of courses are available at FÁS, PLC and third level. *(Check the relevant sections of the Yearbook for details)*.

Software: The software sector currently comprises more than 550 companies, 80% of which are Irish. The sector is growing at the rate of 15% a year, with annual exports of more than three billion pounds. At least 4,500 additional recruits are needed annually, and everyone with a decent qualification is virtually guaranteed a job.

There are a great range of jobs in the software industry, these include:

Programming: Involves writing instructions for a computer to accomplish tasks. Programmers must display logic, imagination and have good interpersonal skills. There are two basic types of programmer; an applications programmer or a systems programmer.

Systems designers: they use computers to improve the way information is processed and communicated within an organisation. They decide what sort of software is needed in an organisation, install and test the system, and make decisions about its maintenance.

Technical writing: Whenever there's a new piece of computer hard/software, there's always a manual, or on-screen literature. You don't need a computing qualification but you do need to understand how computers work. Importantly you need good writing and communication skills, as well as the confidence to work in a technical environment.

Localisation: This means adapting the software/programme to suit the language/country they are being used in. The main parts in need of adaptation are: documentation, software and packaging. A degree in computational linguistics would be an advantage, however there are still openings for language graduates with a good practical knowledge of computer software.

Marketing and Sales: Technical knowledge isn't an essential element to ensuring success, but the ability to impress potential clients with some knowledge will go a long way. Essential skills would include communication, and personality.

Multimedia: A recent report has suggested that the Irish multimedia industry could employ 9,000 people by the year 2000, if the output of programmers and engineers is increased. It says the industry has a minimum requirement for 650 technical staff, 575 creative staff and 525 management staff over the next three years. The sector has been compared to software in the early nineties

Hardware: The term hardware applies to the physical components of the computer. A qualification in electronics is useful for working in the hardware sector of IT. The hardware industry here has attracted some of the major players in the industry worldwide. The market is booming on the back of strong growth in computers, communications and industrial electronics. Many companies in the networking

JOB SPEC

Software Localisation

As you probably know Ireland is the second largest exporter of computer software in the world (after the USA) and there are huge opportunities for computer graduates in Ireland at the moment. Indeed there are worries that there is a skills shortage in the industry and the shortage of computer graduates is driving the salaries upwards.

The availability of skilled workers and our capacity to speak English along with our position within the European Union are the main reasons companies set up here. The majority of these companies are from the USA and wish to sell their products to Europe. To do this they need to adapt them to European consumers and businesses. This is the work done by Software Localiser. This can vary from changing $ to £ or/and adapting spelling and date conventions, to re-recording multimedia programmes to give a more European feel, and changing the emphasis in encyclopaedias from baseball and American football to cricket and soccer for a world market. In other cases it may involve translating whole programmes into another language, not only French and German but also Finnish to Turkish.

As with all computer programming this work demands accuracy, a logical mind and also a capacity to think creatively and find novel solutions to problems. The work is project based in teams and it is really important to be able to work well with others and to meet deadlines and co-ordinate effort. You don't particularly need to be a whiz kid at Maths but you would need to be comfortable with them. You do need to be able to think logically and sequentially, but flexible enough to see solutions by lateral thinking. Skills in languages (especially minority languages) are greatly valued.

There are a huge number of courses available in computer science, programming and applications in universities and Institutes of Technology all of which could lead to work as a software localiser. It is important to realise that while you might love to play games on computers, working with them is a completely different experience. If you like it though, there are enormous opportunities that await you. Click here to begin!

industry are expanding at the rate of 40% per year.

The IT market is volatile and subject to extreme cost-cutting measures, as witnessed by the Seagate plant in Clonmel and Apple Computers in Cork.

SUGGESTIONS

Plague your parents to buy a computer . . . not just for games! Experiment with software packages, e.g. word processing or careers programmes like Qualifax . . . Visit a cyber café . . . Check out the computer facilities in your school or local Youth Information Centre . . . Remember there are two sides to computers . . . Software (programming the computer) and Hardware (electronic and mechanical engineering) . . . Check out the appropriate courses . . . Buy some computer magazines . . . Look at some of the science/computing programmes on TV.

FURTHER INFORMATION

National Software Directorate, Forbairt, Wilton Place, Dublin 2 (01-8082983) email: www.nsd.ie (for a full list of software companies).

Irish Software Association, 84 Lr. Baggot St., Dublin 2 (01-6051566).

All Universities and Institutes of Technology, plus most of the PLC Colleges.

READ VIEW

Careers in Computers, Forbairt.
PCs for Dummies, IDG Books.
The PC Novice's Handbook, H. Kotecha, Computer Step.
Basic Computing Principles, ed. B. West, NCC Blackwell.
How to use Computers, ZD Press.
Simple C, McGregor, et al, Addison-Wesley.
Computer Science, C.S. French, Letts Educational.

Computers and Information Technology Courses

See PLC and FÁS sections for other computer courses.	Business Information Systems	Computational Linguistics	Applied Computing/ Computer Applications	Business (Computing)	Commercial Computing	Computer Aided Engineering	Computer Engineering	Computer Networking	Computer Science	Computer & Languages	Information Technology	Multimedia	Programming	Software Development
Athlone IT								●						
Blanchardstown								●				●		
Carlow IT	●								●	●	●			
Cork IT			●						●	●	●			●
DBS				●										
DCU		●	●		●		●	●						
DIT			●						●					
Dundalk IT			●								●			●
Dun Laoghaire													●	
Galway IT	●		●											●
Griffith									●					
IT Tralee									●					
Letterkenny IT								●		●				
Limerick IT			●		●			●						●
LSB												●		
NCI			●											
NUIG								●				●		
NUI Maynooth									●					
Sligo IT					●		●	●						
Tallaght IT												●		
TCD									●	●	●	●		
Tipperary												●		
UCC	●								●					
UCD									●					
UL												●	●	
Waterford IT			●			●							●	

CONSTRUCTION/TRADES & PROFESSIONAL

Skills famine in construction trades

CAREERS IN THIS CATEGORY
Many of the careers listed below are outlined on the FÁS Gairm Database

Mason; Steel erectors; Fireplace builder; Bricklayer; Carpenter; Electrician; Construction plant fitter; Glazier; Plumber; Pipe layer; Welder; Pipe jointer; Gas fitter; Slater and roof tiler; Thatcher; Steeplejack; Cabinet maker; Wood machinist; Upholsterer; Wood finisher; Tile layer; Raker (asphalt etc.); Heating and Ventilation Technician; Tamperman; Building operative-/helper; Stone cleaning/preservation; Driver — crane, earth moving equipment, road roller, mechanical shovel, bull dozer, dumper etc; Land surveyor; Valuation surveyor; Architect; Architectural Technician; Civil/structural engineer; Civil Engineering Technician; Draughtsperson; Building Technician; Quantity Surveyor; Quantity Survey Technician; Interior designer; Auctioneer; Painter and decorator; Signwriter; French polisher; Plasterer; Quarry Manager; Estimator; Maintenance/Servicing; Production co-ordinator. Waste removal/Skip operators; Drain layer; Insulation layer; Stone Cutter; Town Planner; Builders Providers/D.I.Y.; Plant-Hire Workers.

Construction employment has increased from 100,800 in april 1996 to 136,300 in May 1998, representing almost 10% of the total labour force. Construction output is set to reach £9 billion this year, up 9% on last year. This follows a record 12% growth last year when a record of almost 39,000 houses were built.

The annual survey of the construction industry, by the Department of the Environment shows that between 1994 and 1997 building output has grown by 65%. The growth rate was unprecedented in the history of the State and had not been matched by any other EU member in recent years.

This year the construction sector will account for one-fifth of national income, up from 14%. Average weekly earnings in the construction sector increased by 11 per cent last year. There was also a significant increase in the numbers at work.

News on the construction industry is not all good; by its nature, the building industry is unpredictable and cyclical with a boom or slump generally lasting a few years. But while Ireland continues to experience this economic boom the construction industry will grow.

There are skills shortages in the trade areas within the construction industry. In the future it is predicted that the most notable shortages will be for electricians and painters. Major skills deficits are also projected for plasterers, bricklayers and plant fitters over the next five years. To deal with the shortage more people have been taken on in apprenticeships. FÁS figures showed a 5% increase in registrations for apprenticeships.

Operative Level: Steel erectors, pipe layers, brickwork cleaners and restorers, drivers and machine operators, demolition strippers, scaffolders and concretors. With increasing mechanisation, new areas of work are open to the operative. Sometimes this involves on-site training but a number of courses are offered by FÁS including general engineering for operatives, fork truck operator and heavy goods vehicle driver.

Up to 20,000 general operatives are now employed in the construction sector. In the past, these jobs would have been regarded as unskilled, but increasingly workers are acquiring qualifications and competency standards.

Non Designated Semi-Skilled Construction Workers: These include very important jobs, some of which offer opportunities to young people with the initiative and determination to set up their own business: they include cladders; roofers/asphalters; floor/wall tiler; dry liner; rigger/steel; erector/scaffolder; insulator/lagger; steelfixer/concretor and pipelayers.

Construction Designated Trades — Craft Level (See FÁS for further details): FÁS has introduced a new, standards based apprentice scheme which involves on-the-job training with an employer and off the job training in a FÁS training centre or educational college. Apprenticeships in the construction trade include: bricklayer, carpenter/joiner, construction plant fitter, electrician, fitter, painter/decorator, floor/wall tiler, plasterer, plumber, wood machinist.

Technician Level: These include engineering and architectural technicians, quantity surveying technicians and site clerks. Many Institutes of Technology and the D.I.T. provide 2-year certificate and 3-year diploma courses. Limerick IT also offer courses. Their work would include the design and preparation of drawings and schedules of construc-

1. For details of courses consult College Propectuses.
2. See index for Post Leaving Certificate Courses.
3. See index for FÁS Courses.

	T.C.D.	N.U.I., Galway	U.C.C.	U.C.D.	U.L.	D.I.T.	Athlone IT	Cork IT	Galway–Mayo IT	Sligo IT	Waterford (WIT)	IT Carlow	Dundalk IT	Letterkenny IT	IT Tralee	Limerick IT	Dun Laoghaire
Architecture			●			●		●			●	●				●	
Auctioneering/Property Management						●			●							●	
Building Maintenance/Management						●			●								
Building Services						●		●									
Construction Economics/Quanity Surveying						●					●					●	
Construction Studies						●	●	●	●	●	●	●	●	●	●	●	
Construction Technician						●											
Engineering/Civil	●	●	●	●		●	●	●	●	●	●	●	●	●	●	●	
Engineering/Structural	●																
Geomatics						●											
Construction Management								●		●							
Model Making																	●
Property Economics								●								●	
Earth Science		●	●														
Furniture Design/Wood Science						●			●								

tion projects and would necessitate the monitoring and inspection of on-site works.

Management Level: A one-year diploma in building management is available at Galway IT. Limerick IT offers a diploma in site management.

Professional Level Jobs: These would normally require degree standard qualifications in areas such as engineering, architecture, planning and costing.

Architecture: The majority are self employed, with just 40% in salaried positions. Degrees at UCD and Bolton St. College of Technology.

DIT offers a degree in Environmental Design. Sligo IT offers a diploma in interior architecture while Tiernan Design School offers courses in both interior architecture and interior decoration.

The DIT, Bolton St., Limerick, Cork and Waterford ITs offer courses preparing students to become architectural technicians – preparing plans to an architect's specifications. Increasingly, this is done by means of CAD or computer-aided design, Most certificate, diploma and degree courses in architecture and engineer-

ing will incorporate this, but there are also a number of PLC options available.

Higher Education Authority figures show that 85% of 1997 graduates of architecture gained employment in Ireland within eight months of graduating and only 1.4% were unemployed compared with 16.1% in 1992.

Chartered Surveyor: Chartered surveyors are employed wherever there is land, property or construction. They work to develop and maintain the visible environments which affect all of our lives – from shopping centres to marinas; from historic buildings to industrial estates.

Civil Engineering: This refers to major projects such as roads, bridges or sanitary services. Up to now, it has been the sector of the construction industry showing the least activity in terms of growth and employment levels. But many EU funded projects which have been in the pipeline for some time are now coming to fruition. This year, civil engineering is expected to grow by 17%, with new contracts of almost £900 million.

Construction Studies: Some ITs offer a two year

certificate in construction studies. It gives a basic knowledge and understanding of the business, including costing, surveying, administration and management. Some specialise more in areas like architectural graphics or construction economics.

Town Planner: Post-graduate courses at U.C.D. Queens University in Belfast offers an undergraduate course leading to a B.Sc. in Environmental Planning. It's possible then to go on to their Diploma in Town and Country Planning. The courses at Queens are recognised by the Irish Planning Institute. DIT runs a diploma in Environmental Resources Management which trains technicians in urban and rural planning.

The majority of planners hold posts in central and local government, but there are significant numbers working in architecture and planning practices.

Building Maintenance: Many large properties such as hotels and educational institutions need maintenance people on a full time basis. The College of Technology, Bolton Street has a Building Maintenance Technician Certificate course, aimed at producing people who can take complete charge of maintenance.

Auctioneering: The Irish Auctioneers and Valuers Institute estimates that the number of queries it received about third level courses almost doubled last year. There are three auctioneering, valuation and estate agency courses at Bolton St., Galway and Limerick IT's, also a property degree at Bolton Street and Limerick IT, which is recognised by the Irish Auctioneers and Valuers Institute.

Ballsbridge College of Business Studies has a PLC course in auctioneering skills recognised by the IAVI.

The IPAV run certificate courses at Cork College of Commerce and Dun Laoghaire Senior College. Graduates may go on to study for a diploma or degree.

The job opportunities for those graduating in the estate agency/auctioneering fields are not very good – only between 15% and 20% get jobs.

Employment outside estate agents includes property management for companies like Aer Rianta, CIE and the IDA.

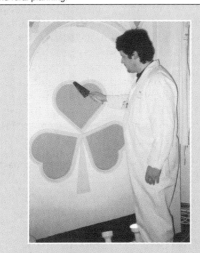

FÁS APPRENTICESHIP SCHEME

There are a wide variety of trades in the construction industry. FÁS trains most of the apprentices in this sector.

During the apprenticeship the trainee will be required to follow a specific course of training and undergo a series of assessments to confirm that they have reached the required standards.

Apprenticeship consists of 7 phases of training both on-the-job with your employer and off-the job in a FÁS Training Centre or Educational College. See Apprenticehip Section in this Yearbook.

SUGGESTIONS

Apprenticeships are very difficult to get; students should be seeking them well in advance of leaving school. Those interested in apprenticeship should seek some kind of practical work experience in the area of their interest whether it be work at home, or helping neighbours at the weekends or during the summer months. If possible, at your school, choose subjects such as building construction . . . technical drawing . . . science . . . woodwork and art . . . Work on a building site . . . offer to do or assist with maintenance in your home, e.g. painting and decorating, electrical work . . . seek work experience in a drawing office . . . note buildings in your locality . . . help with residents associations, conservation groups, etc. . . . for architecture pay special attention to your space relations score in aptitude testing . . . attend Dublin Institute of Technology lectures on Quantity Surveying, trades, etc. . . . Prepare a Portfolio for courses like architecture.

FURTHER INFORMATION

An Taisce, Old Court Hse, Harbour Road, Howth, Co. Dublin (01-8392053).

Construction Industry Federation, Federation House, Canal Road, Dublin 6 (01-4977487).

Electrical Trade Union, 5 Cavendish Row, Dublin (01-8745935).

FÁS, 27-33 Baggot St., Dublin 4 (01-6070500).

Institute of Professional Auctioneers and Valuers, 39 Upr. William St., Dublin 2 (01-6785685).

Irish Auctioneers and Valuers Institute, 38 Merrion Sq., Dublin 2 (01-6611794).

Ordnance Survey, Phoenix Park, Dublin 8 (01-8206100).

Plasterers and Allied Trades Society of Ireland, 13 Blessington St., Dublin 7 (01-8304270).

Royal Institute of Architects in Ireland, 8 Merrion Sq., Dublin 2 (01-6761703).

The Institution of Engineers of Ireland, 22 Clyde Rd., Dublin 4 (01-6684341).

The Society of Chartered Surveyors of Ireland, 5 Wilton Place, Dublin 2 (01-6765500).

Union of Construction Allied Trade and Technicians, 56 Parnell Square, Dublin 1 (01-8731599).

READ

Standard Based Apprenticeships – FÁS.

Build, Construction and Property News, Irish Heating and Ventilating News — periodicals.

Irish Architect, Property Valuer.

Read property sections in newspapers. And some of the many D.I.Y. magazines available.

Training Courses for Adults and Apprentices — FÁS.

DEFENCE FORCES/ GARDA/LEGAL/SECURITY

Recruitment Crisis in the Defence Forces

There has been a dramatic fall in the number of people applying for jobs in the defence forces. In 1998, army applications were just 2,023 compared to 9,306 in 1993. Applications for cadetship were also down from 2,090 in 1994 to 854 in 1998. Ireland has one of the smallest defence forces in Europe. The forces have already been reduced from 12,700 to 11,500. The Department of Finance in its submission on the future of the Defence Forces has proposed cutbacks – costing at least another 3,500 jobs and amalgamating the Air Corps and Naval Service into a "coastguard service". The Defence forces union, the PDFORRA, however, has proposed that there be increased investment in forces and an expansion of the army, so it remains to be seen what the government will decide.

CAREERS IN THIS CATEGORY

Many of the careers listed below are outlined on the FÁS Gairm Database

Barrister-at-Law; Garda and Ban Garda; Prison Officer; Air Corps Apprentice; Air Corps Cadet; Army Apprentice; Army Bandsman; Army Cadet; Soldier; Security Officer; Store and Hotel Detective; Law Clerk; Solicitor; Firefighter; Fire Safety Officer; Private Detective; Security Officer; Patrolman; Park Ranger; Traffic Warden; Naval Service Cadet; Naval Service Rating; Marine Engineer (navy); Judge; County Registrar; Parliamentary Draftsperson; Planning Inspector; Court Messenger; Probate Officer; Taxing Master; Legal Secretary.

So severe is the shortage of personnel the Department of Defence may have to recruit from outside the State to meet a staffing crisis within the Naval Service. Such is the low level of morale within the Naval Service that officers have been leaving just short of retirement to take up more attractive jobs elsewhere. Overall numbers are below strength, at 'around" 1,000, according to the Department of Defence. Although the contract for a new £20 million ship was placed just before Christmas, there are fears that there won't be anyone to crew it.

In the Gardaí there will be a new recruitment drive in 2,000. With a Government commitment to getting numbers up to 12,000 ad an existing force of 10,600, this will mean a larger recruitment drive and an injection of young blood into a force that is undergoing massive change. There is also a £2.3 million expansion plan for the Garda college in Templemore.

There has been much furore about prison officers and pay in recent times. Central Statistics Office figures on public sector earnings show prison officers as the best-paid public servants, earning an average of £675.99 per week. However in the prison services it is claimed that job satisfaction levels are low, sick leave is high and most earnings are made from overtime.

Cadets: Applicants should be aged between 17 and 22, but the upper limit is higher for those with FCA service or a degree. The minimum qualification is the Leaving Cert, with grade C or higher in three subjects and grade D in three others. The subjects must include Irish or English, Maths or Applied Maths, a European Language or Latin or Greek. There is an aptitude test for the Air Corps and Navy, as well as interviews and medical examinations for all three disciplines.

All cadets complete a 21-moth course at the Cadet School in the Curragh. Air Corp Cadets then complete Basic Flying Training Wing in Baldonnel. After initial training and a 16-month period with a military unit all army cadets do a degree course, normally at NUI Galway. Cadets in the Naval Service train in the Naval Base in Cork after initial training in the Curragh. They too have the option to take a degree in NUI Galway usually in areas such as Oceanography, Meteorology, Maritime law and Marine Biology.

Apprentices: The army takes on people as trainee carpenters, electricians, fitters, motor mechanics and radio mechanics. Vacancies in the navy are as engine room artificer, electrical artificer and shipwright. The Air Corps takes on aircraft technicians. Applicants should be aged between 16 and 19. The minimum standard is Junior Cert and there are two interviews.

Army Recruit: Applicants between 17 and 22. Education to a satisfactory general standard. Initial training period of 16 weeks followed by a fixed term of 5 years.

Gardai: This year will see a major recruitment drive by the Gardaí, the first in three years. As in other years it is expected that there will be a huge number of applicants so competition will be very stiff. Selection is by means of written tests, medical examination and interview. Candidates are selected on the basis of their capacity for preforming the basic functions of police work and for having a general aptitude for working with people. Social changes have changed the work of the Garda and this is reflected in the two-year training at the Garda College in Templemore. Trainees study law, procedure, social science and communications, first aid and self-defence as well as Irish and a foreign language.

Recently, the requirements for applying for a place at The Garda College, Templemore have changed. Candidates no longer need five D's in the Leaving Cert. – a merit grade in the Applied Leaving Cert. will now suffice, and foundation level in Irish. Applicants must also sit an aptitude test, and go for an interview.

Applicants should be not less that 5'9" for men or 5'5" for women, they should also be between 18 and 26, although extensions are allowed in some cases for applicants who have spent some time in the FCA or the Defence Forces.

Prison Service: The minimum requirement for prison officers is the Inter or Junior Cert and applicants should be aged between 18 and 30. Both men and women are recruited – women prison officers are employed in Limerick and Mountjoy prisons. Advertisements are placed for these jobs as the need arises.

Work is underway on new prisons or cell units at Castlerea, Wheatfield and Mountjoy, which will create 600 more cells for prisoners. This should create some new job opportunities for prison officers.

Private Security: Crime and security costs £160 million a year to businesses in Dublin alone, so it's hardly surprising that private security is a growth area.

Ringsend Technical Institute offers a certificate in security studies, while both Dun Laoghaire Community College and Cork College of Commerce have diplomas in business management and security studies.

The College of Marketing and Design also runs a two year course in Security Studies with an option of a third year to reach diploma level. The Security Institute of Ireland and the International Professional Security Association also run courses.

The Legal Profession: Law is still a very popular career choice for school leavers, despite the poor employment prospects and financial hardship in the early years for those who do persevere. However, many students do law as a good, basic degree for a career in business, for example. Some Law degrees combine law with other subjects such as business, accountancy, European studies, and languages.

Solicitors: Aspiring solicitors, take a law degree, followed by an apprenticeship combined with further study at the Incorporated Law Society.

In the past, holders of certain designated law degrees, such as the original 'pure' law degrees offered by the universities, were exempt from having to sit the entrance exam set by the Incorporated Law Society. This has recently changed however, and now the holders of such degrees must sit the exam along with non-law graduates, and people with hybrid law degrees.

There is also quite a long wait – sometimes 18 months – for an available course, and the required apprenticeship to a solicitor can prove difficult to secure.

Non law graduates tend to do a course such as DIT's diploma in legal studies to prepare for the exam. Everyone who passes the entrance exam is entitled to train as a solicitor but must wait until a place becomes available on a training course.

Other courses are available at ITs which qualify people as law clerks and legal secretaries.

Barristers: On completing an approved law degree it is necessary to complete a two-year barrister-at-law degree at the King's Inn. Admission is very competitive, 50% of the places are reserved for graduates of approved degrees.

Along with the pure law degrees at the various universities, the King's Inns also recognises some hybrid law degrees, such as Law/Accountancy and Law/European studies at UL, also Law/French and Law/German at TCD and UCD, but admission is not guaranteed, and usually depends on the results achieved in the primary law degree.

At present, holders of other degrees must first take a two year legal studies diploma at the King's Inns and then apply for the degree course. But this situation may change, and it's wise to keep in touch with Kings Inns on requirements.

Lesley Walsh
Soldier

Growing up in Newbridge, County Kildare, close to the Curragh Camp, meant that Corporal Lesley Walsh always had a fair idea what life in the army involved.

Lesley was keen to be a part of it. The army held a recruitment drive when she was in fifth year at the Holy Family Secondary School in Newbridge. She applied, but, at 16, was too young. After the Leaving Cert she took a two-year PLC in recreation and leisure management in Inchicore. In 1994 she applied to the army again, and was accepted.

"I started off with six months basic training at the Curragh to become a two star private. After another ten weeks I progressed to three stars. It was very physical, and there were no set hours. We lived in the barracks, and there were often late lectures, or night navigation after a full day."

Lesley has completed quite a lot of training in the use of weapons - rifles, machine guns and anti-tank weapons. "Then in late '97, I was accepted for an Non Commissioned Officer's course. You have to be recommended for it - It's a big career development course to get."

The course involved five and a half months of training. "Some of it is the same as a management course you'd do outside the Defence Forces, " she says. It qualified Lesley, now 25 and promoted to Corporal, to instruct new recruits. She hopes to take another course to become a sergeant.

The army, she says, is a more popular career choice for women now. "When I started, there were only four women in my unit. Now there are 15."

Life as a fledgling barrister can be very precarious. After qualifying and a year of "devilling" for a master, getting enough briefs to sustain yourself in the law library can take years, during which you will probably have to be subsidised.

SUGGESTIONS

Join the FCA, Order of Malta, St. Johns Ambulance, Civil Defence or Red Cross . . . get involved in youth clubs, debating societies, schools debating competitions . . . become more interested in civic matters . . . read the Constitution . . . read newspapers regularly and brush up on current affairs . . . for intending Army apprentices get summer or weekend experience in your desired trade area . . . likewise for those who wish to join the Army equitation unit or Army band, you should have already developed some of your skills in these areas.

Talk to local gardai, including liaison officers . . . visit your local fire unit . . . spend some time in court — observing of course!

Take more of an interest in physical education and games . . . If you are seventeen, get a driving licence.

FURTHER INFORMATION

Public Relations Office, Garda Siochana Headquarters, Phoenix Park, Dublin 8 (01-6771156).

Civil Defence School, Phoenix Park, Dublin 8 (01-8042000).

Dept. of Defence, Colaiste Caoimhin, Glasnevin, Dublin 9. (01-8042000).

Dept. of Justice Prisons Division, 72/76 St. Stephens Green, Dublin 2 (01-6789711).

Honourable Society of Kings Inns, Henrietta St., Dublin 1 (Barristers) (01-8744840).

Incorporated Law Society of Ireland, Blackhall Place, Dublin 7 (Solicitors) (01-6710711).

Legal Aid Board, St. Stephens Green House, Dublin 2 (01-6615811).

Look up "Security Services" in Golden Pages.

Prison Officers Association, 18 Merrion Square, Dublin 2 (01-6625495).

READ/VIEW

Air Corp Video.

An Cosantoir — Dept. of Defence.

Becoming a Solicitor — Inc. Law Society.

Defence Forces Handbook — Essential reading for those interested in the Army, Navy or Air Corps. Available for £4 (including P & P) from Editor, An Cosantoir, Defence Forces H.Q., Parkgate, Dublin 8.

First Rights (FLAC).

Law Quarterly Review, Irish Law Report Monthly.

Naval Service Video.

The Irish Constitution — Government Publications Office.

45

EDUCATION/ TEACHING/NURSERY

New Teachers to tackle educational disadvantage

The Minister for Education and Science announced a £57 million funding initiative to tackle educational disadvantage. Two hundred and twenty-five new primary teachers will be employed in September 1999 in remedial and home school liaison posts. At second level a further 225 teachers will be appointed in an effort to move towards the provision of an automatic remedial resource in all schools, and home/school/community liaison in all disadvantaged schools.

A package of measures aimed at providing thousands of children with disabilities with an automatic right to an education for the first time will also result in new posts in primary schools. It will provide a formal system of both education and childcare for primary school children with special educational needs. Increased resources for children with special needs will require 200 child care positions and 65 teaching posts.

At the moment, the pupil-teacher ratio in Irish primary schools – one teacher for every twenty three pupils – is the highest in the EU. It's estimated that more than 4,000 extra teachers will be needed over the next five years, to reduce this slightly and keep up with the increasing demand.

Permanent employment at second level is difficult to access. Figures form April 1998 show that only 3% of Higher Diploma graduates obtained permanent teaching positions in Ireland, 56% obtained part-time, temporary or substitute teaching posts, 19.5% were in non-teaching jobs, and 3.5% were still seeking employment. This figure compares unfavourably with overall graduate unemployment of 2%.

£1.5 million has recently been allocated by the Department to establish and provide initial staffing for the new National Educational Psychology Service. It is expected that 30 new educational psychologists will be employed for the service.

PreSchool/Childcare: There is a virtual crisis in childcare supply. There is a huge demand for crèche and playschool places, particularly in the bigger towns and cities, where getting a suitable place means long waiting lists and being very lucky. The regulation of nurseries, crèches and other pre-school services catering for children under six by the Health Boards resulted in many having to close down because they could not afford to adapt their premises or employ enough qualified staff to meet regulations.

Ireland has one of the poorest State childcare records in the EU, but it is currently trying to clean up its act. A new report by the expert government group on childcare has recommended a new pay scale for childcare workers, all childcare providers including childminders to be registered and tax relief towards childminding costs.

UCC has a degree in Early Childhood Studies and DIT has a new degree courses in Early Childhood Care and Education.

Other courses include those run by the Irish Pre-school Playgroups Association,The School of Practical Child Care (01-2886994), The Portobello School, 40 Lr. Dominick St., Dublin 1.(01-8721277) and the National Childcare Institute in Herbert Place. The Institute runs a Certificate in Childcare which is recognised by the British

Nursery Nursing Education Board. FÁS runs training courses in childcare, and these are also offered by some ITs, as well as at post-Leaving Cert levels in certain secondary/vocational schools.

Nursery Schools: Generally run by Montessori teachers. One, two and three year training courses are available at the Montessori College, Mount St. Mary's, Milltown, Dublin; the St. Nicholas Montessori College in Dun Laoghaire, and the Montessori Education Centre on North Great Georges Street in Dublin.

A 2 year Diploma in St. Peter's College, Killester is linked to St. Nicholas Montessori College in Dun Laoghaire.

Primary Schools: Primary school teachers train for 5 years in one of he 5 teacher training colleges. About 4,000 people each year apply for a place. The minimum requirement for primary school teaching still includes Leaving Cert. honours Irish.

Last year the Department of Education and Science increased the number of places on teacher training courses to 1,000 to offset the current shortage of primary school teachers. 280 of these places were on the 18-month teacher-training course for graduates. School leavers should not bank on the postgraduate course as an option because there is no guarantee that the course will be run again. Because of the shortage of primary teachers job prospects are currently good; 22% of 1997 graduates had permanent teaching positions a year after graduating. a further 70% were in part-time, temporary or substitute teaching, and less than 0.5% were still seeking employment.

Second Level Schools: Students interested in becoming teachers in second level schools will need a degree in a relevant subject followed by the one year higher diploma in education, more commonly known as the H.Dip. Vocational schools don't require the H.Dip but in practice most applicants won't even be interviewed without one. For the past number of years places on the H. Dip have been limited to 800. The Minister raised the cap from 800 to 940 last year. 100 of these additional places were for people with Science, Irish, RE, Italian, and Spanish degrees.

Students who take concurrent teaching degrees do not need to take the H.Dip as the concurrent degree incorporates academic and teacher training in a 4-year course. Concurrent degrees are available in areas such as: home economics art, science, religion, PE, engineering technology and wood/building technology. Graduates from concurrent degrees tend to do better in the jobs market, UL statistics of graduates from its concurrent degrees in the technology area found that they were all in teaching positions within a year of graduating.

Science graduates tend to fare well, and there's also a demand for teachers of Irish and Maths. Normally, there's a surplus of English, History and Geography teachers.

The demand for teachers of art and home economics continues to exceed supply. Religion teachers have few problems getting jobs. The Mater Dei Institute of Education offers a four year Bachelor of Religious Science, with the option of either English, History or Music as a second subject. The B.A. in Theology in St. Patrick's College, Maynooth also qualifies graduates to teach Religion in secondary schools.

The introduction of new subjects at junior level, such as Civic, Social and Political education and the new Junior Certificate Elementary programme, should create more employment for teachers, while at senior level, demand is increasing for Transition Year, Leaving Cert Applied and Vocational programmes.

Guidance and Counselling: Students who want to work as guidance counsellors in secondary schools will need a degree, a H.Dip and further post-grad diploma in guidance and counselling. There are now six guidance and counselling courses – UCD, UCC, Trinity College Dublin, Maynooth, Limerick University and Marino Institute of Education.

The Institute of Guidance Counsellors maintains that their numbers should be trebled so that they can provide an adequate service to students. Experts agree there ought to be one guidance counsellor for every 250 students. But this is far from the case in our schools where many guidance counsellors are striving against the odds to deliver a full and efficient service.

Third Level Colleges: For universities, and more academic courses, a post-graduate degree, probably a Ph.D, is often required. But there is generally greater flexibility in more practical or job orientated courses, which often tend to take on people who have experience or are still working in the relevant industry.

The proportion of school-leavers participating in third level education and training continues to increase. There has also been an increase in mature students and part-time students participating in third level education. However the number of school leavers will fall by 2,000 per year for the next 15 years form the present 75,000 to 50,00 by 2010. While there has been some growth in the numbers employed in third level, the Irish Federation of University Teachers says staffing is inadequate and a large proportion of lecturing jobs are part-time.

Special Needs Education: Children with special

Computer teaching – just one of the specialist areas in second level education.

needs include those with a physical or mental disability, serious behavioural problems, specific learning disabilities such as dyslexia, speech and language disorders, hearing and visual impairment. There are at least 18,000 such children in primary schools. Under new department measures children assessed as having a special educational need would have an automatic entitlement to special extra teaching or school-based childcare or both. These new measures will provide an extra 65 teaching posts and about 200 child care jobs.

Remedial teachers in primary schools are trained in St. Patrick's College in Drumcondra. At second level there is a higher diploma in remedial and special education in UCC. UCD and St. Angela's for qualified second level teachers. To work with the visually impaired, qualified primary teachers may follow a prescribed course leading to a Certificate from the College of Teachers of the Blind in Britain, or take a one year course at Birmingham University. To work with the deaf, primary teachers with a year's experience may attend a one year course at UCD. A special one year course for teachers of handicapped children is held at St Patrick's College, Drumcondra.

A one year PLC course in Care of the Special Child is jointly run by the Central Remedial Clinic and Liberties Vocational School in Dublin.

SUGGESTIONS

Join a youth organisation and try to get leadership experience . . . help with summer projects and community games . . . acquire other skills besides purely academic ones, e.g. sport, music, art and crafts . . . participate in activities to improve your confidence in dealing with crowds, e.g. debating . . . choose subjects carefully — there is a greater demand for teachers of technical or specialist subjects than teachers of other subjects . . . get involved in a local playschool . . . particular requirements are necessary for certain specialist areas, e.g. for P.E. teaching, involvement and commitment in a range of sporting activities. . . honours Irish is essential for entry to National teaching — go to the Gaeltacht . . . if you are interested in teaching the handicapped you should locate and visit some of their special schools.

FURTHER INFORMATION

Association of Secondary Teachers in Ireland, Winetavern St., Dublin 8 (01-6719144).

Dept. of Education, Marlborough St., Dublin 1 (01-8734700).

Institute of Guidance Counsellors, 17 Herbert Street, Dublin 2 (01-6761975).

Irish National Teachers Organisation, 35 Parnell Sq., Dublin 1 (01-8722533).

Irish Preschool Playgroups Assoc., Spade Enterprise Centre, Dublin 7 (01-6719245).

Montessori College, Mount St. Mary's, Dundrum Road, Milltown, Dublin 14 (01-2692499).

Montessori Education Centre, 41–43 Nth. Great Georges St., Dublin 1 (01-8780071).

National Childcare Institute, 7 Herbert Place, Dublin 2.

National Centre for Guidance in Education, 189 Parnell St., Dublin 1. (01-8731411).

Portobello School of Childcare, 40 Lr. Dominick St., Dublin 1. (01-8721277)

School of Practical Child Care, Blackrock Campus, Carysfort, Blackrock, Co. Dublin. (01-2886994)

St. Nicholas Montessori Society, St. Nicholas House, 16 Adelaide St., Dun Laoghaire, Co. Dublin (01-2806064).

Teachers Union of Ireland, 73 Orwell Road, Dublin 6 (01-4922588).

READ

An Tuarascáil and An Múinteoir Náisiúnta (INTO).
ASTIR and Secondary Teacher (ASTI).
TUI News (TUI).
The prospectus and/or calendar of courses provided by each college (see college addresses in index).

ENGINEERING/TECHNOLOGY/ INDUSTRY

More jobs, more "mobiles"

CAREERS IN THIS CATEGORY
Many of the careers listed below are outlined on the FÁS Gairm Database

Fitter; Hosiery Mechanic; Junior Telephone and Telegraph Mechanic; Metal Fabricator; Trainee Installer, Bord Telecom; Trainee Technician Bord Telecom; Sheet Metal Worker; Toolmaker; Turner; Welder; Foundry Craftsman; Production Process Worker; Estimator, Industrial Engineer, Fork Lift Operator; Packer; Refrigeration Craftsman; Apprentices in Bord na Mona; E.S.B. and Sugar Co.; Hosiery factory operative; Industrial Inspector; Purchasing Officer; Electrician; Brassfinisher; Coppersmith; Boilermaker; Blacksmith; Patternmaker; Instrument mechanic; Engineer — mechanical, production, electronic, structural, electrical; Electronics technician; Mechanical Engineering technician; Engineering and draughts-person; Industrial designer; Industrial safety officer; Industrial engineer; Metallurgist; Glass technologist; Quality control officer; Watchmaking and Repair. There is also a huge variety of jobs at operative level in this sector, e.g. assembly work in electronic factories, or machine operators in the manufacture of mechanical equipment. Biomedical, Ceramic, Environment, Geological, Mining, Nuclear, Textile, Transportation, and Petroleum engineers.

One of the most rapidly changing industries of the past few years has to be telecommunications. The enforcement of EU regulations has meant that many existing and new operators have been granted licences in a newly liberalised market, and the public demand for new services appears insatiable.

At the moment, for example, the mobile phone market is growing at a phenomenal rate. One fifth of the population now has a mobile phone, and predictions are this will continue to rise, perhaps to the extent where many people will have two mobiles – one for business and one for personal use.

The revolution which the Internet has meant to communications has also been very significant for Ireland. The Industrial Development Authority has targeted this as a prime job creation opportunity, saying it wants Ireland to become the Internet capital of the world. The IDA believes 25,000 new jobs could be created in electronic commerce on the Internet over the next ten years.

Even in the Celtic tiger economy, the news is, as ever, dominated by job losses when they happen. But the reality is that we're creating far more jobs than we're losing – at the moment, it's running at about 1,000 extra jobs a week. In fact, experts are predicting a skills shortage in the coming years which could threaten the growth of the economy. They say that as well as the average 8,000 technical specialists – in areas like engineering and computing – who are coming on to the jobs market every year, at least another 2,000 will be necessary to keep pace with demand.

For the most part, Ireland appears to be weathering the worst of the global slowdown in the electronics sector. More than 35,000 people are employed in multi-national electronics companies, and this is set to grow. Dell Computers is taking on more people for its operations in Wicklow and Limerick, while Xerox, despite looking for 9,000 redundancies worldwide, is creating 2,200 new jobs in Dundalk and Blanchardstown.

Opportunities for civil engineers continue to be among the best in the engineering field. Ireland currently has the fastest growing construction industry in Europe.

Electronic Engineering: Involved in the design of radio and television equipment, and computer hardware and control systems.

Lately, students seem to be heading more towards software and computers, with hardware and electronics not as popular as previously.

Industrial Engineering: Responsible for such diverse areas as the improvement of safety at work and design of the working environment, to the improvement of decision processes and reduction of cost. A broadly based qualification which allows the graduate to work in various areas of industry. It's very business orientated, and geared towards the management of company resources. Degree course available at UCG and the University of Limerick, as well as Galway IT and Limerick IT.

Chemical Engineering: Chemical and process engineers deal with manufacturing processes involving plastics, pharmaceuticals, mining, oil and gas.

Civil Engineering: A wide variety of

employment areas including sanitation, environmental engineering, structural engineering, building and road maintenance. About half of civil engineers working in Ireland are employed by the public sector. The remainder work for private consultancy firms and contractors.

Marine Engineering: Involves the design and maintenance of ship structure and power plants; may be land-based (shipyard) or at sea.

Mechanical Engineering: Provides the machines and power for manufacturing machinery. Involved in the design of cars, ships, planes, and household appliances, among a variety of machines.

Sligo IT is now offering Bachelor of Engineering (Design). It's a two year add-on degree available to diploma students, which will focus on industrial design from an engineering perspective.

Technicians: No matter how many people are needed to engineer and design products, there is always a need for technicians to back up the team. ITs around the county offer electronic engineering technicians courses; seven offer civil engineering; production engineering at Dundalk and Waterford; Agricultural Engineering at Tralee; Marine Engineering at Cork; Plastics Engineering at Athlone; Water Engineering at Sligo and Electronics Technology at Cork — see NCEA guide and IT Colleges ('Best Guide').

Apprentices: The ESB usually takes on up to 50 apprentices each year. Applicants are expected to have their Junior Cert, with Irish or English, Maths, Science or Mechanical Drawing and Woodwork or Metalwork.

Electrical apprentices work at one of the ESB's twenty five power stations or outdoors on the distribution system. **Mechanical** apprentices are normally based in the power stations, installing, maintaining and repairing equipment.

Telecommunications: There are huge developments in this area at the moment, and there's plenty of potential for exciting careers for those who decide to enter this rapidly changing work environment.

While the market has been slowly becoming more liberalised over the past few years, it's only now that the monopoly held by Telecom Eireann is being dented, with other phone companies being allowed to compete for domestic accounts, using their own network. The next few years will see alliances between various companies, and more entrants into the mobile phone market.

But as well as such service providers, there'll also be an increase in the number of companies supplying products and new ideas to them. One such company is Tellabs in Shannon, which is increasing its workforce by 200.

Certificate and diploma courses for communications technicians are available at Kevin Street, Limerick IT and Cork IT. Other ITs offer general electronic technician courses.

Oil and gas exploration/mining: The first mining for gold in Ireland in almost two centuries is to be carried out near Omagh in County Tyrone, and there's also potential for commercial gold mining at Clontibret in County Monaghan.

Test drilling of the Enterprise Oil gas discovery off the west coast has indicated the highest levels of gas ever recorded in a find in Irish waters. This may be enough to supply Ireland's gas needs for a number of years, and even some of Britain's.

In addition, two European companies have been awarded licences to explore for oil and gas off the south coast.

UCC and UCG offer earth sciences as a separate science option. It's mainly geology, but UCG has hydrology and oceanography as well.

Athlone IT is the country's only centre for mineral engineering. It offers a chance to study a National Diploma in Mining Engineering, with the possibility of transferring to degrees in the UK.

SUGGESTIONS

Avail of any opportunity to maintain or repair equipment – hi-fi, bikes, cars, etc . . . pay particular attention to technical and scientific subjects . . . get involved in motor and machinery preservation societies . . . visit trade exhibitions . . . attend DIT lectures on trades, mechanical and electronic engineering and science . . attend annual lecture organised by the Institute of Electrical Engineers in TCD . . . visit airports . . . ESB Power Stations . . . Born na Mona factories and bog developments . . . alert yourself to new developments in technology . . . watch out for special TV reports and programmes such as "Tomorrow's World" . . . arrange a visit to a local factory, perhaps you could obtain a summer job there . . . arrange a trip to a local industry . . . buy an advanced electronic kit . . . attend various college open days.

FURTHER INFORMATION

Irish Business & Employers Confederation, 84 Lr. Baggot Street, Dublin 2 (01-6601011).

Engineering Careers Information Service, 54 Clarendon Road, Watford, Herts. W1 1IB UK.

Forbairt (Irish Science and Technology Agency), Glasnevin Road, Dublin 9 (01-8082000).

Federation of Irish Chemical Industries, 140 Pembroke Road, Dublin 4 (01-6603350).

FÁS, PO Box 456, 27–33 Upper Baggot St., Dublin 4 (01-6070500).

Institute of Chemistry, RDS, Ballsbridge, Dublin 4.

Institute of Industrial Engineers (01-2943131).

Institute of Physics, c/o Physics Dept., UCD, Dublin 4.

Institute of Electrical Engineers, 6 Tivoli Close, Dun Laoghaire, Co. Dublin.

Institute of Engineers, 22 Clyde Road, Dublin 4 (01-6684867).

Irish Institute of Purchasing and Materials Management, John Player House, SCR., Dublin 8.

Irish Production and Inventory Control Society, 14 Herbert St , Dublin 2 (01-0765197).

Irish Productivity Centre, IPC House, 42 Lr. Mount Street, Dublin 2 (01-6623233).

DIPLOMA IN WATCHMAKING

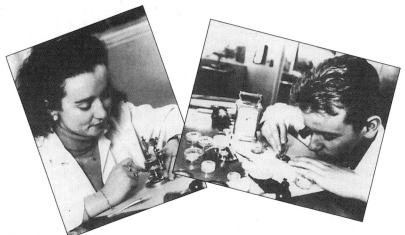

Diploma in Watchmaking
The Diploma Course in watchmaking has been conducted at the Irish Swiss Institute of Horology in Blanchardstown, Dublin 15 since 1965. In a recent survey the Swiss Watch Industry identified the necessity of training 25,000 watchmakers over the next ten years to service their top quality watch products.

Best Overall Student Scholarship
At Diploma presentation the best Overall Student is awarded a scholarship to Switzerland for a three-week further training period in the After Sales Service departments of three top quality watch manufacturers. This scholarship is generously sponsored by E.T.A. – the world's largest manufacturers of watch movements.

Entry Requirements
Candidates should have Leaving Certificate with Grade D in five subjects including Mathematics and one Applied Science/Science subject or equivalent.

Application Procedure
Application forms (available from address below) should be completed and returned by the first week in June. Interviews are held towards the end of August and the course commences in September.

IRISH SWISS INSTITUTE OF HOROLOGY,
Mill Road, Blanchardstown, Dublin 15.
Telephone: (01) 821 3352   Fax: (01) 820 7627

1. For details of courses consult College Propectuses.
2. See index for Post Leaving Certificate Courses.
3. See index for FÁS Courses.

	T.C.D.	N.U.I. Galway	U.C.C.	D.C.U.	U.L.	U.C.D.	D.I.T.	N.U.I. Maynooth	Athlone IT	Cork IT	Galway Mayo IT	Sligo IT	Waterford IT	Carlow IT	Dundalk IT	Letterkenny IT	Tralee IT	Limerick IT	Tallaght IT	Portobello	Blanchardsto. IT
Civil Engineering	●	●	●			●	●		●	●	●	●	●	●	●	●	●	●	●	●	
Engineering – Aeronautical					●																
Engineering – Agricultural					●												●				
Engineering – Automobile						●				●							●				
Engineering – Biomedical/Medical Mechanical		●	●	●							●										
Engineering – Chemical						●				●											
Engineering – Computer	●	●		●				●								●		●			
Engineering – Electrical	●		●			●	●	●										●			
Engineering – Electronics	●	●	●	●	●	●	●		●	●	●	●	●	●	●	●	●	●	●		●
Engineering – Environmental													●	●							
Engineering – Industrial		●		●									●	●			●				
Engineering – Manufacturing Technology				●	●						●				●						
Engineering – Mechanical	●	●		●	●	●	●		●	●	●	●	●	●	●	●	●	●	●		
Engineering – Mineral/Plastics										●											
Engineering – Nautical										●											
Engineering – Production				●		●									●						
Engineering – Telecommunications				●																	
Engineering – Transport										●											
Mathematical Physics		●	●			●															
Mathematics	●	●	●	●	●	●										●		●			
Mechatronics (Electronics/Mechanical)				●											●		●				

Irish Quality Association, Merrion Hall, Strand Road (01-2695255).
Irish Swiss Institute of Horology, Mill Road, Blanchardstown, Dublin 15 (01-8213352).
The various 3rd level colleges and their engineering departments.

READ/VIEW
Chemistry is Everywhere – Inst. of Chemistry, RDS.
Chemistry and Careers (from Institute of Chemistry).
Careers with Physics, Institute of Physics
Irish Engineering Directory (Eolas)
Technology Ireland (Eolas).
The Shannon Basin – ESB.

ENTERTAINMENT/CULTURAL /MUSIC/SPORT

Irish talent tops U.K. charts

Last year, U2 clinched one of the most lucrative deals in the history of the music industry. Under the fifty million dollar agreement, the band will release three 'Best of U2' albums.

The deal is seen as a real testament to their continued popularity and success. But it's also clear that there's plenty of room on the international music scene for other Irish talent too. The past year has been perhaps the most successful so far for Dundalk siblings The Corrs, while Dublin quartet B Witched have been topping the charts. The undiminished popularity of Boyzone has spawned a whole new generation of similar bands, such as Westlife – managed by Boyzone lead singer Ronan Keating.

Music is one of the biggest employers among the culture industries, providing almost 42% of employment in this sector. But another area which is really beginning to bloom is theatre, especially in Dublin. The rebuilt and expanded Project Theatre in Temple Bar has been one milestone, and in the suburbs, the Tallaght Civic Theatre is set to be followed by others in Blanchardstown, Coolock and Dun Laoghaire.

This is good news for anyone aspiring to a career in theatre – backstage or treading the boards. Increasingly, there is more work for Irish actors at home, between theatre, television and film. But they're continuing to make their mark in Britain too, with Victoria Smurfit, James Nesbitt and Liam Cunningham winning valuable television roles. Irish comedians like Dylan Moran, Graham Norton and, of course, Ardal O'Hanlon have all been given their own series.

At the time of writing, the Government remains committed to setting up an academy for the performing arts in Dublin city centre. This would offer programmes in classical music, opera, traditional music and dance to degree level.

Acting: The Gaiety School of Acting provides a two year intensive course as well as part time lessons. TCD has a four year degree in drama and theatre studies – aimed mainly at those who want to become playwrights, managers, directors and screenwriters. There is also a two year diploma for actors. There are no academic requirements – entry is by audition. Andrews Lane Theatre also offers courses.

Other people move into acting through drama societies in colleges. Some schools also offer post-Leaving Cert courses such as theatre studies or drama and dance.

Stage Manager: Co-ordinates the running of the show and props on stage.

Set Designer: Creates the set for different shows and plays. Set design is incorporated as part of the course in Environmental Design at the College of Marketing and Design in Mountjoy Square, Dublin.

Useful courses include those provided in University of Limerick, and Waterford IT.

Dance: Some good news for aspiring dancers — the Arts Council has allocated one million pounds to a purpose built centre for dance. This, combined with the proposed academy for the performing arts, will considerably enhance the prospects for dancers in this country. A number of courses are already available, including a two year ballet and contemporary dance course at Sallynoggin Senior College, Dublin. Some graduates become professional performers or choreographers, others go into teaching. Entry is by audition and interview. Other PLC courses are available at Colaiste Stiofain Naofa in Cork (Performing Arts/Dance), and in Dublin, Inchicore Vocational School (Theatre/Dance), and Marino College (Drama/Dance)

Music Industry: About 10,000 people work in the music industry. Traditionally, holders of music qualifications went into teaching. But over the past

Gordon Brett
Athlone Institute of Technology

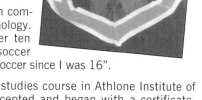

When twenty four year old Gordon Brett was getting ready to sit his Leaving Cert at the Marist College in Athlone, his preference was for a career in leisure management. Six years on, it seems his original instinct was the right one for him.

After the Leaving, Gordon started a degree in computer studies in Waterford Institute of Technology. "But it wasn't for me. I de-registered after ten weeks, and started a FÁS course in soccer coaching. I'd been playing League of Ireland soccer since I was 16".

Gordon re-applied to CAO for the business studies course in Athlone Institute of Technology the following year. He was accepted and began with a certificate, moving on to a diploma and a degree. It took four years.

"The course was interesting; I felt it looked to the needs of industry", he says now.

Gordon had continued playing sport, particularly soccer, right through college, and knew he wanted to get into sports management. "The sports officer in Athlone recommended a year long M.Sc in Sport and Recreation Management in Sheffield. I applied and was accepted. It's exactly what I wanted".

And his career options? "I'd like to come back to Ireland. The area is starting to open up. There are opportunities on national governing bodies such as the Irish Sports Council, and I could always lecture."

ten years their horizons have expanded into public relations, arts management and production.

Courses in Ballyfermot Senior College and Scoil Stiofain Naofa in Cork are among the few available. Both cover the management of bands, as well as production and performance.

The Higher National Diploma in Music Management at Ballyfermot concentrates on management. Studies include the domestic and international music industry, production of music events, operation of recording studios, and negotiation of recording, publishing and merchandising deals. Also business and computing skills, as well as marketing, PR and legal studies.

There is also a professional musician training certificate course at Newpark Music Centre in Dublin, which caters for all instruments, plus voice training. In addition, Newpark is running a diploma in jazz studies.

Classical music training is available at the College of Music, Dublin, the Cork School of Music or the Royal Irish Academy of Music. Also B.A. or B.Mus. degrees at UCD, UCC and Trinity and Maynooth

Students can also study music as part of an Arts Degree in many other colleges.

DIT conservatory of Music and Drama has a one year music foundation course.

Sport: Irish politicians are campaigning to hold the Olympics in Dublin sometime in the next twenty years. There are major stadium developments being carried out by the GAA, the FAI and the IRFU, and the Government is also working on proposals for Ireland's first ever national stadium.

Soccer contiues to be a huge attraction for those who dream of following in the footsteps of Niall Quinn, Roy Keane and Shay Given. Under the direction of Brian Kerr, a system has been put in place to make sure that our best youngsters are given every chance to make their mark with major English and European clubs.

Increasingly sports sponsorship means that top athletes like Susan Smith, Sonia O'Sullivan and

Catherina McKiernan can make a career without having to hold down full time or part time jobs to supplement their income.

Irish rugby is also becoming more professional, and players like Keith Wood, Paul Wallace and Malcolm O'Kelly are now among the biggest earners in Irish sport. However, with more money becoming available, there is also increased pressure on Irish youngsters who may be tempted to pursue a career in sports. The bottom line is that less than one in ten will make the grade, and it is essential that sport continues to be treated first as a hobby rather than as a career path. Don't forget too that teaching sport is another option, and there are plenty of opportunities in the burgeoning leisure industry.

Generally speaking, students who have a future in professional sport will be identified at school, as training starts at an early age. One of the most structured forms of training is in soccer, and most professionals have gone through the youth training system in Britain. Big clubs and others take on youths aged 16 or 17 for a standard two year training programme. PLCs are available in schools like Colaiste Íde, Finglas. FAS also runs a training scheme, usually with less than 20 vacancies per year.

UCD offers soccer scholarships and other colleges such as UCC and TCD offer significant sports scholarships. Applicants must, however, obtain the necessary points for the degree they want to study. Scholarships are also available from some American colleges, who maintain contact with some Irish schools as part of their search for new talent to train in football, basketball etc. Some leading Australian Rules football clubs maintain similar links. (See Grants Section).

Teaching sport is another option open to people who reach a certain level. There aren't many job openings for P.E. teachers at the moment, but there are opportunities for holders of more specialised qualifications i.e. tennis coaches. FÁS offers a 40 week course in conjunction with Tennis Ireland. It qualifies people to coach in schools, clubs and public park programmes.

Leisure Management: It's estimated that there are 8,000 jobs in the sports industry, and the publication of the National Sports Strategy identifies more opportunities in coaching and leisure management.

There are more than 100 hotels with indoor leisure clubs, and the list of such clubs and leisure centres is growing. Within the last few years, at least three 'super gyms' have been built around the country, with more in the pipeline.

A wide variety of courses are available, from one year certificates to three year diplomas, incorporating skills as sports and fitness instructors.

Some are more sport orientated than business.

At junior level, jobs would include attendants at sports clubs, reception and lifeguard duties and maintenance of equipment. At more senior level, the co-ordination of services to the customer, and implementation of policy.

SUGGESTIONS

Avail of the many part-time classes in acting and dance . . . enter competitions for young bands . . . spend some time at an adventure sports centre such as the Tiglin Adventure Centre, Ashford, Co. Wicklow . . . Investigate leisure and sport courses available in many second level schools, e.g. Colaiste Íde, Finglas . . . enter feiseanna . . . Slógadh . . . amateur dramatics . . . school drama and sport . . . participate in National Association for Youth Drama annual summer school . . . "practice makes perfect" . . . enquire about sporting scholarships . . . for other cultural activities contact the Arts Council.

FURTHER INFORMATION

Abbey Theatre, Lower Abbey St., Dublin 1 (01-8748741).

AFAS (Association for Adventure Sports), Tiglin Adventure Centre, Ashford, Co. Wicklow (0404-40169).

Community Games, Sports and Cultural Organisation, 5 Abbey St., Dublin 1 (01-8788095).

Dept. of Theatre Studies, Trinity College, Dublin 2 (01-6772941).

Dublin Youth Orchestras, 62 Ailesbury Grove, Dublin 16 (01-2980680)

Dublin Youth Theatre, 23 Upr. Gardiner St., Dublin 1 (01-8743687).

Football Assoc. of Ireland, 80 Merrion Square, Dublin 2 (01-6766864).

Gaiety School of Acting, Meeting Hse. Square, Temple Bar, Dublin 2. (01-6799277)

Information Centre, The Sports Council, 70 Brompton Road, London SW3 IEX.

Institute of Leisure and Amenity Management, 65 Crumlin Road, Dublin 12 (01-4540399).

Irish Cycling Federation, 287 Castletown, Leixlip, Co. Kildare.

Irish Federation of Musicians, 63 Gardiner St., Dublin 1 (01-8744645).

Irish Film Institute, 6 Eustace, Dublin 2. (01-6795744).

Olympic Council of Ireland, 27 Mespil Road, Dublin 4. (01-6680444)

Professional Golfers Association, Dundalk Golf Club (045-21193).

Students interested in dance should contact: Irish Ballet Co. Emmet Place, Cork (021-20112) or College of Dance, Blackrock Town Hall, Co. Dublin; National Association for Youth Drama, 23 Upper Gardiner St., Dublin 1.

The Arts Council, 70 Merrion Sq., Dublin 2 (01-6611840).

The Irish Actors Equity, Liberty Hall, Dublin (01-8740081).

University of Ulster (sports degree, sport courses are also available in U.L., Cork, Waterford and Tralee ITs, Cathal Brugha. St. (D.I.T.) and D.C.U.

READ/VIEW

Your local library has in stock a variety of books relating to sport and culture.

"Careers and Course in Leisure – Finding your Way" published by ILAM (address above)

Health & Sport – a handbook for organisers in Community Games.

Writers & Artists Yearbook (A.&C. Black Ltd.).

Hot Press, Jazz News, Theatre Ireland, Gaelic Sport, Gaelic World, The Title, Sporting Press — periodicals.

FASHION/BEAUTY CARE/ HAIRDRESSING

Job losses in Rag Trade

The last ten years has brought huge success, at home and abroad, to Irish designers such as John Rocha, Louise Kennedy, Lainey Keogh and Paul Costello. Thanks to the continued fostering of the home talent at the Design Centre at the Powerscourt Centre in Dublin, Mary Gregory, Miriam Mone, Deborah Veale and Aliano have become the natural successors to those household names. Irish labels, you would think, are doing very nicely.

But the reality is very different. Despite the acclaim for the current darlings of the designer world, the rag trade in Ireland has been almost brought to its knees. More than fifteen internationally owned clothing companies have closed their Irish operations over the past five years, with the loss of more than 2,000 jobs. About 15,000 people are currently at work in the clothing industry, but it's estimated that jobs will be lost at the rate of 2,000 a year for the foreseeable future.

Much of the problem stems from the fact that garments can be produced far more cheaply in African, South American and East European countries, and the industry in Ireland is simply going through the same experience as other countries in Europe, such as Denmark, where the number of people employed in clothes manufacturing has halved over the last decade.

In other, related fields, however, the opportunities are much better. The health consciousness of the nineties seems likely to be even more pronounced in the new millennium – and that's good news for anyone planning to work in the health and leisure field. And there's also a huge demand for people to train as hairdressers.

Fashion Design: Some graduates find employment here, others go further afield in search of new ideas and have got jobs in Italy, America and Britain. As well as designing in-house or as freelance consultants, they may go into design management, journalism, teaching, merchandising, or film, TV and theatre design.

The National College of Art and Design, Limerick IT, the VECs and ITs run courses, as do some privately run schools, such as the Grafton Academy of Dress Design and the Bourke College in Dublin, the Cork College of Fashion Design and the Mallow College of Design and Tailoring. The Grafton Academy of Dress Designing offers a three year diploma course, while the Bourke College in Dublin holds courses in fashion design and fashion merchandising – including fashion journalism, advertising, public relations and fashion show production. Some Post-Leaving Cert courses also available i.e. at the College of Commerce, Cork and the Senior College, Sallynoggin, in Dublin.

General Clothing Industry: FÁS runs courses for sewing and knitting machinists – but the overall level of formal training in the clothing industry is very low, with only one in three companies undertaking training. Jobs in the industry are still poorly paid. Irish manufacturers are facing stiff competition from Eastern Europe particularly, and are under pressure to keep costs low.

Modelling: There are about 70 full-time, professional models in Dublin. Another 400 only do modelling work now and again, but call themselves models.

Some agencies reckon there's only room for maybe four new faces a year. A top Irish model can earn up to £600 a day at the peak of a career which will only last about seven years – that's a long way from the £10,000 a day fees commanded by the so-called "supermodels".

However, Ireland has, in recent years, been producing its own supermodels. Names like Erin O'Connor, Linda Byrne and Jane Bradbury may not be too well known here – but that's because they've broken through at an early stage to the international circuit, and have been strutting the catwalks of New York, Milan and Paris.

Modelling schools and agencies generally offer grooming and training courses to suitable women and men who have the potential to earn a living in the business. The minimum height is usually 5'8" for women and 6' for men. Go for a reputable agency with a proven success record, and carefully check out the expenditure involved before committing yourself.

Agencies take a cut of about 20% of the fees which a model earns.

Health and Fitness: Evidence that the health and fitness craze shows no sign of abating can be seen in the number of large gym and fitness complexes opening in recent years. Health farms are also on the increase, and are becoming more sophisticated, aiming to cater for those who previously would have gone abroad to avail of the treatments on offer.

Hairdressing: Shortage of staff has reached crisis point in the hairdressing industry. Everybody needs a haircut or colour, but, it seems no one wants to do it anymore. A lot of people perceive hairdressing as something people do to get out of school early, and they don't want to spend their time washing hair or sweeping floors during a long and badly paid training period. Yet, at the top end, hairdressing can be a very glamourous career, with opportunities for travel or opening your own salon.

There are four ways to enter this profession. Traditional four year apprenticeships are run by salons like Peter Mark. FÁS has introduced a standard system of training whereby graduates will be awarded official qualifications – for the first time, hairdressing is being recognised as an official trade.

Many of the top salons run courses. These can be expensive, but some guarantee a fees refund if the student fails to gain employment afterwards.

Some PLC courses are available, combining hairdressing with cosmetic and beauty studies. Dun Laoghaire Institute of Further Education, Dublin, and Crumlin College of Business Studies both run one year courses.

Beauty Therapy: This is an expanding field which offers plenty of job opportunities. One indication of the extent of this expansion is a look at the membership of the professional body, the Society of Applied Cosmetology – from ten members in 1976 to nearly 900 today. Beauty therapists work in beauty salons, health farms, keep fit centres and gyms, large hotels and department stores, the cosmetic industry and TV, theatre and film. There are many courses on offer. The internationally recognised CIDESCO course is available at schools such as the Kilkenny School of Beauty

Therapy, Coogan Bergin School of Beauty Therapy, the Bronwyn Conroy School and Dun Laoghaire Institute of Further Education.

Make-up Artist: Make-up artists work in film, television, commercial, advertising and fashion. Courses are available in some PLC colleges and beauty salons. In addition, Dun Laoghaire IT runs a two year certificate course in make up for film, TV and theatre. The emphasis is on art rather than beauty, and graduates work in these areas as well as catalogues and magazines.

Colour Analysis: This is a growing area of the beauty industry. It involves advising women and men on what colours and styles suit them best so that they can avoid making costly mistakes in the future.

SUGGESTIONS

Attend one of the grooming courses run by the modelling agencies . . . develop an interest in healthcare . . . careful diet, good grooming, deportment (dance, gymnastics, etc.) . . . an eye for fashion — attend fashion shows, read fashion magazines, etc. . . . seek temporary work in boutique or fashion department and for hairdressing seek temporary work in a salon . . . As well as keeping an eye on new products and trends in hair and beauty magazines. . . There is work to be had for young models (both male and female) and you should contact a modelling agency close to you for further details. . . . For beauty therapy studying biology would help . . . visit local crafts industries in your area. Many young designers start up making fabrics, garments and knitwear for their local communities . . . Attend a hairdressing summer school.

FURTHER INFORMATION

Clothing Manufacturing Federation, Confederation House, 84/86 Lr. Baggot Street, Dublin 2. (01-6601011).

Bourke College, Pembroke Road, Dublin 4 (01-6607576).

Check "Golden Pages" under Model Agencies.

College of Chiropody, 43 Paul St., Cork (021-273200).

Cork College of Fashion Design, 6 Anglesea St., Cork (021-311350).

Grafton Academy of Dress Designing, 6 Herbert Place Dublin 2 (01-6767940).

Irish Hairdressers Federation, 19 Broadford Ave, Ballinteer, Dublin 16 (01-4946907) Enclose S.A.E.

Mallow College of Design and Tailoring, 161, West End, Mallow, Co. Cork (022-22768).

National College of Art and Design, 100 Thomas St., Dublin 8 (01-6711377).

Society of Chiropodists & Podiatrists (IR), Medical Centre, Balbriggan (01-8413350).

Society of Applied Cosmetology, 47 Sth. William St., Dublin 2 (01-6798018). Send S.A.E.

The Crafts Council of Ireland, Powerscourt Townhouse Centre, Dublin 2 (01-6797368).

The Society of Chiropodists, 8 Wimpole Street, London WIM 8BX.

READ/VIEW

Any of the many glossy women's magazines, particularly high fashion international publications such as Vogue, or Irish magazines like Image, also magazines dealing with health and fitness.

Hairdressing — video from Colaiste Dhulaigh, Coolock, Dublin 5.

HOTEL/CATERING/BAR & TOURISM

Getting a Job in the Tourism industry: it's a dead CERT

There's very good news for anybody interested in a career in the hotel/catering and tourism industry. It is estimated that at least one in seven people employed in Ireland are now working in the tourism and hospitality business. With revenue generations of on average, 2 billion pounds a year it is fast becoming Ireland's number one industry. The number of new hotel beds grew by 12.45 per cent last year and since 1994 over 500 new restaurants have opened nationwide.

All 2,000 CERT graduates enjoyed 100% employment last year. Despite the fact that training in the tourism industry virtually guarantees a job school leavers are turning away in large numbers. The widespread perception of tourism as an industry with low pay, long and unsociable hours according to the chairman of CERT Mr. James Nugent, were "hitting recruitment hard". So hard that the Irish times reported in August last that a number of Dublin hotels were using a Madrid agency to recruit Spanish staff.

CERT run more than 80 programmes at 18 centres nationwide, with an element of languages and tourism skills now incorporated into every course.

Courses run by CERT include chef, hotel and catering management, reception, hospitality, bar operations, diningroom assistant, house assistant and tourism studies. Grants are available through CERT for some of the courses and these provide the student with free training, free accommodation and meals, payment during training and a book and uniform allowance.

Tourism: LSB has a BA in Tourism Studies which is a Business degree focusing on the Tourism Sector. There are tourism courses in the Cork, Tralee, Sligo, Galway and Dublin Institutes of Technology and many PLC colleges. Graduates can pursue careers in travel agencies, heritage centres, local tourist offices, or indeed in Bord Failte, Aer Lingus or the Regional Tourism Centres. They would aspire to managing such operations and would be qualified to pursue Post Graduate Studies.

Tourism Information Assistant: The aim of this one year full time course is to equip people with the skills necessary to work in a variety of tourist businesses, from heritage centres to historical sites and information centres. A European language is taught as part of the course, which is on offer at Tralee, Waterford and Athlone ITs and selected CERT centres. Applicants must be aged 17 with a Junior or Leaving Cert. New Courses are available in Portobello School (Tel: 8721277) and LSB College (6794844).

Hotel and Catering Management: Courses on offer at the Dublin College of Catering (B.Sc. TCD), Galway IT (B.A. NCEA), Athlone IT (NCEA Dip.), and Shannon College of Hotel Management (Diploma). Students at Shannon now have the option to graduate with a B.Comm from UCG. These two Shannon college courses have now been approved for participation in the CAO for the year 2000. Also the CERT Management Development Programme offers on-the-job management training. Exact entry requirements vary from college to college, but Leaving Cert. would be the minimum. Degree holders can now go on to do a Masters in Hotel and Hospitality Management at DIT Cathal Brugha Street.

Waiter/Waitress: More than 28,000 people work in restaurant service, with more than half in hotels, a third in restaurants, and the rest in areas like industrial or fastfood catering. It's one of the few courses which CERT has no difficulty filling. CERT offers a multi-skills course in either diningroom/bar service or diningroom service/housekeeping.

Training is at the Dublin College of Catering, as well as ITs in Cork and Galway Mayo. Also contact CERT for locations of its hotel training centres. Minimum age 17 with a Junior or Leaving Cert.

Bartender: Either a one year full time course or obtain employment in a bar and attend college one day a week over three years. Training includes the study of alcoholic and non-alcoholic beverages, bar food, bar service, stock and cash control and licensing legislation.

Courses are available at ITs in Athlone, Galway Mayo and Cork – contact CERT for other locations. Minimum age 18 with a Junior, Senior or Leaving Cert.

Chef: Full time two year training course or obtain employment and attend college on one or two days each week. Training includes all aspects of cookery as well as kitchen operation, menu planning and food costing.

Training is at the Dublin College of Catering, and ITs at Athlone, Cork, Galway, Tallaght, Tralee, Dundalk, Limerick, Waterford and Sligo, as well as Killybegs Hotel Training & Catering College. Also the CERT Centre in Limerick. (*Contact CERT for locations of other centres*). Minimum age 17 with Junior, Senior or Leaving Cert.

Last year 1,600 applied for 500 places – 200 are reserved for applicants who've successfully completed a Vocational Preparation Training course.

Other specialised cookery courses are also available – most notably at the renowned Ballymaloe Cookery School in Cork.

Hospitality Assistant: Hospitality assistants must be multi-skilled and move easily into different areas as required. Their days work could include time in reception, in the kitchen, bar, bedrooms and diningroom – so they must have a basic training in all these areas. CERT runs a two year, full time hospitality skills course, and last year all graduates found employment. The courses are held at ITs in Athlone, Tallaght, Cork, Tralee, Galway-Mayo, Waterford, Limerick, Dundalk, Killybegs Tourism College and CERT hotel schools. Up to 300 places are available nationally.

Course in ITs at Athlone, Tralee, Waterford, Galway Mayo and Cork, as well as Killybegs Hotel Training & Catering College. Minimum age 17, with Junior, Senior or Leaving Cert.

Receptionist: One-year full-time course including work experience held in Donegal and Galway. Employed in hotels and large guesthouses. Work would include greeting guests, room reservations, registering guests, accounts and cash transactions and operating switchboards.

Applicants must be 18, and educated to Leaving Cert. with grade D or higher in five subjects, including English and Maths. The International Hotel Career Centre in Dublin runs both diploma and certificate courses in hotel reception.

Other Courses: Certificate in Hotel Front Office Administration, Athlone IT. Covers hotel and catering industry studies, office and accounting procedures, reception, language studies and marketing. Two year Certificate in Business Studies-Tourism at Cork IT, Diploma in Business Studies in Applied Tourism at Sligo IT, and two year course in tourism and travel at the College of Catering. FÁS also run a course in tourism enterprise at Shannon. Heritage Studies is on

offer at Galway Mayo and Tallaght ITs and applied cultural studies in Dundalk IT equip students to work in heritage centres.

PLC courses are available in a variety of areas in this sector. Hotel, Catering and Tourism is on offer at Monaghan Institute of Further Education and Training, Tralee Community College, and Ballyfermot Senior College, which also runs a course in Tourism, Reception and Craft Retailing.

SUGGESTIONS

Relevant work experience is essential for employment in this industry . . . obtain summer work in hotels, bars, summer camps and restaurants . . . experiment in your own kitchen . . . get to know more about food preparation, preservation, menus and budgeting . . . Learn a language . . . talk to people already working in catering, discover their main job likes and dislikes, relate these findings to yourself . . . arrange visits to local hotels etc . . . . enter cookery competitions, e.g. BIM's Fish Cookery Competition . . . check out CERT's Preliminary Course in Hotel and Catering Studies . . . learn how to drive . . . avail of school trips abroad . . . study Home Economics, Biology or Chemistry.

FURTHER INFORMATION

Athlone RTC, Dublin College of Catering, Galway RTC, Sligo RTC, Waterford RTC. See third- level section of this Directory.
Ballymaloe Cookery School, Barn Kinoith, Shangarry, Co. Cork (021-646785).

Bord Failte, Baggot St. Bridge, Dublin 2 (01-6024000).

CERT, CERT House, Amiens St., Dublin 1 (01-8556555).

Hotel Training School, Killybegs, Co. Donegal (073-31120).

International Hotel Career Centre, 44 Dawson Street, Dublin 2 (01-6798942).

Irish Hotels Federation, 13 Northbrook Road, Dublin 6.

Irish Travel Agents Association, 32 South William Street, Dublin 2 (01-6707679).

Licensed Vintners Association, Anglesea Road, Dublin 4 (01-6680215).

LSB College, 6-9 Balfe Street, Dublin 2 (01-6794844).

Northern Ireland Hotel & Catering College, Portrush, Co. Antrim. (08-0265-823768).

Portobello School, 40 Lr. Dominick Street, Dublin 1 (01-8721277).

Shannon College of Hotel Management, Shannon Airport (061-475075).

Look up "Hotels". "Caterers", "Restaurants", in Golden Pages Directory.

READ/VIEW

"It's the Business" — CERT (Video)

McDonnells Good Food Kitchen have produced a video and wallchart for schools.

Hotel and Catering (Career vision). A video on the Shannon College of Hotel Management is also available.

CERT – Free brochures, bar, waiting, chef and hotel management.

MARITIME/FISHING/ AQUA BUSINESS

Multi million investment to create 500 extra jobs

A recent study by Bord Iascaigh Mhara, the organisation which oversees the development of the fishing industry, has said that a doubling of EU and State spending on the marine sector could increase employment by twenty per cent. The bulk of this would be generated in remote regions which have been lagging behind the rest of the country in experiencing the current economic benefits.

Some 60,000 people, including 16,000 direct employees, are currently dependent on the seafood industry, which is worth more than £300 million annually in sales.

Employment in the industry is already on the increase, thanks to the £50 million investment package in the whitefish fleet. Many of the existing fishing vessels were old and unsafe, and have contributed to a number of accidents at sea over recent years.

However, this multi-million pound investment package is expected to benefit 400 vessel owners over a three year period, and allow new entrants into the industry – with the spin off of about 500 additional jobs.

Training in the industry is improving too. This year saw the opening of the State's second national fisheries training school at Castletownbere in County Cork. The new £500,000 regional fisheries centre will be run by Bord Iascaigh Mhara, along with its existing centre at Greencastle, County Donegal.

In addition, work on the establishment of a new national maritime college in Cork harbour is also continuing. It will service the needs of the merchant marine and Naval service.

The Cork Institute of Technology currently trains seafarers at its nautical studies department, but demand for qualified personnel had been exceeding supply. The new maritime college would accommodate 120 students annually – more than double the current capacity.

Fishing: Just 13% of fishing deckhands have had any formal training, and there's a huge shortage of trained crew in this country.

Training is at the BIM centre at Greencastle, Co. Donegal, or the newly established centre at Castletownbere in Co. Cork. It will accommodate 150 students each year. BIM offers intensive courses in seafaring, safety and survival, navigation, wheelhouse electronics, fish farm husbandry, fish handling, hygiene and quality control. The duration of the courses is from 30 to 400 hours.

There are no specific educational requirements for the courses, which are free with accommodation provided. Applicants should be aged between 16 and 21, and physically fit with good eyesight.

Aquaculture: The BIM blueprint for the next six years has advised the Government that increased investment in the fishing industry could more than double the output from aquaculture or fish farming – from £59 million to £123 million annually.

Farmed salmon and trout are perhaps the best known among these enterprises, but the industry has been diversifying, with shellfish becoming more common.

A one million pound cross-border investment programme has been put in place, so that counties north and south can share expertise in fish and shellfish farming.

Meanwhile, a recent report on aquaculture in the Shannon estuary has identified the potential to create 500 new jobs. It says the oyster harvest could increase in the next decade, from less than 450 tons to 4,000 tons. And it says the estuary could also have a significant mussel industry of up to 13,000 tons if current trials are successful. It also recommends developing seaweed, and species such as eels, sea urchins, halibut and turbot in the region.

The range of work required in fish farming is immense. Farm workers, divers, boat handlers, fish pathologists, environmental maintenance people and financial handlers are all employed in the industry, along with processing and packaging workers. The attractions of aquaculture are quite similar to those of farming.

BIM runs a 34 week training course at its centre in Greencastle. Galway IT has certificate and diploma courses, while Tralee and Letterkenny IT have certificate courses in aquaculture technology UCC runs a one year diploma course, and UCG offers an undergraduate degree in marine science.

Navy: The Minister for the Defence has promised 70 extra recruits for the Naval service. Normally, a small number of cadetships and apprenticeships are offered every year. Cadets undergo three months basic military training at the Curragh, then go on to the Naval Cadet School at Haulbowline in Cork before going out to sea. Later there are a number of career paths. As a seaman/executive officer you would be responsible for the smooth running of a ship. An engineering officer would manage and maintain the equipment – after completing a three year diploma in marine engineering and a nine month post-graduate course abroad. These jobs would both be at sea, but if you wanted to be land based, you could aim to be a supply and administrative officer – responsible for keeping ships supplied with equipment.

Marine Engineer: Maintains the machinery of the vessel, and ensures that it can be operated efficiently and safely. Can move into shore based employment, as the skills adapt to machinery in factories, power stations etc. Training is at the National Marine Training centre at Cork IT.

Minimum entry requirements are five Leaving Cert subjects, grade D at ordinary or higher level, including Maths, English or Irish and a science subject. Applicants must also pass medical, fitness and eyesight tests.

Once in a shipping company, the chances of promotion are very good. Graduates could reach chief engineer by their late twenties.

Deck Cadet: The deck cadet course run by the Nautical Studies Dept. at Cork IT prepares people to be ships' navigation officers on a variety of vessels – from cruise ships to oil tankers.

Job prospects for Irish cadets elsewhere in the EU are set to grow, because of the increased emphasis on vessel safety by the international shipping authorities.

Harbour Workers: The Government appears to be committed to the upgrading of ports and harbours around the country. In the last budget, funding for fisheries harbours was up almost 150%, with Killybegs, Dingle, Burtonport, Greencastle ad Kilmore Quay identified as priorities. In addition, over the last number of years, some £35 million has been invested in the development of Waterford Port.

Jobs would include seamen, dockers, clerical and administration staff. Other shore-based jobs include some filled by people with deck officer qualifications – such as pilots, harbour masters, marine surveyors and superintendents. There are also jobs in shipping companies and in marine insurance.

SUGGESTIONS

Join Sea Scouts — Sail in Asgard II (15 year old's are invited to sail on programmes from March to October) . . . visit local harbours, docks seloot subjooto carefully, e.g. biology/chemistry for marine studies or physics for naval cadet . . . join Slua Muiri . . . participate in water sports, swimming, boating, diving, etc. . . . . try to get a summer job aboard a ship, holiday cruiser or fishing boat. Visit fish farms. Do project on the fishing industry for the Young Scientist of the Year Competition.

FURTHER INFORMATION

Asgard Coiste An Sáil Training Scheme, Infirmary Road, Dublin 7 (01-6792169).

Bord Iascaigh Mhara, Crofton Road, Dun Laoghaire, Co. Dublin (01-2841544).

British Shipping Careers Service, The General Council of British Shipping, 30-32 St. Mary's Ave., London EC 3A 8ET.

Department of Marine, Leeson Lane, Leeson St., Dublin 2 (01-6785444).

Marconi International Marine Co., Tolka Quay Road, Dublin 1 (01-8555157).

Marine Port and General Workers Union, 14 Gardiner Place, Dublin 1 (01-8726566).

Marine Rescue Co-ordination Centre, Shannon Airport.

Naval Base, Hawlbowline, Cobh, Co. Cork (021- 811246).

Naval Service, Department of Defence, Parkgate Street, Dublin 8 (01-6771881).

Royal National Lifeboats Institution, 15 Windsor Terrace, Dun Laoire, Dublin 2 (01-2845050).

Royal Navy Careers Service, Old Admiralty Building, Whitehall, London SWIA 2BE.

The Merchant Navy Training Board, 30-32 St. Mary's Avenue, London EC 3A 8ET.

The National Fishery Training Centre, Greencastle, Co. Donegal.

READ/VIEW

The Naval Service produces a variety of literature, posters and a video.

Aquaculture Explained — BIM.

Irish Offshore Review, Irish Skipper and *Irish Fishing Industry* in periodicals.

Marconi Marine Careers — address above.

Fisheries Training — BIM.

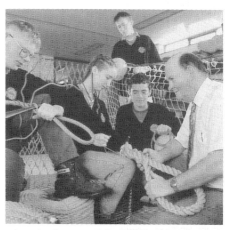

Learning the ropes at the fisheries training centre.

MEDIA/COMMUNICATIONS/ PRINTING

Broadcasting Revolution Coming

Some enthusiasts believe it'll be the biggest change since the advent of colour television. Others say it's the greatest broadcasting revolution since television itself. It is, of course, digital television, which, over the next fifteen years, will fundamentally alter this medium for a worldwide television audience.

Ireland will be no exception. Thirty channels will be on offer here, with RTE getting an extra three on top of RTE 1 and Network 2. One is likely to be a twenty four hour news channel; another an educational channel, and there'll be lots of scope for regional programming under the new system.

All of this will mean many more opportunities for people who want to work in television. Although much of the new programming will be bought in from abroad, it's likely there will be some rules laid down which will set a minimum target for home produced news and entertainment.

Even in the last few years, there have been huge changes in the broadcasting environment here. TV3 and Telefís na Gaeilge have generated several hundred new jobs in televisionk while Today FM and local radio stations have been consolidating their audience, and look as if they're here to stay. And more jobs in radio are coming on stream with RTE's new Limerick based music station, Lyric FM.

The film industry continues to thrive here. The success of 'Saving Private Ryan' has been followed by films like 'This is My Father'. The Film Board has received an increase of £750,000 to go towards helping indigenous Irish film projects, and an industry think tank has been working on how to develop this growing industry to its full potential.

Cinemas and video outlets are doing well too. A recent EU survey found that the Irish rent three times as many videos as our nearest rivals, the Danes, and we're also top of the filmgoing league – with cinema attendances up more than 50% in the last five years.

Communications: DCU offers a degree in Communications Studies, which covers everything from broadcasting, writing, graphics, and film theory to marketing and economics. DIT Aungier St. has a four year communications degree, which is practical, with a view to the film and video industry. DIT and Tallaght IT provide courses at technician level. Communications has proved very popular at post-Leaving Cert level, and a number of VECs, e.g., Marino College, Colaiste Dhulaigh and Senior College Ballyfermot now have courses. All these courses are now certified by NCVA.

Film: More than 2,000 people are employed in the film industry, which appears to be flourishing. In the independent film and TV sector this year, six out of every ten companies increased their staff numbers.

Film and video are part of the communications degrees at DCU and DIT Aungier St. Training is also available at Mayo, Dun Laoghaire and Galway IT's. UCD has an MA in Film Studies, which has a practical element, and Film Studies is also available through its arts degree. The organisation Filmbase provides facilities, equipment, information, training and support for 200 filmmakers and lobbies on their behalf.

TV Producer/Director: Usually degree standard of education with experience in current affairs, drama, education, sport etc. the tendency is to recruit people in their late 20's or older, and often from other grades in RTE such as researcher or production assistant.

Animation: Ballyfermot Senior College runs three animation courses at certificate and diploma level. The courses are very well respected internationally, and are one of twelve worldwide officially linked to the biggest name in world animation, Walt Disney.

Graduates tend to secure employment immediately, and there are good travel prospects, as there's a worldwide deficit of animators, particularly in the US.

At home the industry is also quite healthy, with computer games and television, rather than film, the main areas of expansion.

The Chicago-based games company TerraGlyph Interactive has set up here - employing many Don Bluth staff, and Norwegian company Funcam has also located in this country, attracted by the numbers of suitably trained artists.

Journalism: DCU offers a BA and MA in journalism, and also an MSc in Science Communications, with the aim of training students to become communicators in the news media, industry, government and public affairs.

Journalism students at DIT Aungier Street now have the option of a diploma or degree. UCG offers a one year post-graduate diploma which teaches broadcast journalism skills through Irish. Dun Laoghaire IT offers a Certificate in Radio Broadcasting in alternate years. At Ballyfermot Senior College there's a Higher Diploma in Radio and Journalism, also Print Journalism and Media Management, which covers journalism, PR, current affairs, advertising and financial planning and control. Dun Laoire Community College (01-2809676) have a diploma in media, print, radio and T.V. Graduates receive City & Guilds, R.S.A. and certification from the Irish Institute of Journalism & Theatre. G.C.D. (Griffith College, Dublin) offers a range of courses. Post-Leaving Cert and FÁS courses are also available.

Researcher: RTE advertises for researchers every couple of years and a panel is formed to fill any further vacancies. Candidates are usually graduates with experience in research, journalism, or some area of programme making, i.e. music. Researchers work closely with programme producers, gathering information and conducting interviews for items, assessing the suitability of guests and finding interested parties to contribute from the audience.

Production Assistant: The PA is responsible for timing and calling all shots in a production. A Leaving Cert. is the minimum requirement but in practice most candidates have a third-level qualification as well as a broad range of interests. The job used to be seen as a secretarial position but increasingly it is viewed as a stepping stone to directing.

Operator: This covers areas like sound, lighting and video tape recording. Ballyfermot Senior College and Colaiste Dhulaigh run two post-Leaving Cert. courses in radio and tv operation and radio production and studio operation.

Music industry: It should be stressed that only a handful will ever make it as performers. With only one in ten records released making a profit, there's little or no reward for those who fail to make a breakthrough on the international market.

However, the prospects are steadier for people who opt for production or management.

Courses in Ballyfermot Senior College and Scoil Stiofain Naofa in Cork are among those available. Both cover the management of bands, as well as production and performance.

Studio training is also provided by the Sound Training Centre.

Photography: Kevin Street has a three year, full time diploma, and a degree course is planned. Commercial photography courses in Dun Laoghaire IT and Marino College, Dublin 3 (01-8339342). Photographers can find work in the medical, industrial, fashion and journalistic fields.

Multi-media: The print, electronics, TV and film industries are merging, with newspapers already available on our computer screens. Multi-media involves combining text, sound, pictures and video on one interactive device.

Colaiste Dhulaigh and Tallaght IT offer courses in multi-media. Students can move into graphic design, computer aided design, publishing, advertising, digital sound or TV editing, and the devising of multi-media software packages. DIT Aungier Street have introduced an MA in Interactive Multimedia and Dun Laoghaire IT has an add-on degree year for holders of a Diploma in Communication Design.

Writing: It seems there's never been a better time to be a young Irish writer, with publishers prepared to hand over massive advances to encourage talent. Cathy Kelly, John Connolly, Antonia Logue and Eamon Sweeney are some of the more recent arrivals on this thriving scene, while others like Joseph O'Connor and Marian Keyes have now produced several novels and are well establshed.

Publishing: There are about a hundred and forty publishing firms in this country. But the workforce is very small – 80% have four or fewer people working in them. Most jobs are in marketing and sales, but in the smaller companies, you'd be expected to do just about everything. Many begin with jobs in bookshops to learn the market.

Printing: Printing today is a multi-faceted industry, employing some 16,000 people. The production of high quality, printed material is an increasingly high-tech production process, involving typesetters, graphic and layout artists, graphic reproducers and plate makers, as well as printers. Cork IT offers a National Certificate in Technology – Printing and publishing. Also available in Bolton Street.

SUGGESTIONS

Journalism: Write to and for newspapers, magazines, etc., even if it is only to the letters column, making sure you keep a copy of anything published . . . learn typing and shorthand . . . try to develop special writing skills . . . offer to act as PRO for organisations to which you belong . . . read all daily papers (local library, newspaper offices, etc.) and compare the different treatment given by each to similar stories . . . Set up a school or community magazine . . . Try to organise a visit to a newspaper office . . . Go on one of the regular tours given in RTE.

Communications: look critically at television programmes, advertisements, etc . . . pursue hobbies like photography and recording . . . visit radio and television museum . . . act as disc jockey for local discos . . . send "demo" tapes to studios . . . get work experience with your local radio station or hospital radio . . . Photography: Visit Irish Film Centre . . . attend their junior film festival. Join a camera club . . . develop your own photographs . . . visit photographic exhibitions, e.g. Camera Circle's 100 Best Press Photographs.

FURTHER INFORMATION

BBC, Broadcasting House, London WIA IAA.

Irish Book Publishers Association, 34 Nth. Frederick Street, Dublin 1 (01-8729090).

Griffith College Dublin,South Circular Road, Dublin 8 (01-4545640).

Independent Broadcasting Authority, Crawley Court, Winchester, Hants SO21 2QA.

Irish Film Centre, Eustace St., Dublin 2. (01-6778788).

Irish Print Union, 35 Lower Gardiner St., Dublin 1 (01-8743662).

Irish Professional Photographers Association, 5 Knocklyon Road, Dublin 16. (01-4939488).

National Union of Journalists, Liberty Hall, Dublin 2 (01-8748694).

RTE, Donnybrook, Dublin 4 (01-2083111).

Sound Training Centre, Temple Bar Music Centre, Curved St., Dublin (01-6709033)

See "Golden Pages" under "recording studios", "news-papers", "publishers", and "publications".

READ/VIEW

Every newspaper, journal and publication you can read.

Media Careers (Best Guides).

Making Your Mark — producing your own publication. Women's Community Press.

Writers and Artists Yearbook (published by A. and C. Black).

Doing it in Style, by Leslie Sellers (Pergamon Press).

The Successful Author's Handbook by Gordon Wells.

MEDICAL/PARAMEDICAL/ NURSING

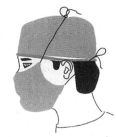

Six applicants for every place but employment prospects are excellent

The demand for health professionals is strong. Career prospects for occupational therapists, physiotherapists and opticians are excellent. There is a shortage of speech and language therapists and therapeutic radiographers.

Entry into medical and paramedical courses is very competitive, however, with cut off points consistently high. The number of places on the courses are limited, and this coupled with the popularity and high status of many of the jobs, results in far more applicants than there are places. At degree level alone there are on average 6 applicants for every place.

Employment prospects for nurses are very good but again demand outweighs supply, there were four applicants for each place last year. The demand for psychiatric and mental handicap nursing places was far lower than for general nursing places. Of the 117 mental handicap places last year only 72 were filled while 92 of he 201 psychiatric places were filled.

Nursing: Nursing education is still in a state of transition having moved from the old apprenticeship styled model to a 3-year college associated diploma. Once qualified there is an option to take a further year's study for a degree. There have been changes since last year and the foreign language is no longer required for entry to nursing.

Trainee nurses are no longer part of the hospital workforce, but divide their time between college and hospital, doing hospital work as a learning exercise. After completing a three year diploma, students are eligible to register with An Bord Altranais. There is then an option to take a further year's study to obtain a degree.

Doctor: The career path is a long haul – graduating from university is only half way there. Further study and exams are needed to get into just about any field, including becoming a GP.

More than three hundred people qualify with medical degrees every year, yet in the State sector, no more than seventy positions – in general practice, hospital consultancy and public health – come up each year.

Those lucky enough to secure one of the 150 training places in a hospital will have to face working very long hours – on average, 70 per week, sometimes 100.

Radiographer: There are two courses, at UCD and TCD, with 30 places between them. The UCD degree is concerned with diagnostic radiography; TCD's course is therapeutic radiography – one of the main methods used in treating people with cancer. The TCD course has been upgraded from diploma to degree standard.

There is also a course at the University of Ulster which has up to 40 places. The majority of applicants last year were from the Republic.

Currently there are about 700 radiographers

working in Ireland. There is world-wide shortage of therapeutic radiographers so graduates have no trouble in getting employment, A survey of UCD's diagnostic radiography graduates found that 50% were in permanent employment and the remainder in temporary employment.

Optician: There are two different streams. Ophthalmic opticians (now called optometrists) who test eyes and prescribe glasses, and dispensing opticians, who measure and fit glasses according to prescription. The former involves a four year degree course at the DIT in Kevin Street. The dispensing optician also trains at Kevin Street. There's no shortage of employment - last year all graduates secured jobs here. The new walk-in chainstore opticians have created some new opportunities.

Medical Laboratory Science: Although this was listed in the CAO handbook as a three year certificate course available at the DIT Kevin St, and Galway and Cork IT, in practice 99% of graduates have gone on to take another two years to bring their qualification up to degree level.

The Department of Health won't recognise the certificate as a suitable entry requirement for hospitals under its control, so prospective students must bear in mind that it's really the degree they'll have to do. Biomedical Science can be studied at degree level in NUI Galway. An aptitude for science and interest in medicine is necessary. The job involves disease diagnosis and monitoring, and also an element of preventive screening.

The job scene for medical laboratory science graduates is reasonably good, most find jobs in temporary and locum positions but it may take a while to secure a permanent position. They find jobs in diagnostic labs in hospitals, research labs, the food and pharmaceutical industries. A qualification in biomedical science also offers opportunities to work in diagnostic labs.

Pharmacists: More pharmacists are due to begin coming on stream in a few years, now that Trinity has doubled the number of places on its degree course from 50 to 100. However, the shortage of pharmacists should ensure that there will still be jobs for all who qualify.

Because competition for places in Ireland is so stiff many students apply to colleges in Britain and Northern Ireland.

A Post-Leaving Cert. course, retail pharmacy aide, is available at Colaiste Ide, Cardiffsbridge Road, Dublin 11, and FÁS runs a Pharmacy Sales Assistant course at Loughlinstown.

Physiotherapy: Physiotherapists work in a variety of situations in hospitals, clinics, patients' homes or in their own practice. They work with children helping to treat spina bifida, cerebral palsy and cystic fibrosis; with outpatients who've had accidents, sports injuries or arthritis; in intensive care keeping limbs mobile and chests cleared, and in maternity giving ante and post natal classes.

UCD and Trinity College both have four-year degree courses. Up to 5 places will be offered to Irish students on the new physiotherapy course at the RCSI. Training is largely hospital based. There appears to be no unemployment in this career, and Irish physiotherapists who choose to travel have earned worldwide recognition.

Hospital Administration Staff: Many of the management in hospitals come from the ranks of the medical or nursing staff, but there are a number of positions at clerical and administration level. These would generally require some secretarial/office administration qualification, and an additional secretarial dimension, such as medical reception skills, would be an advantage.

Dentist: Dentistry is still a popular career choice. TCD and UCC both have Dental Science degrees, turning out between 70 and 80 graduates each year. The salary and prospects are good - the main problem is getting a place on one of the courses. Twelve colleges in Britain, and Queen's university in Belfast also offer dentistry, but they're also difficult to get into. A large proportion of newly qualified graduates enter the public dental service operated by the health board as they need to be able to invest a substantial amount to buy into a practice. Many go abroad for a few years after graduating.

For the following dental careers applicants apply through the admissions office in the relevant institution and not through the CAO.

Dental Nurse: There is a one-year certificate course in dental nursing at TCD. However many dental nurses are taken on and trained on the job.

Dental Technician: TCD dental school offers a 3-year diploma course in dental technology.

Dental Hygienist: UCC and TCD offer 2 year diploma courses in dental hygiene, only a limited number of places are open to school leavers.

Speech and Language therapists: There are 26 first year places on the clinical speech and language degree in TCD. the University of Ulster also offers a four-year degree course in speech and language therapy.

Applied Physiology and Health Sciences: Carlow IT has a 2 year certificate course in applied physiology and health sciences, most graduates of the course get onto paramedical courses in Britain and Northern Ireland i.e. physiotherapy, occupational therapy, speech and language therapy, radiology and dietetics The cut off points in 1998 were 415, a good deal lower than any of the paramedical courses.

Dietician: Advises on the adaptation of menus for individual diets and the provision of meals of good nutritional value in hospitals. Communicates with doctors, nurses and other health professionals in the course of this work.

There are up to 25 places at the DIT Kevin St.

There are 30 places on the University of Ulster's BSc in Human Nutrition. UCC also offers a nutritional science degree, which trains nutritionists for the food and healthcare industries.

Holistic Medicine: This form of "alternative" medicine concentrates on prevention rather than cure. The underlying principle is that there's a basic energy within us which can be released to enhance well-being.

Pearse College, Dublin and Bray Senior College offers a one year post-leaving cert course in Holistic Health Studies. Subjects include holistic philosophy, nutrition, massage and organic cooking.

Entry requirements are an interest in the area. Job prospects would include health store or health food department management, sales rep for nutritional specialists, gym and leisure management, and consultancy.

Ambulance Personnel: Recruitment is through the health boards. Dublin Corporation has an ambulance service and there are some private services.

Training for this job is changing. From now on, drivers and attendants will be known as emergency medical technicians, and will train over two years at the National Ambulance Training School, combined with on-the-job experience.

Minimum requirements are a pass Leaving Cert. with English, Maths and a science subject. Prospective applicants are advised to join voluntary ambulance organisations, which will introduce them to the basics.

 # MEDICAL/HEALTH COURSES in CAO

1. For details of courses consult College Prospectuses.
2. See index for Post Leaving Certificate Courses.
3. Nursing Studies are run in association with colleges listed. You apply through the National Application Centre not CAO.

	T.C.D.	N.U.I. Galway	U.C.C.	U.C.D.	Athlone IT	Dundalk IT	Letterkenny IT	D.I.T.	Cork IT	Galway Mayo IT	R.C.S.I.	University Limerick	Carlow IT	Sligo IT	D.C.U.	Waterford IT	Letterkenny IT	Dundalk IT	St. Angelas, Sligo
Applied Physiology/Health Science												•							
Clinical Speech	•																		
Dental Science	•		•																
Environmental Health								•						•					
Health Care Technology								•											
Human Nutrition/Dietetics			•					•											
Medical Laboratory Science								•	•	•									
Medicine	•	•	•	•							•								
Nursing	•	•	•	•	•	•	•					•		•	•	•	•	•	•
Occupational Therapy	•																		
Optometry								•											
Pharmacy/Pharmaceutical	•										•		•						
Physiotherapy	•		•								•								
Radiography	•		•																
Sports Science												•			•				
Biomedical Science		•																	
Biomedical Engineering		•										•							
Medical Chemistry	•																		
Medical Mechanical Engineering																•			
Occupational Safety														•					·

NURSE TRAINING

An Bord Altranais Minimum Educational Requirements

Applicants for admission to the Registration/Diploma programmes must:

(a) be at least 17 years of age on June 1 of the year of application

(b) have obtained in the Leaving Certificate examination a minimum grade of C3 in two higher level papers and a minimum grade of D3 in four ordinary or highr level papers in the following subjects:

- English or Irish (not Foundation level Irish)
- Mathematics (not Foundation level)
- A Laboratory Science subject (Biology, Physics, Chemistry, Physics and Chemistry [joint] or Agricultural Science)
- Three other subjects (may include Irish or English and a Laboratory Science subject not included already, or other subjects)

or

- Have equivalent second level educational qualifications to the foregoing

(c) meet the minimum educational requirements specified by the third level institution concerned for entry to the programme.

The minimum educational erquirements referred to in the foregoing paragraph may be accumulated over not more than two sittings of the Leaving Certificate examination or an equivalent examination.

Read *Nursing, a Career For You*, available from An Bord Altranais, 31-32 Fitzwilliam Square, Dublin 2 (includes details of some special 3rd level requirements).

GRANTS/FEES/OTHER BENEFITS

- An annual non-means-tested maintenance grant will be paid by the health board/hospital to students.
- Students are responsible for their own accommodation.
- Diploma programme fees are paid.
- Uniforms, meals, and principal textbooks are also provided free of charge.

NURSING DEGREES

A one year programme leading to a degree in nursing is available from third level institutes. The degree programme is an optional post-registration qualification. Entry to the degree programme will be open to nurses who successfully register with An Bord Altranais and gain the Diploma in Nursing. Since the degree programme is optional, nurses will be responsible for making their own arrangements for admission to, attendance at and the costs associated with such programmes.

NURSING APPLICATIONS AND INFORMATION

Application forms for general and psychiatric applicants are available from the Nursing Careers Centre P.O. Box 6703, Dublin 2.

Mental Handicap: The National Applications Centre – Mental Handicap, PO Box 3017, Dublin 15.Telephone: 01-821 7266.

General Information on Nursing is available from An Bord Altranais, 31/32 Fitzwilliam Square,

NURSING COURSES

Students may apply for three types of nurse training: **1. General Nursing 2. Psychiatric Nursing 3. Mental Handicap Nursing.** Successful completion of the Programmes will lead to registration in the General/Psychiatric/Mental Handicap Divisions of the Register of Nurses maintained by An Bord Altranais and to the award of a Diploma in Nursing from the third level institute associated with the School of Nursing.

Registration/Diploma Programme Centres Schools of Nursing, Nursing Disciplines and the linked third level institution

Linked third Level Institution	Discipline	Schol of Nursing
Athlone Institute of Technology	General	• Midland Health Board School of Nursing

Dublin City University	General
	
	Psychiatric
	
	Mental Handicap
		• Beaumont Hospital
		• James Connolly Memorial Hospital
		• St. Vincent's, Fairview
		• Eastern Health Board (North)
		  St. Ita's Hospital, Portrrane
		• Eastern Health board
		  St. Ita's Hospital, Portrane
		• St. Joseph's, Clonsilla

Dundalk Institute of Technology	General Mental Handicap	• Our Lady of Lourdes Hospital, Drogheda • St. Mary's, Drumcar
Letterkenny Institute of Technology	General Psychiatric	• Letterkenny General Hospital • North Western Health Board

National University of Ireland Galway	General
	
	Psychiatric
	Mental Handicap
		• University College Hospital,
		• Portiuncula Hospital
		• Sligo General Hiospital (via
		  St. Angela's College of Education,
		  Sligo
		• Western Health Board
		•Cregg House (via St. Angela's
		  College of Education, Sligo)

University College Cork	General Psychiatric Mental Handicap	•Bon Secours Hospital • Cork University Hoispital • Cork Voluntary Hospitals • Southern Health Board • COPE Foundation
University College Dublin	General Psychiatric	•Mater Hospital • St. Vincent's Hospital, Elm Park • St. John of God Hospital, Stillorgan
University of Limerick	General Psychieatric Mental Handicap	• School of Nursing, Limerick • Mid-Western health Board • St. Vincent's Centre, Lisnagry

University of Dublin, Trinity College	General
	
	Psychiatric
	
	Mental Handicap
		• Adelaide School of Nursing
		• Meath School of Nursing
		• St. James's Hospital
		• Eastern Health Board (South),
		  St. James's Hospital
		• St. Patrick's Hospital
		• Stewart's Hospital, Dublin
		• St. Anne's, Moore Abbey,
		  Monasterevin

Waterford Institute of Technology	General Psychiatric	• Waterford Regional Hospital • South Eastern Health Board

SUGGESTIONS

Study science subjects . . . also Irish, English and a 3rd language to satisfy new National Application Centre (nurse entry requirements) . . . join voluntary organisations like Civil Defence, Red Cross or St. John's Ambulance . . . see list of helping agencies in this Yearbook . . . seek vacation work in hospitals - attendants, kitchen staff . . . attend DIT lectures on para-medical careers . . . join your Mental Health association . . . Is there a voluntary organisation in your locality you can assist? e.g. remedial clinics; wheelchair association; meals on wheels; community welfare organisations; Simon Community . . . many hospitals patients never have visitors - could you befriend a patient? . . . Check our Pre-Nursing courses available countrywide (see the PLC Section of this Yearbook).

FURTHER INFORMATION

Academy of Medical Laboratory Science, R.D.S., Ballsbridge, Dublin 4.

An Bord Altranais, 31/32 Fitzwilliam Square, Dublin 2 (01-6760226). (Controlling Body for Nursing)

Department of Radiography, UCD, Belfield, Dublin 4 (01-2693244).

Dept. of Health, Hawkins House, Dublin 2 (01-6714711).

Environmental Health Officers Association of Ireland, 9 Aston Quay, Dublin 2 (01-6712266).

Irish Association of Dental Surgery Auxiliaries, 18 Farmhill Park, Goatstown, Dublin 14. (01-2985810).

Irish Association of Speech Therapists, Mater Hospital, Dublin 1.

Irish Dental Assoc., 10 Richview Office Park, Clonskeagh, Dublin 14. (01-2830499)

Irish Medical Organisation, 10 Fitzwilliam Place, Dublin 2 (01-6767273).

Irish Nutrition and Dietetic Institute, Dundrum Business Centre, Frankfort, Dundrum, Dublin 14 (01-2964247)

Irish Red Cross Society, 16 Merrion Sq., Dublin 2 (01-6765135)

Irish Society of Chartered Physiotherapists, Royal College of Surgeons, 84–85 Harcourt St., Dublin 2 (01-4022148).

Nurse Application Centre (Mental Handicap) P.O. Box 3017, Dublin 15 (01-821 7266).

Nursing Careers Centre (General Psychiatric Nursing) P.O. Box 6703, Dublin 2.

Opticians Board, 18 Fitzwilliam Sq., Dublin 2 (01- 6767416).

Order of Malta, 32 Clyde Road, Dublin 4 (01-6684308).

Royal College of Surgeons in Ireland, 123 St. Stephen's Green, Dublin 2 (01-4022100)

School of Radiography, St. Luke's Hospital, D. 6 (01-4974552)

St. John's Ambulance Brigade, 29 Upper Leeson St., Dublin 2 (01-6688077).

St. Joseph's College of Occupational Therapy, Rochestown Ave., Dun Laoire (01-2852677)

The Irish Dental Association, 10 Richview Office Pk., Clonskeagh, Dublin 14. (01-2830499).

The Mental Health Association of Ireland, 6 Adelaide St., Dun Laoghaire, Co. Dublin (01-2841166).

The Pharmaceutical Society of Ireland, 37 Northumberland Road, Dublin 4 (01-6600699)

Royal College of Surgeons in Ireland

MEDICAL SCHOOL

123 St. Stephen's Green, Dublin 2, Ireland

The College prospectus and all details concerning admission to both the medical and physiotherapy programmes may be obtained from the Admissions Office at the College. Please note that application to the Royal College of Surgeons in Ireland is via the C.A.O., Tower House, Eglinton Street, Galway.

Medical Scholarships

The Royal College of Surgeons in Ireland awards full and partial scholarships on the Leaving Certificate and on the Scholarship Examination in General Education.

For further details contact the Admissions Office.

The Admissions Officer, Royal College of Surgeons in Ireland
Tel: 402 2228 Fax: 402 2451
e.mail: admission@rcsi.ie World Wide Web: http//www.rcsi.ie

READ

Nursing a Career For You – An Bord Altranais
The Pharmacist and the Pharmaceutical Technician — The Pharmaceutical Society of Ireland, 37 Northumberland Road, Dublin 4.
Caring in the Fullest Sense, a pamphlet prepared by regis-

tered nurses of Mentally Handicapped.
Careers pamphlets obtainable from your local Health Boards, e.g. *Careers with the Eastern Health Board.*

HEALTH BOARDS

Eastern Health Boards, Dr. Steven's Hospital, Dublin 8 (01-1800 520520)

Mid-Western Health Board, 31-33 Catherine St., Limerick (061-31665)

North Western Health Board, Manorhamilton, Co. Leitrim (072-55123)

Western Health Board, Merlin Park, Galway. (081-751131)

Midland Health Board, Tullamore, Co. Offaly. (0506-21868)

North Eastern Health Board, Kells, Co. Meath. (046-40341)

South Eastern Health Board, Dublin Road, Kilkenny. (056-51702)

Southern Health Board, Wilton Rd, Cork. (021-545011)

MEDICAL AND PARAMEDICAL COURSES IN THE U.K.

Because of the level of competition for medical nursing courses (from radiography to physiotherapy) in Ireland many students look to the U.K. for a real alternative. Students should check carefully their maintenance grant/fee eligibility for paramedical courses in the U.K as funding comes from a variety of sources. In the case of medicine there are no maintenance grants available for Irish students to study outside Ireland.

NURSING

English National Board for Nursing, Midwifery and Health Visiting – Careers Section, PO Box 2EN, London, WIA 2EN,

(Careers Information)

National Board for Nursing Midwifery and Health Visiting for Scotland – 22 Queen Street, Edinburgh, EH2 1NT

(Careers Information)

National Board for Nursing, Midwifery and Health Visiting for Scotland – Catch, PO Box 21, Edinburgh, EH2 1NT

(Application Package)

Welsh National Board for Nursing, Midwifery and Health Visiting, – 2nd Floor, Golate house, 101 St. Mary Street, Cardiff CF1 1DX

(Careers Information)

Degree Courses Application to: – UCAS, PO Box 28, Cheltenham, Gloucestershire, GL50 3SH

Diploma Course (Project 2000) Application to: – NMAS, UCAS, PO Box 28, Cheltenham, Gloucestershire, GL50 3SH

NORTHERN IRELAND – National Board for Nursing, Midwifery and Health Visiting for Northern Ireland, R.A.C. House, 79B Chichester Street, Belfast BT1 4JR. (08-01-232 238152) (Careers Information)

NORTHERN IRELAND

Application Forms:
Queen's School of Nursing and Midwifery, Queen's University, 1-3 College Park East, Belfast BT7 1LQ (08-01-232 245133)

WALES
Apply directly to colleges.

NURSING SEMINARS

The Irish Chaplains Association, 57 Parnell Sq., West, Dublin 1 (01) 8723655 will:

• answer queries on nursing in the U.K

• arrange seminars on nursing in the U.K. throughout Ireland every October. Please enclose S.A.E. for useful booklet and information.

A very useful source of information on such courses and grants is the British Council, Newmount House, 22 Lr. Mount Street, Dublin 2. (open to public 2.30–5.00pm, Mon. to Fri.)

LSB
COLLEGE
LIBERAL ARTS · SOCIAL SCIENCES · BUSINESS

COLLEGE CHOICES FOR SCHOOL-LEAVERS

LSB College offers school-leavers in 2000 the following full-time Degree, Diploma and Certificate courses, validated by the NCEA, ICM or LSB:

3 Year NCEA Degree Programmes

LS101	Anthropology
LS201	Arts (General) – Three first-year subjects from Anthropology, Art History, Economics, French <u>or</u> German, Literature and Drama, Philosophy, Politics, Psychoanalysis
LS202	Arts (Psychology)
LS203	Arts (Sociology)
LS301	Psychoanalytic Studies
LS401	Business (Computing)
LS501	Business (Marketing)
LS502	Business (Psychology)
LS601	Tourism (Language)
LS602	Tourism (Marketing)

2 Year NCEA National Certificate Programmes

LS421	Information Technology/Computing
LS422	Business Studies (Office Information Systems)
LS521	Business Studies

1 Year Programmes

LS211	Certificate in Arts in Cultural Studies
IT251	Diploma in Business and Computer Skills
BS241	Diploma in Marketing, Advertising and Public Relations
BS242	Diploma in Tourism Studies

Notes:
1. Applications for Degree, National Certificate and Certificate programmes are through the CAO admissions system.
2. Applications for Diploma courses should be made directly to the College.
3. Tuition fees are payable for all courses.

For further information and a Prospectus call in or telephone:

LSB College, Balfe Street, Dublin 2

A Bonded College and a Member of HECA

Tel: 01 679 4844 Fax: 01 679 4205

e-mail: admissions@lsb.ie   Web Site: www.indigo.ie/lsb

Where Third-Level is First-Class

OFFICE/BUSINESS/ SECRETARIAL

Banks recruiting in large numbers again

The past few years have been somewhat nervous ones for those employed in any form of commerce in this country – from currency dealing to small businesses. For, despite the benefits of the booming economy, all have been waiting to see just how European Monetary Union will work – how the new currency will perform on the international markets, and what effect the more centralised European economic control will have on Ireland's fortunes, particularly if the boom times come to an end.

But despite a degree of uncertainty, things have rarely looked so good for the financial community. Business leaders, particularly, are confident of increased sales and economic growth, and, most importantly, greater employment in their own companies.

Ireland's current success has owed a great deal to the deliberate creation of a business-friendly culture, and this is particularly evident at present. There has never been a better time to be an entrepreneur, and small businesses in particular are taking advantage of low interest rates and the willingness of the banks to lend money for expansion purposes. In fact, their main complaint is the difficulties of recruiting suitable staff for these larger businesses.

Almost 5,000 people are now employed in the Financial Services Centre, in a development which could, to all appearances, be part of the City of London. Most of the world's major financial institutions are now represented there, and many of the Irish institutions either have branches in the centre, or have relocated their main office to it. Always regarded as an exciting and glamorous place to work, it's particularly so now, as people here are at the cutting edge of the latest developments on the Euro front.

After a period of somewhat piecemeal recruitment over the last few years, the banks are starting to take on people in large numbers again. AIB, for example, is recruiting 500 staff who will work at branch level and in customer and support services.

Financial Services: This involves treasury management, accounting and control management, stock broking, investment analysis, taxation and personal financial planning, as well as mergers and acquisitions.

Fund management/administration is predicted to be the biggest growth area over the coming years.

Dublin City University is offering a two year day release Masters in Investment and Treasury which is opened to business and economics graduates and people already working in the area. Their Business Studies degree also incorporates a finance option.

There are Finance degrees at St. Patrick's College, Maynooth, and UCC, while the Language Secretarial and Business Centre in Dublin has a two year diploma in Languages and Financial Services.

U.C.D. also offers certificates, diplomas and degrees in Financial Services. These are run in association with the Institute of Bankers.

Stockbrokers: Engaged by buyers or sellers to acquire or sell stock. Under Irish Stock Exchange rules, they're obliged to get the best possible deal for

John O'Connor
LSB College graduate

John O'Connor grew up in Glenageary in Dublin, and did his Leaving Cert at St Conleth's College, Ballsbridge in 1986. "After a terrible Leaving Cert, I worked as a sales rep for various companies, and I thought to myself, there must be something better than this."

John enrolled at LSB for a BA in Business Studies, specialising in psychology. It was a three-year, full time course. "It was tough to go back, but I was able to work as a consultant to various companies right through college, so that helped."

He has great praise for the LSB course. "While academically very good, it was also very practical as well."

John graduated in 1997 with a first class honours degree. He went on to do a Masters degree, socialising in Human Resource Management, at the Michael Smurfit Graduate School of Business at UCD. Again he graduated with first class honours. "When you go back to college at my age, you have to make it worth your while," he says.

Now 30, John works as a business consultant. "I hope to build up a small company of like minded people, advising organisation on how to develop the softer skills within their workforce - like team building, networking, communications. These are some of the most important skills within business, yet are the most neglected."

their client. Insider trading isn't common, and contrary to popular perception, it's not an especially glamorous job, although the more successful stockbrokers make a very good living. A business qualification is important.

Insurance: Around 10,100 people are currently employed in this sector. Of these, more than half work in life insurance. It's one of the big financial forces in our economy, along with banks and building societies. It offers protection against the expected and the unexpected – from old age to robbery and sudden death. Job areas include underwriting or drafting policies, checking and processing claims as well as selling insurance. Insurance companies train their own staff, generally recruited at Leaving Cert level.

UL offers a degree in insurance and European studies, while both it and UCD have business courses which offer specialist insurance options.

Actuary: The employment prospects in this area are good. Until recently, actuaries worked mainly in two areas, life assurance and pension funds, mainly concerned with making forecasts and assessing risk potential. But increasingly, they're becoming more involved in general insurance, and trying to open up other areas like banking, stock broking, investment analysis and financial services.

The traditional route was to join a company from school, for which an A in Honours Maths was the basic requirement. However, there are now also degree courses in DCU and UCD.

About two thirds of graduates go into trainee actuarial positions, about 20% go into banking and finance while the remainder tend to go into accounting and management consultancy.

Banking: Despite the increasing use of credit cards and electronic banking, it seems the demand for across the counter banking services is as strong as ever. In response to this, AIB is one bank which is phasing in six and seven day retail bank opening at selected branches over the next two years.

The bank has also launched a recruitment campaign to take on 500 general banking staff, and has recently taken on more than 200 graduates to fill other vacancies.

Currency Dealing: Ireland's currency dealers came to prominence during the currency crisis and devaluation. Most are employed by the major banks – Bank of Ireland and AIB have roughly 60 each, while Ulster Bank has 40. Other organisations such as the National Treasury Management Agency and a handful of semi-state and private companies also operate on foreign exchange markets.

Dealers must be numerate and able to act quickly and calmly under pressure. Opportunities for job mobility are few compared to the bigger financial centres. There is no set path to the job of currency dealer. Those who work in the treasury departments at Bank of Ireland and Ulster Bank tend to be graduates, while AIB generally recruits from within it's own personnel.

Accountancy: Ten years ago, there was a glut of accountants on the employment market, and emigra-

tion, at least on a temporary basis, was the only realistic option for many.

Now unemployment among accountants has been virtually wiped out. Demand for accountants in all areas of Irish business is very healthy, and salaries have been rising steadily. Accountants working in the financial services sector are paid more and have more attractive fringe benefits than those in industry and commerce. Both fare better than accountants in private practice – unless they are partners or sole practitioners.

The hours are long, and the exams notoriously difficult, but the job satisfaction and financial rewards compensate. Accountancy with a language is increasingly attractive to employers, especially in the International Financial Services Centre.

Although it is still possible to join straight from school, more and more students are opting for graduate entry.

Some accountants work in public practice – which involves working with other accountants in a large firm or management consultancy. The Institute of Chartered Accountants and the Institute of Certified Public Accountants train students for practice or industry. Graduates of the Chartered Association of Certified Accountants generally work in industry and commerce or management, while Chartered Institute of Management Accountants are geared more towards people working in management accountancy. Students can train for each of these bodies by:

(a) Getting a third level qualification, for which they'll get exemptions from professional accountancy exams.

(b) Doing a foundation course in some of the IT's, universities or in D.I.T. Aungier St.

(c) Joining straight from school. Students must have a minimum of five Leaving Cert subjects – including English and Maths – and three honours for both the Chartered Association of Certified Accountants and the Chartered Institute of Management Accountants. The Institute of Certified Public Accountants and the Institute of Chartered Accountants require six subjects – including English and Maths.

The traditional route for school leavers into the Institute of Chartered Accountants in Ireland, the commencement course, has ceased with effect from Autumn 1998. In a unique partnership with the Institute of Accounting Technicians in Ireland a new route for school leavers has been developed. This will be available from Autumn 1999 – consult the Institutes for further information.

Accounting Technician: Accounting Technicians are skilled support staff who work in accounting and finance. They deal with accounting, aspects of auditing and related areas of law and data processing. The Institute of Accounting Technicians in Ireland and the Association of Accounting Technicians provide qualifications in this area. Accountancy Technician courses

BUSINESS STUDIES COURSES IN C.A.O.

STUDENT YEARBOOK & CAREER DIRECTORY

1. For details of courses consult College Prospectuses.
2. See index for Post Leaving Certificate Courses.
3. See index for FÁS Courses.

Course	T.C.D.	NUI, Galway	U.C.C.	D.C.U.	U.L.	U.C.D.	D.I.T.	Athlone IT	Cork IT	Galway Mayo IT	Sligo IT	Waterford IT	Carlow IT	Dundalk IT	Letterkenny IT	Tralee IT	Limerick IT	Tallaght IT	NCI	NUI Maynooth	L.S.B.	Portobello	American College	Griffith College	Blanchardstown IT	DBS	Tipperary RBDI	Dun Laoghaire IADT
Accountancy & Finance			●			●			●			●		●					●	●	●	●		●				
Accountancy		●					●	●	●		●	●	●			●			●	●		●						
Accountancy/Law				●	●																							
Accountancy/Technician													●		●													
Business Information Systems		●					●			●			●							●								
Business Studies/Accounting							●	●	●	●		●		●		●										●		
Business Studies/Agribusiness										●													●	●				
Business Studies/Commerce	●	●	●		●	●	●	●	●	●	●	●	●	●	●	●	●	●		●		●	●	●	●	●	●	●
Business/Commerce/Language	●	●	●	●	●	●	●				●	●	●	●	●	●				●			●					
Business Studies/Front Office								●		●																		
Business Studies/Management								●														●						
Business/Marketing/Language			●					●				●	●		●	●	●	●		●	●					●	●	
Business Studies/Office Admin.									●							●												
Bus. Studies/& Retail Proprietorship								●													●							
Business Studies/Secretarial							●	●	●	●	●		●	●	●						●							
Business Studies/Security								●													●		●					
Business Studies/Tourism								●		●	●	●				●					●		●					
Chartered Sec. & Admin.														●														
Economics	●	●	●			●																						
European Studies	●		●	●	●															●								
Finance			●	●		●																	●					
Insurance				●																								
Public Relations							●							●														
Public Administration/Government		●	●			●																						
Stadéir Gnó/Airgeadas			●							●											●							
Staidéir Rúnaíochta															●						●							
Business/Legal				●	●																							
Entrepreneur																												●
Electronic Commerce Systems																												●
Rural Development																											●	

First Steps ...

in finance and management

If you are looking for a career which will enable you to work at the heart of business and operate at the centre of the decision-making process, ACCA has the answer

ACCA Accounting Technician

- no formal academic qualifications necessary to register
- nine exams ranging from cost accounting systems to managing finances
- no time limit

Chartered Certified Accountancy

- A professional qualification which enables you to work in all aspects of finance once qualified
- three stages of examinations follow a modular approach, allowing you to progress as quickly as you wish, or your circumstances dictate
- Broad syllabus covering IT, management, accounting and taxation topics

**The Association of
Chartered Certified Accountants**

For more information contact:
ACCA Ireland
9 Leeson Park
Dublin 6
Tel: +353 1 496 3144
Fax: +353 1 496 3615
E-mail: recruit.dublin@acca.org.uk

are now on offer in many schools and colleges country-wide.

Taxation consultancy: Tax consultancy is one of Ireland's fastest growing and best rewarded professions. Qualified tax consultants are now being recruited by all the major taxation/accounting firms, financial institutions and legal firms as well as many multi-national corporations and government departments. Tax consultants have access to the key decision makers in the organisations they advise and are seen as central to the success of these organisations. As Ireland's tax system operates on a self-assessment basis there is a strong demand for quality taxation advice. Tax Consultants are recognised as crucially important to the successful operation of the self-assessment system. The Institute of Taxation's AITI qualification is Ireland's only dedicated professional taxation qualification.

Careers in business: There are plenty of courses to choose from in this area. The advice seems to be to combine business and another subject, such as a language, computers or law. There are many courses which suit these requirements, and it's possible also to take language modules in many of the mainstream business/commerce degrees. As well as the obvious French and German, there are more unusual and potentially useful options such as Russian at TCD or Japanese at UL.

Post-Leaving Cert. courses on offer usually combine business studies and computers. FÁS runs a number of business and book-keeping courses including Enterprise Development, Entrepreneurial Skills and Management Development. Many private colleges also run business skills programmes, while third-level institutions offer qualifications from certificate to degree level in specialised areas of business or general Business Studies and Commerce. The career opportunities are good at home and abroad.

SECRETARIAL AND RECEPTIONIST COURSES

Any student thinking of embarking on a secretarial course would be well advised to consider a specialisation. It may seem at first that you're narrowing your job prospects – that by, for example, combining legal studies with secretarial skills, you can only get a job in a solicitor's office, but that's not the case. You'll also be qualified as a general secretary, so it opens up opportunities rather than narrowing options.

Taking legal studies, medical reception skills or languages will give secretaries an edge in the jobs market, as most employers are looking for multi-skilled job applicants.

Many of the private colleges offer specialised secretarial courses. A number of the IT's run courses in Office Information Systems, and report that it's one of their most popular and expanding courses. The course structures acknowledge that the work of the secretary has changed. The traditional office skills are still included, but they take account of the computerised office, where familiarity with word processing packages, spreadsheets and databases is essential.

At certificate level, most graduates find jobs as secretaries, whereas holders of degrees tend to work as administrators, PA's or in information technology.

FURTHER INFORMATION

See Third Level Section for Colleges and Courses.

Association of Accounting Technicians, Monarch House, Lesson Pl., Dublin 1 (01-4963260).

Association of Chartered Certified Accountants, 9 Leeson Park, Dublin 6 (01-4963144).

Dorset College, 64a Lower Dorset Street Dublin 1. (01-8309677)

Institute of Accounting Technicians of Ireland, 87/89 Pembroke Rd., Dublin 4 (01-6602899).

Institute of Bankers, Nassau House, Nassau St., Dublin 2 (01-6793311).

Institute of Certified Public Accountants, 9 Ely Place, Dublin 2 (01-6767353).

Institute of Chartered Accountants, 87 Pembroke Rd., Dublin 4 (01-6680400).

Institute of Public Administration, 59 Lansdowne Rd., Dublin 4 (01-6686233).

Institute of Taxation in Ireland, 19 Sandymount Ave., Dublin 4 (01-6688222).

Insurance Institute of Ireland, 39 Molesworth Street, Dublin 2 (01-6772753).

Irish Insurance Federation, 39 Molesworth Street, Dublin 2 (01-6761820).

NCEA (National Council for Educational Awards), 26 Mountjoy Sq., Dublin 1 (01-8556526).

Society of Actuaries in Ireland, 5 Wilton Place, Dublin 2 (01-6612422).

Stock Exchange, 28 Anglesea St., Dublin 2 (01-6778808).

The Chartered Institute of Management Accountants, 44 Upper Mount St., Dublin 2 (01-6761721).

Secretarial/Computer Training – *see PLC section, our advertisers and consult the Golden Pages.*

SUGGESTIONS

If possible do some commercial subjects at school, e.g. book-keeping, accountancy, business organisation, economics, typing, shorthand, computer studies . . . gain practical experience in an office during the summer . . . learn typing/word processing . . . visit the stock exchange . . . check the educational requirements for entry to various courses and professions as they vary a lot . . . sometimes working with a company that ties in with your own interests may be more satisfying, e.g. those interested in travel may prefer to seek employment with a travel, shipping or tourism company . . . don't wait for advertisements! . . . many companies have no set advertising strategy so get together your letters of application and C.V.s . . . participate in some of the business competitions for school — C.I.M.A. and "Business and Finance" are just some of the organisers.

READ/VIEW

Information pack from Business Studies Teachers Association.
Many of the professional institutes supply their own careers literature, and in some instances, lists of vacancies.
Sunday Business Post
Business and Finance, Management, Accountancy Ireland — Periodicals.
Also *business sections* in newspapers.
Administration Yearbook — IPA
"Clerical Work" — CDC (01-8474399).

SALES/MARKETING/ ADVERTISING

Shopping staff shortages

A recent report has shown that the number of people shopping in Dublin city centre is at an all time high. Shoppers in Grafton Street are up fifty per cent. In the city's other main shopping area, the revamped Henry Street, the number is up sixty five per cent.

All of this is happening despite a huge growth in the number of out of town centres – such as the Blanchardstown and Liffey Valley Centres – which it had been thought would eat into the profits of city traders. In fact, the survey concluded that the Dublin retail market was on the verge of being over shopped.

With the completion of phase two of the Blanchardstown Centre and the creation of 500 new jobs, the centre is now one of the biggest employers in the country, with more than 3,000 people working there.

But it's not all boom and bloom for the retail sales industry, which currently provides more than 150,000 jobs – that's about 11.5% of the entire workforce. Critical staff shortages are predicted in the next few years unless employers do more to keep their staff and attract new workers. They're being told to address issues like pay and hours and promotion, and there are moves to upgrade training in this sector.

With other developments such as weekend and twenty four hour opening at some of the major supermarkets, there's plenty of scope for those who want to make a career in this area.

As the economy remains healthy, demand for communications services has soared, and the marketing, PR and advertising sectors have all benefited. The greater number of broadcasting outlets, and the arrival of TV3, have led to more work for those in this business. And more ads are being placed in newspapers. The money spent on such advertising amounted to more than £160 million last year – up 25%.

Ireland continues to hold its attraction for the providers of teleservices. More than 5,000 people are employed in this area, in a variety of call centres, including many of the important multinational companies such as American Airlines, Hertz and Best Western Hotels.

Sales: Efforts are currently underway to try to make sales a more attractive career for school leavers, as increasingly it's seen as a part-time or stop-gap job. To really make a career out of sales, it's essential to be able to get on with people, whether the job is an over the counter sales assistant, or a sales rep on the road trying to convince a prospective client to buy a product.

FÁS runs a number of courses including Sales Representative, Sales Training and Retail Sales. They cover training in sales skills, customer care, personal development and advice on clothing, as well as routine financial transactions. There are also post-leaving Cert courses in sales. The DIT at Mountjoy Square offers courses in retail foodstore management, export management, sales promotion management, retail meat management, distributive management, retail display, floristry, bookselling, grocery and bacon.

The Sales Institute of Ireland has also begun running courses at Mountjoy Square, mainly aimed at senior sales people already working in the industry.

Trainee Managers: Most big stores run in-house training programmes – sometimes taking on as many as 80 trainees in a year – and have a policy of promoting from within. More and more they're recruiting third level students. Superquinn now has its own graduate training programme.

Marketing: Jobs in marketing are many and diverse. It stands to reason, as just about everything can be marketed, providing the marketing plan itself is sound. The basic elements are market research, which aims to match a product to a market, and then the marketing itself – making sure that the product or message reaches that target market. The higher your qualifications, the better your job prospects. With a variety of marketing courses available, there is a large number of trained people on the jobs market.

Manufacturers of consumer goods no longer need to be convinced of the merits of marketing, but the service industries are way behind. Future opportunities may arise in charities, semi-state companies and healthcare.

As many companies tend to recruit from within, it can be difficult to get that first job. Here again, experience abroad can be useful, with Britain being identified by those in the business as the most similar marketing base to Ireland. Obviously it's also a good idea to think about combining marketing with a language – as many courses now do – to be equipped for export marketing opportunities.

The DIT boasts a wide range of courses, and they're also available at Tallaght, Dundalk, Carlow and Galway ITs. International marketing courses are on offer at the Dublin City University, Waterford and Sligo ITs and many private colleges e.g. LSB's most popular 1-year programme is a diploma in Marketing, Advertising and PR. FÁS and post-Leaving Cert courses are another option.

SECTOR SPEC

TELESERVICES
People in this area, range from those providing hotel/airline reservations to individuals selling computers or insurance. They use a phone, computer and normally their language skills. Not all of the jobs in this sector involve languages, but companies in the business of servicing Europe from an Irish base are looking for people with a good spoken knowledge of at least one European language. They're not necessarily interested in academic qualifications – just an ability to communicate effectively.

The IDA says there's still a shortage of people with languages skills, with German, French, Italian and Dutch most in demand.

The Department of Education and Science are meeting the needs of this sector with the provision of up to 1,000 training places on courses in over forty schools. Some of the features of the courses are:

Content Content
- Languages
- Information Technology for Teleservices
- Communications
- Customer Care
- Business Mangement
- Teleservices
- Transnational Work Placement

The emphasis is placed on language training. Students have at least 9 hours per week language classes in Year 1 and in Year 2 of the programme.

It is a two-year full time training programme, which includes an extensive work experience placement overseas.

Tuition is free, and a student support scheme provides substantial assistance (of up to £2,000 per person) towards the cost of the overseas placement.

Applicants for the course are expected to have a minimum of a grade B in pass level English and one continental language in the Leaving Certificate, – or equivalent.

Further information from your Local Centre listed on page 276/277.

MAKE YOUR MARK ! ...

THE
MARKETING
INSTITUTE

South County Business Park
Leopardstown, Dublin 18.
Phone: 01-2952355
Fax. 01-2952453
E-mail: education@mii.ie

Please send me details of a Career in Marketing

Name

Address

Tel

Most marketing courses involve the study of core business subjects (e.g. finance, law) as well as those specific to marketing (eg. buyer behaviour, market research).

The Marketing Institute is the examining body for professional marketing courses which are offered in DIT and IT colleges at night for those in employment. The same courses are available to schoolleavers (fulltime) at Colaiste Dhulaigh and Dun Laoghaire VEC in Dublin, and the College of Commerce in Cork. The Foundation Certificate in Marketing is awarded after two years, the Diploma after three and the Graduateship of the Institute (which is degree-equivalent) after four years. At certificate level there is a selling option. Students may take the certificate fulltime and continue the course to diploma and graduateship while in employment.

Advertising Agencies: People work in such diverse areas as graphics, copywriting, photography and filming – as well as sales, marketing, accounting, space buying etc. This is one of the hardest areas of the media to break into, and those who do find work generally do so through sheer persistence, and a willingness to accept low pay in the first few years.

The academic route to a career in the industry is through the one year certificate course in advertising at the DIT Aungier Street. It is organised with the involvement of advertisers themselves, the media and advertising agencies – and is closely geared towards meeting the needs of the industry. The course has a good record of placing its graduates in jobs.

You'll find marketing, business studies, arts and other graduates going into advertising, as well as those from an art and design background.

FÁS also run some short term advertising courses, leading to permanent employment in over 75% of cases. The courses are certified by FÁS and the Association of Advertisers in Ireland.

Advertising Jobs in the Media: This is the other end of the advertising spectrum – selling newspaper and magazine space, or airtime. Recruits to this area come from a wide range of backgrounds, and are promoted within the industry. Relies largely on contacts, so experience and personality are the main factors. Some training in sales or marketing would be an advantage. Increasingly, graduates apply for these jobs.

Public Relations: Around 500 people are employed in public relations. However, the industry is doing well at the moment, and that number is expected to increase by about 20% over the next three years. People who work in this area are employed either in a PR firm – handling publicity for a client and dealing with media queries – or for an individual company, dealing only with its public relations.

It's a job which requires great attention to detail. An ability to write and identify a news angle which will attract press coverage must be combined with organisation skills.

Don't wait for jobs to be advertised, contact companies yourself and try to get work experience. Public relations is an element of the Communications degree at DCU, Dun Laoghaire Community College and the DIT Aungier Street offer one year diplomas, and part time courses are run at Tallaght IT, UL and the Public Relations Institute of Ireland.

It can be a good idea to do a degree of your choice, and specialise in PR later. This is increasingly the case as PR becomes more specialised. Some companies will only handle financial PR for example, as it becomes more difficult for the PR consultant to be an expert on everything.

SUGGESTIONS

Take part in your school's "Mini Company" projects . . . If you are interested in selling, talk to people already involved — sales assistants in shops, direct salespersons, etc. . . . try to get a part-time job dealing with the public, preferably in sales . . . take an interest in the organisation of your local "Sale of Work" . . . develop more of an interest in talking to different people — learn to relate to all ages and types . . . observe various marketing and advertising strategies — billboards, newspaper and television ads.

Get involved in the marketing of your local community newsletter or school magazine —perhaps you could raise advertising revenue as well . . . Help out with publicity for voluntary organisations.

Choose some business subjects for your Leaving Cert. programme . . . Do a project designing, marketing and selling a product . . . Study art at school.

FURTHER INFORMATION

Advertising Standards Authority for Ireland, IPC House, Shelbourne Road, Dublin 4 (01-6608766).

Institute of Advertising Practitioners in Ireland, 8 Upper Fitzwilliam St., Dublin 2 (01-6765991).

Institute of Professional Auctioneers, Valuers and Livestock Salesmen, 39 Upper Fitzwilliam St., Dublin 2 (01-6785685).

Insurance Institute of Ireland, 39 Molesworth St., Dublin 2 (01-6772582).

Irish Auctioneers and Valuers Institute, 38 Merrion Square East, Dublin 2 (01-6611794).

Irish Institute of Purchasing and Materials Management, 5 Belvedere Place, Dublin 1 (01-8559257).

The Marketing Institute, South County Business Park, Leopardstown, Dublin 18 (01-2952355).

Public Relations Institute of Ireland, 78 Merrion Sq., Dublin 2 (01-6618004).

See "Golden Pages" under "insurance brokers"; "marketing"; "auctioneers"; "advertising agencies"; "sales training"; "public relations"; "cash and carry wholesalers"; etc.

READ/VIEW

Various business magazines such as "Business and Finance"; "Irish Marketing Journal" — provide an annual list of all P.R. advertising and related agencies, "Sunday Business Post"

Mapps which gives a complete list of advertising agencies.

A Career in Marketing — A video from the Marketing Institute.

Sales and Advertising CDC — (01-8474399).

SCIENCE

Top chemical companies manufacture in Ireland

Sixteen of the world's top twenty ranked chemical and pharmaceutical companies now manufacture in Ireland. The country has become the world's 15th largest exporters of these products, which comprise 18.6% of total exports. The main products are fine chemicals, drugs and hospital products, medical equipment, cosmetics and toiletries. There is an increasing emphasis on research and development. IBEC has called for a increased supply of third level science and engineering graduates for the pharmaceutical and chemical-manufacturing sector.

Half of the 1997 science degree graduates were in employment by April 1998. Thirty one per cent went on to further academic study and 2.2% were seeking employment.

Choosing a science course can be confusing – there are so many courses on offer. Common entry courses allow students to try out many of he sciences and specialise in second year. You should check with the college prospectus to see what subjects are on offer. Most of the ITs offer certificates and diplomas in the applied sciences, many with follow on degrees.

The plastics or polymer industry is another area which is thriving at the moment. About 16,000 people are employed, up to 20% of them in the technical area. About 30 graduates and 40 technicians are needed each year, and plastic engineering graduates are virtually guaranteed jobs.

The expansion of the physics-based electronics industries has generated jobs for physics graduates, but the prospects for biology students are less certain. The rapidly developing biotechnology section is an exception.

Chemistry: IBEC has expressed concern at the decline in the number of Leaving Cert. students taking chemistry and feels that this could have a dramatic effect on future technology based developments in Ireland. In the past decade employment has increased by 85% in the chemical and pharmaceutical industry. In the past 18 months there's been a 12% increase in the number of jobs. Pure chemistry is offered by UCD, UCC, UCG, TCD and Maynooth, and is taken as an option in science. Practical applied chemistry courses are on offer at DCU and the University of Limerick, Kevin St. College of Technology and various ITs. In recent years, the jobs placement rate for applied chemistry graduates has been higher than that for pure chemistry degrees. UCC has introduced a new honours degree in the chemistry of pharmaceutical compounds and Athlone IT has a national certificate in toxicology.

Polymer Technology: Athlone IT offers a number of courses, from certificate to degree level. UL also offers a degree in material science which includes the study of polymers. The UL course reports almost 100% employment for its graduates.

Physicist: Employed in all branches of industry, but the major employers are the high technology and defence related industries involving electronics, optics, aerospace applications, computing and telecommunications.

Applied physics is often combined with instrumentation or electronics at certificate, diploma and degree level.

Employment prospects for applied physics graduates are good with many going into software development. NUI Galway offers degrees in applied physics and electronics and experimental physics. Many ITs offer courses at certificate and diploma level.

UL and DCU offer applied physics and DCU offers it with a language.

Microbiologist: Involves protecting the public from micro-organisms which may endanger health.

Most common entry science degree courses in the universities and applied biology courses in ITs offer microbiology as a subject.

Biotechnology: Many people equate biotechnology with the controversial development of genetic engineering, but it's about a lot more than that. In its broadest sense, it is about the control and manufacture of biological systems, such as the fermentation of barley to produce alcohol. It is thought that biotechnology could be worth as much as £200 billion to the EU by 2005.

Ireland now has 170 biotech companies, employing 45,000. This includes 55 Irish companies staffing almost 5,000. The overseas companies are mainly in the pharmaceutical and healthcare areas, while indigenous companies are predominantly in brewing, distilling, dairy and other agribusiness sectors.

Four year undergraduate courses are available at DCU, NUI Maynooth and NUI Galway – the latter includes business and a language. The longest established biotechnology course is the diploma at Waterford IT. Other courses are available in overlapping areas such as applied sciences, industrial microbiology and chemical engineering, while biotechnology is incorporated into most broad based science degrees. An interesting development is the new biotechnology course in St. Tiernans, Balally, Dublin 16. The course links St. Tiernans with D.C.U.

Quality Control: The usual route to this career is a primary qualification in a technological or scientific area, followed by a quality assurance qualification, available at TCD, NUI Galway, and ITs at Sligo and Waterford.

The biotechnology degree courses at NUI Galway, DCU and NUI Maynooth would also prepare a student for a career in quality assurance.

Environmental Science: DIT offers a three-year diploma in environmental resource management, there is a certificate at Limerick IT and Dundalk IT. Sligo IT has a three diploma in Pollution Assessment and Control and a B.Sc. in Environmental Science. UL also has a degree course in environmental science.

Food Science: The food industry is one of the biggest in Ireland, and provides jobs for science graduates at degree and diploma level. The jobs are in quality control, research and management. UCC has four degrees – Nutritional Science, Food Science, Food Technology and Food Business.

Dundalk, Sligo and Letterkenny ITs have courses available in food science. Some common entry science courses as well as the agricultural science degree in UCD offer food science as an option.

Science Technicians: Qualified in a field of science to assist scientists. Openings in all modern manufacturing industry, such as chemical/pharmaceutical, the food industry, health care, instrumentation and semi-conductor manufacturing, as well as in aquaculture, mining and geo-chemical exploration, in research institutes and semi-state bodies.

Two or three year courses available at ITs and DIT colleges.

SUGGESTIONS

Pay particular attention to technical and scientific subjects . . . visit trade exhibitions . . . attend D.I.T. lectures on trades, mechanical and electronic engineering and science . . . enter Esat "Young Scientist & Technology" competition . . . attend annual lecture . . . visit airports . . . ESB power stations . . . Bord na Mona factories and bog developments . . . alert yourself to new developments in technology and science . . . watch out for special T.V. reports and programmes such as "Tomorrow's World" . . . arrange a visit to a local factory, perhaps you could obtain a summer job there.

Visit places of special scientific interest, e.g. Botanic Gardens open days every May . . . perhaps a science teacher could arrange a trip to a local chemical or pharmaceutical plant . . . buy an advanced chemistry set . . . attend various open days in agricultural colleges and other research institutes . . . budding biologists or zoologists should not miss the Natural History Museum, Merrion St., Dublin, or the Zoological Gardens, Dublin, or Fota Island, Cork.

INFORMATION

Irish Business & Employers Confederation, 84 Lr. Baggot Street, Dublin 2. (01-6601011).

Forbairt (Irish Science and Technology Agency), Glasnevin Road, Dublin 9 (01-8082000).

Federation of Irish Chemical Industries, 140 Pembroke Road, Dublin 4, Dublin 2 (01-6603350).

Institute of Biology of Ireland, R.D.S., Ballsbridge, Dublin 4.

Institute of Chemistry, R.D.S., Ballsbridge, Dublin 4.

Institute of Physics, c/o Physics Dept., U.C.D., D. 4.

Irish Productivity Centre, IPC House, 42 Lr Mount Street, Dublin 2 (01-6623233).

Irish Quality Control Association, Merrion Hall, Strand Road. (01-2695255).

Irish Swiss Institute of Horology, Mill Road, Blanchardstown, Dublin 15 (01-8213352).

The various 3rd level colleges and their engineering departments.

READ/VIEW

Chemistry is Everywhere — Inst. of Chemistry, RDS.
Chemistry and Careers (from Institute of Chemistry).
Careers with Physics, Institute of Physics.
Technology Ireland (Eolas).
Chemistry Innovations (BASF).

1. *For details of courses consult College Propectuses.*
2. *See index for Post Leaving Certificate Courses.*
3. *See index for FÁS Courses.*

	T.C.D.	NUI Galway	U.C.C.	D.C.U.	U.L.	U.C.D.	D.I.T.	Maynooth	Athlone IT	Cork IT	Galway IT	Sligo IT	Waterford IT	Carlow IT	Dundalk IT	Letterkenny IT	Tralee IT	Limerick IT	Tallaght IT	Portobello
Science – Applied Biology		●	●				●		●	●	●	●	●	●	●	●	●	●	●	
Science – Applied Chemistry		●		●	●		●			●	●	●	●	●	●	●	●	●	●	
Science – Applied Physics/Electronics		●		●	●	●	●		●	●	●				●	●		●	●	
Science – Applied Science	●	●	●	●	●	●	●	●	●	●	●	●	●	●	●	●	●	●	●	
Science – Biotechnology		●		●				●												
Science – Earth		●	●																	
Science – Environmental		●				●							●		●	●		●		
Science – Food/Food Technology			●		●	●	●						●			●	●	●		
Science – Marine/Aquaculture		●									●	●					●	●		
Science – Mathematical				●		●														
Biomedical Science		●																		
Medical Chemistry	●																			
Agricultural								●						●						
Science – Computer	●		●			●	●	●		●										
Science – Equine					●															
Theoretical Physics	●					●														
Science – Wood						●														

Rory has Plans for the Millennium

Who is Rory Layden?

Rory grew up in Carrick- on-Shannon with his twin brother and two sisters. He went to school in Rockwell, Co. Tipperary, and came to Dublin after the Leaving Cert in 1986. For five years he worked in the bank, and did a B.Comm. by night. He enjoyed tennis, and was a keen golfer. By 1992 he felt called to a different kind of service, and left the bank to become a priest. After two years with the Spiritans (a missionary order), he chose Diocesan priesthood, and completed his studies at Clonliffe College in 1999.

Rory already has a wide circle of friends. Now he joins a team of 800 priests, and thousands of committed lay people. He is part of something which goes back two thousand years, but his focus is on the future. Whatever that future holds, wherever he is sent; Rory knows that Jesus lives still and loves still. Through his ministry as a priest, God will continue to heal and console, to reconcile, and to give life. Rory has already experienced this in his work with prisoners, among others with whom he has worked during his years of preparation.

What are you doing for the next fifty years?

If you are:

- a good team person;
- with natural leadership qualities;
- willing to serve others
- confident enough to be different
- committed to the truth;
- ready to take God at His word

then you may be just the man we want.

Would you consider joining Rory?

Dublin Priests work in

- parish ministry;
- chaplaincy to schools and colleges;
- hospital chaplaincy;
- prison and army chaplaincy;
- youth services;
- the promotion of justice and peace.

For further information, check out the Vocations web-site at:
http://homepage.tinet.ie/~vocations
or contact

Fr. Kevin Doran at the Diocesan Vocations Centre CYC Arran Quay, Dublin 7 Tel: (01) 8725055

DIOCESAN VOCATIONS CENTRE

SOCIAL WORK/PSYCHOLOGY/ COUNSELLING

Difficult but rewarding work

Health boards have been advertising social work posts in the UK because of they can't find enough staff in Ireland. Social workers work with people who are vulnerable i.e. children who have been abused and children in care, people with disabilities or mental health problems, the elderly, the homeless. They have the difficult job of trying to meet people's needs with the limited resources that are available. Social workers employed by the Health Boards usually work in teams and are based in health centre, hospitals or separate welfare offices.The main employment area at the moment is in child protection work and statutory child-care. There are also openings in mental health. Voluntary organisations also employ social workers in support roles in residential care and community care services for people who are elderly and people with disabilities.

Another area where jobs may become more plentiful is the probation and welfare service. A report from the Department of Justice has recommended that more than 75 new probation officers should be recruited to the probation and welfare service.

The number of vocations has fallen dramatically in the last decade. On average 100 priests are lost to the Church every year through retirement and death while only 40 are ordained. Some smaller parishes in rural areas have had to be amalgamated with other parishes because of the shortage of parish priests. Dublin parishes have also had difficulties as a result of the collapse in the numbers going forward for the priesthood. Similarly there has been a devastating collapse in the numbers entering convents. Many convents have been closed down and lands sold as the ageing religious community move into smaller houses.

Social Workers: Social workers are involved in fieldwork i.e. working with families and individuals in the community, residential work, hospital work and working in support/resource centres. They assess individual and family needs and devise packages of care to help support people and enable them to live their lives with more freedom, dignity and autonomy. they are often involved in multi-disciplinary work with nurses. health visitors,psychiatrists, psychologists, the police and other care professionals.

Most social work posts require applicants to be professionally qualified and registered with the National Social Work Qualifications Board. To be professionally qualified they will need to have completed a degree in one of the social sciences along with a two-year postgraduate master's degree in social work in UCD or UCC. People without a social sciences degree can do a post-graduate diploma in social policy followed by the two years master's in social work. The only direct entry professionally qualifying course for school leavers is the 4-year degree course in TCD.

Social Care Workers: Care workers usually work with people with disabilities, children with special needs and the elderly in residential and day care centres. Sligo, Waterford, Cork and Athlone ITs run certificate and diploma course in social care. The DIT in Cathal Brugha Street has a degree in social care. There are also a number of PLC courses in social care and community care.

Youth and Community Workers: With the youngest growing population in the EU and increased youth unemployment, this area has developed rapidly. St. Patrick's College in Maynooth offer a 2-year diploma in Community Education. There are also post-Leaving Cert courses in Youth Leadership at Clogher Road Vocational School, Dublin 12 and Cólaiste Íde, Finglas, Dublin 11.

Probation Officer: There are currently 200 probation officers employed in the probation service, which is supposed to manage 5,500 offenders in the community. The work involves providing reports on offenders to the courts, supervising and monitoring those allowed to return home, helping offenders and their families to cope with a term of imprisonment and providing after care for those released or on parole. A social science degree or relevant qualification is required and entry is through the Civil Service Commission.

Politician: Aspiring politicians usually get involved first at branch level, whether locally or at college. Few people start off as full-time public representatives, so another career or job is virtually essential.

Psychology: Psychology is the scientific study of thought, emotion and behaviour. Psychologists examine various aspects of human experience and apply their understanding of people to a variety of professional setting, including clinical, counselling, educational, organisational and research settings.

To become a psychologist you will need a degree in psychology followed by postgraduate training. There are very few jobs and a master's degree is crucial. The vast majority of people who study psychology end up using it as a broad general qualification.

£1.5 million has recently been allocated by the Department to establish and provide initial staffing for the new National Educational Psychology Service. It is expected that many new educational psychologists will be employed for the service.

Counsellors: Ten years ago there were just a few dozen counsellors — now there are hundreds who are trained and certified. Interest in the area is growing. The interest is reflected in the number and variety of courses available e.g. LSB have a BA in Counselling and Psychotherapy, Master's degree in counselling is available in U.C.C. or addiction counselling in T.C.D. There are other specialist courses in Gestalt or Reality Therapy and Adlerian Counselling.

For people who intend getting into an area such as guidance counselling there are six courses - U.C.C., U.C.D., N.U.I. (Maynooth), UL, Masters in T.C.D and Marino Institute of Education.

People interested in becoming professionally qualified counsellors should contact the Irish Association for Counselling and Therapy to find out if their course is recognised.

Occupational Therapist: Helps people to recover some or all of their original functions and movements following an accident or illness. Work is both in hospitals and in the community. T.C.D. offers the only occupational therapy course in Ireland.

Priesthood/Religious Life: Their ministry is as varied as the needs of the people they serve. Most priests in Ireland are based in parishes and try to be with the people, especially in the significant moments of their lives; Baptisms, weddings, funerals. From day to day their routine can vary from celebrating mass to visiting someone who is sick to going for a pint with a young couple after a wedding practice. Training towards Priesthood usually takes six to seven years and the major seminary is in Maynooth.

95

Social Worker

Social workers work with individuals, families and groups who are experiencing difficulties and problems in their lives. These problems can arise from a variety of sources: unemployment, conflicts and problems in marriage, drugs, drink and substance abuse, emotional, physical or sexual abuse, violence, illness etc. The interventions taken may be individual or group counselling, information on services, supply of resources or place of safety orders for children at risk. At all times you are working with individuals to help them, but you tend to meet them when they are at their lowest point or behaving at their worst. The job places huge demands on you emotionally and physically and it can be hard to leave the work behind. It is strongly advised that you have your own life in order and that you have some activity orsport to give you an outlet away from the demands of the work.

Employment could be in Community Care (with the local Health Board), Medical Social Worker (with hospitals and caring institutions), Psychiatric, Local Authority (Housing welfare officer, travellers), Probation and Welfare Officers, Occupational Social Work (industry) or with Voluntary Organisations.

Courses: Pre-professional training is by means of the Degree in Social Science in UCD or UCC or a one year conversion course for those who do not have those degrees in the form of the Diploma in Social Policy (UCD). You then proceed to the Diploma in Applied Social Studies or the Masters in Social Science (Social Work) at UCD. In UCC you can do the Masters in Social Work or the Higher Diploma in Social Work Studies. All of these courses are two years in duration and include work placement practice.

TCD runs a Bachelor of Social Studies Degree that is four years long and includes work placement, so graduates are ready to begin work on completion of the course. UCC also offers a three year Bachelor of Social Work degree but this is for mature students and is not open to school leavers.

Job prospects are excellent, but remember the work is very emotionally demanding and calls for maturity, judgement and compassion.

Religious life usually means to live in a community as a brother, sister, monk, nun or priest. They live in all types of places from monasteries to council estates, from islands to inner cities, from slums to bright lights. Their work can vary from AIDS projects to retreats, from workshops to filming, from health care to missionary work. In religious life people take vows of poverty, chastity and obedience after living for a number of years in community and experiencing the work.

Men and women seeking ordination to the Church of Ireland are trained at the Church of Ireland Theological College and Trinity, where they take a diploma or degree in Theological Studies.

Speech Therapists: Deal with disorders of communication, including problems with voice, speech and language. Some of these may be the result of physical disability, such as a cleft palate,while others may be acquired through illness, such as a stroke. Degree course in Trinity College Dublin.

Child-care: There is a huge demand for crèche and playschool places, particularly in the bigger towns and cities, where getting a suitable place means long waiting lists and being very lucky. the regulation of nurseries, crèche and other pre-school services catering for children under six by the Health boards resulted in many having to close down because they could not afford to adapt their premises or employ enough qualified staff to meet regulations.

UCC has a degree in Early Childhood studies and DIT has a new degree in Early Childhood Care and Education.

Child care professionals and nursery nurses find employment in nurseries, child daycare facilities, crèches and privately with families. There are excellent opportunities for self-employment and travel.

Colleges offering training in this area include the Portobello School, 40 Lr. Dominick Street, Dublin 1 (01-8721277) and School of Practical Child Care (01-2886994).

SUGGESTIONS

Assist with fund raising in third world agencies like Oxfam or Concern . . . familiarise yourself with the various helping agencies listed in this Yearbook (see index); start by visiting your local community information centre . . . seek voluntary work in youth clubs, Simon Community, "Out-reach", Vincent De Paul, etc. . . . or better still look closely at the help you give at home, in school or to those in need in your neighbourhood . . . for religious life, attend the "live-in" organised by religious bodies; many of these occur around the Easter and Summer holidays ... consider joining a political party ... visit old folk and children in orphanages or residential care.

FURTHER INFORMATION

Agency for Personal Services Overseas, 30 Fitzwilliam Sq., Dublin 2 (01-6614411).

Association of Occupational Therapists, Unit 4, Argus House, Greenmount Office Park, Harolds Cross, Dublin 6. (01-4730320).

Association of Occupational Therapists of Ireland, 29 Eaton Sq , Monkstown, Co. Dublin.

Chief Rabbi's Office, Ephraim Mews, c/o Herzog House, Zion Road, Rathgar, Dublin 6 (01-923751).

Fr. Brian Shorthall
Chaplain

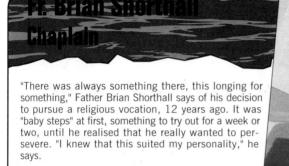

"There was always something there, this longing for something," Father Brian Shorthall says of his decision to pursue a religious vocation, 12 years ago. It was "baby steps" at first, something to try out for a week or two, until he realised that he really wanted to persevere. "I knew that this suited my personality," he says.

After leaving Synge Street CBS in Dublin, Father Shorthall joined a Franciscan order at the age of 18. Settling down to study again "wasn't a cakewalk", he says: "For example, I enjoyed theology much more than philosophy." The training lasts for six to seven years.

Having finally been ordained a priest, Father Shorthall now works as a chaplain in Coolmine Community School in Dublin, and intends to stay there for the foreseeable future. Working with young people is a challenge, but Father Shorthall believes that a spiritual presence is vital: "It's important to help young people to consider something beyond schoolwork, to help them discover the kind of people they will turn out to be, not just academically, but emotionally and spiritually."

To young people thinking about entering religious life, Father Shorthall advises that they work for a few years first: "My one regret is that I started as young as I did." He says young people should talk to parents, guidance counsellor or to the vocations directors established by various orders. He also stresses the need to continue with prayer and other religious practices.

Clerk of the Presbyterian Church, 9 Sandymount Green, Dublin 4 (01-6683316).

Community Information Centres.

Concern, 1 Upper Camden Street, Dublin 2 (01-4754162).

Director of Ordinands, Divinity Hostel, Braemore Park, Dublin 14.

Director of Vocations, Kimmage Manor, Dublin 12. (01-4554994).

DIT School of Social Sciences, Rathmines, Dublin 6. (01-4023000).

GOAL, 9 Norththumberland Ave., Dun Laoghaire (01-2809779).

Gorta, 12 Herbert Street, Dublin 2 (01-6615522).

Institute of Guidance Counsellors, 17 Herbert St., Dublin 2. (01-6761975)

Irish Association for Counselling and Therapy, 8 Cumberland St., Dun Laoghaire, Co. Dublin.

Irish Association of Social Workers, 114 Pearse St., Dublin 2. (01-6774838)

Irish Association of Speech & Language Therapists, Unit 4, Greenmount Office Park, Dublin 6W (01-4730398).

National Centre for Guidance in Education, 189 Parnell St., Dublin 9. (01-8731411)

National Social Service Board, Hume House, Dublin 4 (01-6059000).

Portobello School, 40 Lr. Dominick St., Dublin 1. (01-8721277).

Psychological Society of Ireland, 13 Adelaide Rd., Dublin 2. (01-4783916)

School of Practical Child Care, Blackrock Campus, Blackrock, Co. Dublin (01-2886994).

Secretary, Methodist Church, 3 Upr Malone Road, Belfast BT 96TD.

Social Workers Action Group, 42 Ratoath Estate, Cabra, Dublin 7.

The various health boards are listed in the Medical section of this Yearbook.

Voluntary Services International, 30 Mountjoy Square, Dublin 1.

Lay Missionary

Volunteer Missionary Movement, High Park, Grace Park Road, Dublin 9 (01-8376565).

Viatores Christi, 39 Upr Gardiner St, Dublin 1 (01-8749346).

Irish Missionary Union, Orwell Park, Rathgar, Dublin 6 (01-4965433).

READ/VIEW

Religious orders provide a wide range of literature.

Health Board career information pamphlets.

Summary of Social Insurance and Social Assistance Service (Dept. of Social Welfare).

Current affairs & magazines. Keep up to date with current affairs by reading newspapers and watching relevant documentaries on television.

Child care, (video) produced by Colaiste Dhulaigh, Coolock.

TRANSPORT – AIR/SEA/ROAD/RAIL

Removal of duty free could cost 9,000 jobs

The last few years have seen greater agreement and simplification of laws among the member states of the EU. At the moment, it is in the area of transport that this is most evident, as it has an impact upon just about everybody in the country.

One of the major developments is this abolition of duty free sales. One survey estimates that this is likely to cost 9,000 jobs, most of them within two years. Many of these are not jobs within the travel industry itself, but related employment in tourism and supply services. However, within the industry itself, the study says ferry services will be hardest hit, with 1,800 jobs likely to go.

The greater liberalisation of air travel under EU law has led to a great deal more competition within that market. Aer Lingus has been casting about for a strategic partner airlines to expand and continue to compete. Such a partner would open access to a wide range of international routes, and provide some funding towards fleet replacement and development.

Meanwhile, Ryanair continues to grow, flying to an increasing number of destinations. The company has said it will open ten new routes and create more than 500 jobs, if charges which the airline has to pay at Dublin Airport are reduced.

EU structural funding has meant vast improvements to our road networks in many parts of the country. EU funding also brought about the proposal for the LUAS light rail network. It will be some years, however, before this yields new jobs in the area of transport – initially the main opportunities offered will be in the construction phase.

Some of the EU funding for LUAS has now been reallocated to other transport projects. A total of £56 million has been set aside to improve public transport by providing more buses in Dublin, upgrading mainline rail services, adding extra Dart carriages and enhancing the suburban rail network.

Pilots: Aer Lingus advertises for a small number of pilots from time to time. Some pilot experience helps when applying to the company. Candidates are aged 18 and over with a 'good standard of education'. They have to be physically fit with good hearing – but, contrary to belief, perfect eyesight is not required. Within defined limits, correcting lenses may be permitted, Being colour blind, however, is definitely out. Selection is by application, aptitude test and interview.

Ryanair employs about 165 pilots and is likely to recruit more as its fleet expands.

The Air Corps also trains pilots at their training school at Baldonnell. Unlike most civil airlines, the variety of aircrafts used is very broad.

CAREERS IN THIS CATEGORY
Many of the careers listed below are outlined on the FAS Gairm Database

AIR/AIRPORTS: Air and Ground Hostess-/Steward, Pilot, clerical/management positions in the fields of flight or cargo reservations, Economics, Marketing, Finance, Statistics and Human Resources, airport management staff at all levels, air traffic controllers, airport police, airport fireperson, civil engineers, electrical engineers, mechanical engineers, engineering technicians, architectural technicians, accounting technicians, retail sales, electricians, fitters, plumbers, carpenters.

SEA/SEAPORTS: Deck Officer, Engine Officer, Purser, Radio Officer, Motormen, Electrical Engineer, Cook/Chef, Steward/Stewardess, Able Seamen, Hostess, Reservation Clerks, general management/secretarial/clerical staff in marketing, freight handling, customs clearance, finance, training, human resources.

ROAD: Road transport operator, mechanical and electrical engineer, transport manager, warehouse management, freight despatcher, route planner, general management/clerical staff in the fields of marketing, sales, finance, economics, training, human resources, passenger reservations clerk, driver (including Light and Heavy Goods Vehicles, small and large buses), apprentice mechanic (diesel and petrol), panel beater and spray painter.

RAIL: Management/clerical/secretarial positions in marketing, finance, economics, research, human resources, Electrical/mechanical/civil engineer and technician, fitter, electrician, driver, cook/chef, waiter/waitress.

TRAVEL: Apart from the specific transport modes, there is the tourism sector which touches on all four modes through the network of more than 300 licensed travel agents.

A huge proportion of pilots don't work for major airlines. Many are employed as instructors, or in the private charter business.

Cabin Crew: Advertisements for stewards/stewardesses occur from time to time - and there seems to be plenty of scope with foreign airlines, particularly in the East. At home, many successful candidates have worked for a number of years and/or have third level qualifications, generally with a language element. Good grooming is essential.

Aircraft Maintenance: Much of the uncertainty over the future of the Aer Lingus aircraft maintenance company TEAM has disappeared, following its takeover by the Danish company FLS. Shannon Aerospace is also holding its own. FÁS has been running two year training courses in Shannon in response to the company's demand for qualified aircraft maintenance technicians.

Other jobs with Aer Lingus: The airline advertises each year for seasonal workers. These would include general operatives (baggage loading, aircraft cleaning) and catering staff.

Aer Rianta: Aer Rianta has been preparing in recent years for the loss of duty free sales and the effect that will have on the company, and is likely to seek more opportunities for expansion abroad, in airports, and duty free sales in non-EU areas.

Passenger numbers going through Dublin airport are currently growing at about two million a year. To cope with the increases at this and other main airports, Aer Rianta is to spend £500 million over the next five years expanding and upgrading them.

Rail: CIE will have to invest huge sums in upgrading railway lines to bring them to international standards over the next five years. LUAS, however, should generate some employment.

Vacancies for clerical staff and craftspersons crop up from time to time. Apprenticeships when they're available, are for electricians, fitters, turners, carpenters, plumbers, coachbuilders.

Dublin Bus and Bus Eireann: More than 150 new buses are being introduced in Dublin to help cope with the rush hour traffic gridlock. Both companies advertise for drivers from time to time. Other vacancies are mainly clerical – with permanent and temporary positions advertised from time to time.

Some opportunities also with private operators. At present there are 1,400 private bus operators, running 6,000 buses on provincial routes.

Transport & Distribution: There is an increasing number of companies setting up their European bases in Ireland, and they require access to Europe on a daily basis to deliver their goods. This has had a very positive impact on the road haulage industry. Currently there are 110,000 people employed in road haulage.

With the expansion of Dublin port, many firms from the North have opened offices around Dublin Port, and existing firms have been increasing their staff numbers, with plenty of openings in administration.

Qualifications: Like all industries today, entry can be difficult for a young person without adequate qualification. The Chartered Institute of Transport of Ireland has an established network of centres throughout the country offering part-time and full time educational courses.

The Certificate of Professional Competence is the nationally recognised qualification for those wishing to establish their own transport business and is available in 30 centres throughout the country.

The Institute also oversees the development of full-time Transport Courses at the DIT Aungier Street and Colaiste Ide, Finglas, Dublin 11.

The Institute offers its own professional qualification leading to membership of the Chartered Institute of Transport. This qualification has worldwide recognition within the transport industry.

If you are interested in a career in the transport and distribution sector why not contact their headquarters at No. 1. Fitzwilliam Place, Dublin 2 or phone 01-763188. FÁS runs a course in Transport Management at Loughlinstown. There are also post-Leaving Cert courses in Road Transport Organisation, e.g. Scoil Ide, Cardiffsbridge Road, Dublin 11.

Ferries: Increasingly ferry companies like Irish Ferries, Stena Line and SuperSeaCat are investing in fast ferries as a means of countering competition from airlines on routes to Britain and France.

Travel: The booming economy had been good to travel agents and tour operators – with many people now taking two holidays abroad each year, instead of the traditional one. The market is now dominated by two major players – the Thompson group, which owns Budget Travel, and First Choice, owners of Falcon Holidays and JWT.

SUGGESTIONS

For all apprenticeships some previous form of practical experience is very desirable, even if you can snatch a few hours with a tradesperson on Saturdays or holiday time . . . get a driving licence as soon as you are eligible . . . read motoring magazines . . . attend car rallies . . . service your own bike or friend's motorbike . . . attend motor show.

Enquire about seasonal work at airports . . . watch motoring programmes on television . . . budding air stewards/hostesses should concentrate on languages . . . get vacation work in a garage, e.g. as petrol pump attendant or tyre fitter . . . Aeroplanes — go plane spotting . . . know about the different plane models and various companies that use Irish airports . . . join a flying club . . . Check FÁS courses in this yearbook (see index).

FURTHER INFORMATION

Aer Rianta, Dublin Airport (01-8144111).

Bus Atha Cliath, 59 Upr O'Connell St, Dublin 1 (01-8720000).

Bus Eireann, Broadstone, Dublin 7 (01-8302222).

Chartered Institute of Transport, Irish Section, 1 Fitzwilliam Place, Dublin 2. (01-6763188)

DIT, 30 Upr. Pembroke St. (01-4023445).

FLS Team, Dublin Airport (01-7056000).

Iarnrod Eireann, Connolly Station, D. 1 (01-8363333).

Irish Taxi Drivers Federation, 48 Summerhill Place, Dublin 1 (01-8364166).

Personnel Department, Aer Lingus, Head Office, Dublin Airport (01-8444873).

Personnel Department, C.I.E., Heuston Station, Dublin 8 (01-6771871).

Ryanair, Head Office, Dublin Airport (01-8444400)

Shannon Aerospace, Shannon, Co. Clare (061-370193)

READ/VIEW

Air Corp Video/Defence Forces Video

Irish Aviator, Auto Ireland, Cara, Commercial Transport, Haulage and Distribution, Irish Motor Industry — periodicals.

LEAVING CERT OPTIONS

SUBJECTS & STUDY

Staying in school beyond the Junior Certificate is an option for increasing numbers of students. Two new Leaving Certificates and the revision of the existing Leaving Certificate cater for virtually all levels of student ability. Section 3 explains the subject implications of these courses and helps pupils survive with useful advice on study and examinations.

LEAVING CERTIFICATE OPTIONS

Radical Change

The Irish educational system has changed radically in recent years particularly at Leaving Certificate level. There are now three types of Leaving Certificate examinations catering for students of almost all level of ability and interest.

❖ **ESTABLISHED LEAVING CERTIFICATE**

❖ **LEAVING CERTIFICATE APPLIED**

❖ **LEAVING CERTIFICATE VOCATIONAL PROGRAMME**

ESTABLISHED LEAVING CERTIFICATE

Many Senior Cycle students will continue to choose the established Leaving Certificate taking subjects at either Foundation, Ordinary or Higher levels.

Foundation level is now available at Leaving Certificate in two subjects - Gaeilge and Mathematics - as well as at Ordinary and Higher levels. All other Leaving Certificate subjects are available at Ordinary and Higher levels.

Career and course options are diverse on completion of the programme. Many of these are outlined in Student Yearbook particularly in the 'Subject Matters' section, which follows.

LEAVING CERTIFICATE APPLIED

The Leaving Certificate Applied is a distinct self-contained two-year Leaving Certificate programme aimed at preparing students for adult and working life. It recognises the talents of all students and provides opportunities for development in terms of responsibility, self-esteem and self-knowledge. It is an innovative programme in the way students learn; in what they learn and in the way their achievements are assessed.

EMPLOYMENT PROSPECTS?
Employment prospects for school leavers have seldom been better than they are at present. Students with the range of skills and relevant work experience from the Leaving Certificate Applied will be well placed to avail of these opportunities. Negotiations are currently under way with government agencies and employers groups to widen the career options for Leaving Certificate Applied students.

They are also well placed to compete for the wide range of FÁS and CERT apprenticeship outlined in this Yearbook.

FURTHER EDUCATION?
A student can proceed to Further Education, through the vast majority of PLCs which are described in the Yearbooks PLC section. However, there are a small number of PLC courses where additional requirements are imposed by external professional bodies/associations.

THIRD LEVEL?
Direct access to Third Level Education through the CAO system is not possible immediately on completion of the Leaving Certificate Applied.

However, students who complete the Leaving Certificate Applied and progress on to a NCVA Level 2 award, can become eligible for admission to some third level courses in the Institutes of Technology.

LEAVING CERTIFICATE VOCATIONAL PROGRAMME

The Leaving Certificate Vocational Programme (LCVP) can be described as a Leaving Certificate with a strong vocational dimension.

The LCVP is different from the established Leaving Certificate in strengthening the vocational dimension of the Leaving Certificate by linking subjects into vocational groupings which students take and by adding three Link Modules (Enterprise Education, Preparation for Work and Work Experience).

The Programme balances the virtues of the traditionally academic Leaving Certificate with the development of skills and qualities which will prove relevant to the lives of students on leaving school for further education, the world of work, or the business of making a living.

EMPLOYMENT PROSPECTS?
The content of the LCVP shares common ground with the needs of the business community who expect new employees to be well educated, confident, adaptable, good at solving problems and familiar with a range of technologies.

In a rapidly changing technological world, employers want their new employees to be well educated in the broadest sense, adaptable, multi-skilled, good communicators, capable of making decisions and potential lifelong learners

THIRD LEVEL?
LCVP students have the same opportunity to proceed to universities and colleges as the student of the established Leaving Certificate. Students who successfully complete the Link Modules gain points, which can be used for the purpose of entry into Institutes of Technology. (See 3rd level section in this Yearbook).

SUBJECT MATTERS

What if I drop a subject?
Should I transfer to another subject?
What if I don't get the honours I expect?

These are just some of the questions facing students during their Leaving Certificate years. Subject matters are as relevant now as they were when you made your original choices. Clearly the considerations are different:

- *you have studied the subject for a few months in fifth year and you genuinely can't hack it;*

- *you are pleasantly surprised at how much you like a subject and feel you can transfer from pass to honours;*

- *alternatively the 'Mocks' have exposed some weaknesses and you need to drop some honours.*

Whatever the reasons, it is just as important to reassess your subjects now as it was when you chose them originally.

LEAVING CERTIFICATE SUBJECTS

Whatever choices you have made, or are about to make, from the options available from your school, you should make sure that you:

- *Have the essential subjects for your hoped for course or career;*
- *Can maximise your points, or achieve the grades specified by employers or colleges;*
- *Enjoy and fully participate in the subjects you have chosen.*

Beyond the core essential subjects of English, Irish and Mathematics there are relatively few demands in terms of essential subjects for courses and jobs. If you are considering going to any of the colleges of the National University of Ireland (UCD, UCC, NUI Maynooth, NUI Galway) a third language should be among your chosen subjects. Likewise, if you are considering Medical, Paramedical, Science and Engineering degrees or Nursing you should have a science subject (or sometimes two for some courses). What particular grades you need to have in these or other required subjects will be detailed in the prospectuses from the colleges or employers information sheets. Make sure you consult these.

In the next few pages we will outline the requirements for different subjects but it is important to note some subjects that are not required: Accountancy, Business or Economics are not required for any Business, Commerce or Accountancy course. Technical Drawing is not required for Architecture, Architectural Technician, Engineering, Engineering technician or Construction courses (though it does form part of the study of all of these courses). Art is not required for Art Colleges - but a portfolio is. Science is not required for many of the applied science courses in the Institutes of Technologies. So, whatever your chose as your Leaving Certificate subjects you still have a huge range of options if you wish to do further study.

Here's our summary of what subjects and levels are essential for colleges and courses and what careers they are useful for. Don't just take our word for it - check the relevant college literature and employer details yourself. It's your choice, your responsibility.

> **Leaving Certificate Subjects**
> Subjects are grouped as follows:
>
> *Language Group:* Irish, English, French, German, Italian, Spanish, Latin, Greek, Hebrew Studies, Classical Studies.
>
> *Science Group:* Mathematics, Physics, Chemistry, Physics and Chemistry, Biology, Applied Mathematics.
>
> *Business Studies Group:* Accounting, Business, Economics, Economic History.
>
> *Applied Science Group:* Engineering, Technical Drawing, Construction Studies, Physics and Chemistry, Agricultural Science, Agricultural Economics, Home Economics (Scientific and Social), Home Economics (General).
>
> *Social Studies Group:* History, Geography, Art (including Crafts), Music and Musicianship, Home Economics (General).

MATHEMATICS

Employers tend to expect applicants to have numeric skills and look for at least an OD in Maths. Likewise all the Institutes of Technology require an OD for entry to their Science, Engineering and most of their Business courses. The universities require OC for many of their Science and Business courses reflecting its importance as part of these courses. For Engineering, Mathematical, Theoretical Physics courses and Actuarial Degrees a HC or HB is required, again reflecting the crucial role it plays in these disciplines. For actuarial training you need a HA in Maths. At the other end of the scale Alternative Ordinary Level Mathematics is accepted by very few employers (the Guards will accept a B in it) and very few colleges (usually only for courses where no maths are involved) and it earns no points.

But if your score in Maths is "Nul points" fear not. Chose your college wisely and you can still do an Arts, Law or Social Science degree. You can also do courses in Music, Art, Drama, Sport or Catering.

So, whether you're a Maths hero or zero here's what you need...

HA
• Actuary

HB
• Engineering and Theoretical Physics (UCD),
• Maths and Theoretical Physics, Computational Physics/Chemistry (+HB in Physics/Chemistry or HC Maths + two HB in Physics/Chemistry/Applied Maths) (TCD)
• Medicine (or HB in Science) (RCSI)

HC
• All engineering Courses (UCC, UCG, TCD, DCU, UL IT's)
• Computers/Computers & Languages, Information and Communications Technology (TCD),
• Applied Physics/Languages, Financial & Actuarial (DCU),
• Materials/Mathematical Sciences Applied maths and Computing, Applied Physics, Computer Systems and French, Industrial Chemistry/Biochemistry (a HC or OB/HD+HC from specified Science group). (UL)
• Mathematical Sciences (Maynooth),
• Science (Various options, HC or HC in Science or Applied Maths) (UCC)
• Transport Technology (DIT).

HD or OB
• Financial through Irish (DCU),
• Business/Legal, Commerce/ and Language Science and Computer Science (UCD),
• Computer Systems. Technology Education, Electronic Manufacture, Information Technology & Production Management (UL),, Industrial Design (UL, NCAD),
• Advanced Cert. In Business - Accounting (Cork IT),
• Computer Science and Software Engineering (Maynooth),

OB
• Applied Science, Business Information Systems, Optometry, Telecom/ Electrical/Electrical Engineering Dip, Computer Science, Physics and Physics Technology, Applied Electronics, Industrial Electronics Systems, Geomatics (DIT),
• Communications, (DCU),
• Electronics- Product dev. (Dundalk IT).
• Information Technology (UCG),
• Languages and Computing, Wood Science and Technology, Environmental Science, Food Technology (HC or OB/HD + HC in Science) (UL),
• Computer and Software Engineering (Athlone IT),
• Manufacturing Technology (Galway Mayo IT).

OC or HD
• Accounting & Finance, Analytical Science, Applied Chemistry with a language, Applied Computational Linguistics, Biotechnology, Business Studies, International Business and Languages, European Business Studies, International Marketing and Languages, Science Education, Sports Science, Science (DCU),
• BESS, Business Studies and a language, Economics, Human Genetics, Medicine, Dentistry, Pharmacy, Physiotherapy, Science (TCD),
• Medical Laboratory Science (Galway-Mayo IT)
• Business Studies Degree, Arts Administration (WIT).

OC
• Adv. Cert in Business Studies (IT Tralee),
• Business/Business & a language, Law & Accounting (UL),
• Electronics Technician, Electrical Draughting, Medical Laboratory Science, Photography, Marketing Degree, Tourism Marketing, Hospitality Management, Culinary Arts (DIT),
• Chartered Accountancy and Management Accountancy

OD
• Entry to all IT's, UL, DCU, TCD,
• Law (NUI Galway),
• Primary teaching,
• Philosophy and Theology in Milltown Institute,
• Defence Forces Cadets,
• Nursing,
• Gardai (or Leaving Cert Applied).

No Maths is required for places on Arts, Music, Social Science and Law Degrees in UCD, UCC, NUI Galway and Maynooth unless Maths or some other numerate subject is being studied. Art colleges generally do not require it also. Most PLC courses do not require Maths.

Foundation Maths is less widely accepted. The Gardai will accept a grade B in them for entry. Some colleges will allow it where no maths is involved in the course (e.g. Art and Design) but will not give any points for it. Some employers will accept it for apprenticeships. Most PLC courses will accept it.

Remember to check college information and requirements carefully!

Useful for: Accountancy, Actuary, Air Traffic Controller, Architecture, Astronomy, Banking, Biologist, Clerical Work, Chemist, Civil Servant, Computer Operator, Data Input Operator, Economist, Engineer, Engineering Technician, Geologist, Insurance, Laboratory Technician, Mathematics Teacher, Marketing, Medical Laboratory Technician, Meteorologist, Physicist, Psychologist, Programmer, Quantity Surveyor, Scientist, Sociologist, Statistician, Systems Analyst, Tax Officer, Trades.

Computer Studies though not a full subject can be taken as an optional section of the Mathematics course. However, it is not part of the Leaving Certificate examination, but students who take it and perform satisfactorily will be issued with a statement to that effect by the Dept. of Education.

ENGLISH

Most employers require a pass in English (OD) though some will accept Irish instead. Likewise the majority of third level courses require OD in English though many colleges including the Institutes of Technology, DIT and DCU will accept Irish instead. HC in English is essential for a small number of courses like Journalism (DIT), and Communications and Journalism (DCU).

HC
- Communications -Journalism (DIT),
- Applied Languages, Communications, Journalism (DCU),
- Audio-visual Communications (IT Tallaght),
- Clinical Speech, English Literature (TCD).

HD or OC
- Chartered Accountancy,
- Primary Teaching,
- Management Accountancy,
- Marketing Degree (DIT)(or Irish)
- Arts Administration (WIT).

HD or OB
- Optometry, Business Information Systems (DIT)

OD
- All NUI colleges (UCD, UCC, NUI Galway, Maynooth, NCAD),
- TCD, UL, DCU.
- IT's will accept it or an OD in Irish.
- Defence Forces Cadet,
- Nursing,
- Garda (or LC applied).

Useful for: Acting, Advertising, Broadcasting, Civil Servant, Courier, Librarian, Marketing, Personnel Officer, Politician, Public Relations Officer, Solicitor, Barrister, Speech Therapist, Teacher, Telephonist, Receptionist,Typist, Computer Programmer, Air Steward/Stewardess, Copy Writer, Printer, Proof Reader, Sales Representative, Translator, Interpreter, Secretary.

IRISH

Irish is required for all faculties in the National University of Ireland (UCD, UCC, NUI Galway, NUI Maynooth, NCAD) but you can be exempt from it under certain conditions e.g. being born outside Ireland. If you are exempt from it (or think you could be) then contact the NUI in Dublin for full details of the procedures to adopt if you are applying to any of the colleges. Irish satisfies the requirement of a Modern Language for TCD and the Language other than English requirement for UL and DCU. Primary Teaching requires a HC though the Church of Ireland Training College may accept a HD if sufficient candidates do not present a HC.

HC = Higher paper grade c; OD = Ordinary paper grade D.
C generally refers to minimum grade C₃ and D to minimum grade D₃
The above grades refer to the established Leaving Cert. Programme

HB
- Computer Science and Irish (TCD).

HC
- Primary Teaching,
- Irish -Early and Modern (TCD),
- Home Economics Teaching if taken as elective (St. Catherine's),
- Commerce and Irish (UCD),
- Tourism Marketing (DIT),
- Commerce (European) with Irish (UCC),
- Airgeadas, Riomhaireacht & Fiontraiocht (DCU) or OA.
- Irish Studies (UL)
- Law and Irish Law (NUIG)

OC
- Technology Education (UL).

OD
- All courses in UCD, UCC, NCAD, NUI Galway and Maynooth,
- Some Nursing courses,
- Cadets,
- Humanities (IT -Tralee),
- RTE Continuity Announcer.
- Garda (or LC Applied).

A Special Exam in Irish is required for Secondary Teaching and Solicitor.

Useful for: Acting, Administration Personnel in Irish Voluntary bodies, e.g. Comhaltas Ceoltoirí Eireann, Archivist, Army, Civil Service, Broadcasting, Air Steward/Stewardess, Journalist, Local Government, Politics, Printing, Publishing, School Secretary.

OTHER LANGUAGES

In these days of fast international transport and modern communications knowledge of a foreign language will always be useful. For some areas it is a necessity. You require it for entry to the National University of Ireland (UCD, UCC, NUI Galway and NUI Maynooth). For the other college in the NUI, the NCAD, they will accept Art instead of the third language. The other universities will accept Irish as "a language other than English" for entry. However, many colleges have it as a requirement for specific courses (detailed below) such as European Studies, Languages and Marketing. They also generally require a high standard in it.

There are huge opportunities in the areas of telesales and customer support with many companies locating in Ireland because of our ability with languages. So, for those with ability in languages, never has the study of them been as useful or as important. There are terrific opportunities out there! As they don't say in French: *Le monde est votre huître!*

HB in the appropriate language for:
- Applied languages, Languages and Computing, Computer Systems and French (UL),
- Commerce and Languages, Languages and Cultural Studies (German)(UCC),
- Applied languages (DCU).
- Law and French Law (French) (UCD)

HC in the appropriate language for:
- Business and Languages (HC1), Computers, Linguistics and a language, European Studies, Law and French/German, Information and Communications Technology, Languages, Clinical Speech (or Irish) (TCD),
- Business, Marketing and Languages, Computers and a Language (IT Carlow),
- Languages and Cultural Studies, Business and Languages, Mechanical Engineering and German, Irish Studies (UL),
- Languages and Cultural Studies (or Irish), Law and Languages, European Studies, Commerce (European) with a language (UCC),
- Computational Linguistics, European Electronics Systems, European Business and French/German/Spanish, International marketing, Physics and a Language, Chemistry and French/German (DCU),
- Commerce International (UCD),
- European Business and a Language (NCI),
- International Business and Languages, Travel and Tourism , Tourism Marketing (DIT)
- Tourism and Languages (Galway-Mayo IT),
- French, German/German and Historical Studies (NUI Maynooth)
- Business Studies in Languages and Marketing (or OB) , Business Studies with French (or OB) (WIT),
- Applied Languages (HC in French or German), Applied Languages for Communication and Administration (IT Tallaght)

HD in the appropriate language for:
- Hotel Accommodation and Language Cert. (Galway Mayo IT),
- European Languages and Business (Letterkenny IT),

- Airgeadas, Riomhaireach & Fiontraiocht (DCU) (or OB),
- Business and Languages, Tourism and Languages (or OB) (IT Tralee)
- International Business and French/German (or OB), Office Information Systems and French/German (IT Carlow).
- Tourism and languages (or OB) (IT Blanchardstown)

OC in the appropriate language for:
- Hospitality Management , Culinary Arts (DIT)

OD in a language for:
- Entry to NUI colleges (UCD, UCC, NUI Galway and Maynooth) NCAD will accept Art instead of a language for entry.
- Leisure Management (DIT),
- Cadets,
- Business and Languages, Computing and Languages, Office Information Studies (or OC) (Dundalk IT),
- Medicine (RCSI),
- Hotel Management Dip. (DIT),
- Business and Languages (IT Sligo),
- Front Office Administration (Athlone IT).

NO language required for entry to TCD, UL or DCU apart from the above courses, you could use a pass in Irish instead. It is not required for entry to the Institutes of Technology or the DIT unless it part of the area of study -see above list. Gardai, Apprenticeships or most PLC courses.

CLASSICS

These include, Latin, Greek, Hebrew Studies and Classical studies and like all subjects they aid the development of scholastic skills which are transferable to future tasks. They are seldom mentioned as essential subjects apart from TCD, where HC in Latin or Greek is required for the study of Classics and where OD can be substituted for Mathematics as part of their minimum entry requirements.

CLASSICS are useful for careers in:
Archaeology; Archivist; Barrister; Doctor; Language Teacher; Linguist; Religious Life; Solicitor; Museum work; the Arts; Historian; Journalist.

SCIENCE SUBJECTS

Not all Science courses available at third level require a science subject, but you would be well advised to do one if you were at all interested in anything in the Science, Medical, Paramedical, Nursing, Engineering or Technology areas. On the other hand if you do not find science interesting or have no interest in work or study in any of these areas then you should not fall into the trap of "keeping all your options open" especially if science is not one of your best subjects. Remember also, if you are struggling with it, that the reason it is required in all the above areas is that it forms a large part of the area of study, so if you don't like it at secondary school you may find it unbearable at third level.

With the exception of some courses in some colleges (e.g. TCD, UCC and DIT) most of those courses requiring a Science subject only seek only one and often only at ordinary level.

TCD require two for many of their science based courses e.g. Physiotherapy, Pharmacy and for some courses will accept Mathematics, Applied Mathematics, Agricultural Science and Geography as fulfilling their Higher Science requirement. Their actual requirements are quite detailed and are best checked using the college's Summary of Admission Requirements booklet for the year of entry.

So, for further experiments in Science this is what you will need...

2 Science Subjects required
- For some science based courses at TCD, e.g. Physiotherapy, Pharmacy, Medicine, Dental Science, Science, Human Genetics *(in some cases they require Higher B's or C's, some will accept Maths, Applied Maths and Geography. The requirements are quite detailed so check the Summary of Admission Requirements leaflet).*
- Medicine, Dentistry *(HC in Chemistry and either Physics or Biology) in UCC*

HB in a Science subject for:
- Medicine (+ one HC), Theoretical Physics (HB in Physics) (TCD)
- Medicine (or HB Maths), Physiotherapy (RCSI)

HC in a Science Subject for
- Therapeutic Radiography, Medicine, Physiotherapy, Occupational Therapy, Science, Computational Physics or Chemistry, Pharmacy , Clinical Speech Studies (TCD),
- Electronic and Electrical Engineering (HC in Physics) all Science courses in UCC.

- Material Science, Industrial Chemistry & Biochemistry, Applied Physics, Environmental Science, Food Technology, Applied Maths & Computing, Equine Science (UL),
- Engineering, Human Nutrition (Chemistry), Applied Sciences, Medical Laboratory Science (Chemistry), Optometry, Physics and Physics Technology (DIT).
- Veterinary Science (Chemistry) (UCD)

HD in any Science Subject for:
- Electronic Engineering, Applied Physics, Telecommunications, Mechatronics, Electronics (DCU).

OC or HD in any Science Subject for
- Analytic Science, Pure and Applied Chemistry, Biotechnology, Chemistry and French/German (DCU).
- Environmental Health (DIT)
- Industrial Design, Electronic Manufacturing, Manufacturing Technology, Information Technology, Education (Engineering & Construction), Science Teaching, Sports Science (or OB) (UL).

OD in any Science Subject for

- Architecture, Medicine, Radiography, Physiotherapy, Agriculture, Engineering, Science (UCD),
- Engineering, Medicine, Sciences, Biotechnology, Computing, Information Technology (NUI Galway),
- Food Business/Process Engineering, Civil Engineering, medicine at (UCC),
- Biotechnology, Science, Computer Science (NUI Maynooth)
- All Engineering courses (UL),
- Environmental Health, Food Technology/Quality Assurance, Health Care Technology, Environmental Resource Management, Health Care Technology (DIT),
- Medical laboratory Science (Cork IT)
- Home Economics Teaching (or Home Economics) (Sion Hill & St. Angela's Sligo),
- Industrial Design (NCAD/UL)
- Nursing.

No Science subject required to study any of the Science or Engineering Certificate or Diploma courses at the Institutes of Technology, or for Arts, Commerce, Business Studies, Social Science, Law etc. at Universities. It is not required for most Post Leaving Cert. Courses or for most apprenticeships.

CHEMISTRY

Chemistry deals with the composition of matter, the laws of chemical change and the relation between the properties and composition of substances. In other words it involves everything we use, wear, consume, including medicines, plastics, preservatives, etc. It offers a wide range of options in the scientific field including brewing technology and medical laboratory science.

Although many science courses at third level require a science subject, most colleges are fairly flexible as to which science you present. There are however some important exceptions, for example both Human Nutrition and Medical Laboratory Technician Course in Kevin St. require HC Chemistry. Dentistry (UCC), 2nd Medicine (UCC) will require HC plus HC in either Physics or Biology. Veterinary (UCD) also requires a HC in Chemistry.

CHEMISTRY is useful for careers in:
Agriculture; Animal Nursing Auxiliary; Archaeologist; Architect; Brewing Technologist; Chemist; Chemistry Teacher; Dairy Scientist; Dental Craftsperson; Dental Hygienist; Dental Surgery Assistant; Dentist; Dietician; Doctor; Engineering, especially Chemical Engineering; Food Science Technologist; Forestry Inspector; Fuel Technologist; Health Inspector; Industrial Chemist; Laboratory Assistant; Medical Laboratory Technician; Metallurgist; Nurse; Optician; Patent Work; Pharmacist; Pharmacy Technician; Physiotherapist; Pilot; Polymer Scientist; Radiographer; Science Laboratory Technician; Seed Analyst; Serological Assistant; Speech Therapist;

Textiles; Forensic Science; Photographic Processing; Cosmetic Science; Glass technology; Quality control and Biotechnology.

BIOLOGY

Biology the science of life and living things. Forms a knowledge base for hundreds of careers ranging from oceanography and ecology to medicine and biotechnology. Though not a specific Bord Altranais requirement for entry to nurse training, the vast majority of training hospitals would probably be reluctant to consider a candidate without it, while many specify a pass at ordinary level in it as a minimum requirement, some may even look for a Higher Grade C. Students taking Biology as an elective for Home Economics Teacher Training in St. Angela's must present Biology at OD or higher. St. Catherine's require it if you are not presenting Home Economics. It is an essential requirement for entry to Dental Hygiene (UCC). Maynooth College normally requires students to have obtained a high grade on the Higher Leaving Certificate paper if they wish to take Biology through the Arts Faculty.

BIOLOGY is useful for careers in:
Agriculture; Agricultural Research; Animal Breeder; Animal Nursing Auxiliary; Animal Trainer; Ambulance Driver; Audiologist; Biochemist; Biologist; Biology Teacher; Catering Superintendent; Chiropodist; Conservation Work; Dental Craftsperson; Dairy Scientist; Dental Hygienist; Dental Surgery Assistant; Dentist; Dietician; Doctor; Farmer; Farrier; Fisherman; Food Science Technician; Forester; Forestry Inspector;

Geneticist; Health Inspector; Horticulturist; Kennel Assistant; Laboratory Assistant; Marine Biologist; Medical/Laboratory Technician; Microbiologist; Nurse; Occupational Therapist; Optician; Pet Shop Assistant; Pharmacist; Pharmacy Technician; Physiotherapist; Psychologist; Radiographer; Seed Analyst; Serological Assistant; Speech Therapist; Trout Farmer; Veterinary Surgeon; Wild Life Ranger; Zookeeper; Zoologist; Oceanographer; Cyto-technology.

Subject requirements for science, medical and paramedical courses in TCD are quite complex, so it is essential that your individual requirements are checked against their current prospectus.

PHYSICS

Physics deals with the laws and forces governing natural phenomena, and includes heat, light, electricity and magnetism. It is of key importance in technology and particularly relevant for those interested in specialising in most branches of engineering. In most engineering courses, one will find a high physics content, while some paramedical careers will involve the study of it, e.g. Radiography, Physiotherapy etc.

It is an essential requirement (HB) for Theoretical Physics (TCD) and Electrical Engineering (UCC) – HC.

PHYSICS is useful for careers in:
Architecture; Astronomy; Biophysicist; Computer Careers; Dentist; Doctor; Engineer, especially electrical and electronics at all levels; Geophysicist; Health Inspector; Marine Radio Operator; Medical Laboratory Technician; Metallurgist; Meteorologist; Naval Services; Nurse; Oceanographer; Optician; Patent Worker; Pharmacist; Physicist; Physics Teacher; Photographic Technician; Pilot; Radiographer; Science Laboratory Technician; Telecommunications; various trade apprenticeships; Scientific Research; Heating and Ventilation technicians.

ART

Though some RTC Art Departments require it, it is not always an essential subject for entry to Art Colleges. Yet it is highly recommended that intending students take it at Leaving Cert. level. However, the preparation of a portfolio without the guidance of an art teacher would be most difficult. A portfolio is normally an essential requirement for all art courses and should not be left to your final year to prepare. Some schools of Architecture recommend its study even in preference to Technical drawing. Sligo IT National Diploma in Industrial Design require students to have OD in art and it is recommended for the National Certificate in Print Media Communications in the IT Cork.

ART is useful for careers in:
Advertising; Antiques; Art Teacher; Architecture; Bookbinding; Crafts (leather work, wood carving, etc.); Environmental Designer; Fashion; Florist; Furniture; Gallery and Museum Work; Graphic Design; Industrial Design; Painting and Decorating; Photographer;

Marketing; Merchandiser; Occupational Therapist; National Teacher; Picture Restorer; Printing and Publishing; Sculptor; Signwriter; Video production; Textile design; Poet; Cosmetics; Upholstery; Television and Theatre; Town and Country Planning; Hobby or a Pastime.

MUSIC AND MUSICIANSHIP

Due to its lack of availability in schools, some of the best musicians probably do not take it to Leaving Certificate, despite the fact that valuable points for entry to third level colleges can be achieved by the talented and interested students. Particular standards at the Leaving Certificate or other relevant exams would normally be expected of those applying to read Music at Third Level. At NUI, Maynooth, HC or equivalent is required for taking Music through (MH001) while the denominated courses in Music (MH005) expects HC or equivalent, while UCC, DIT and WIT require all intending students of Music to take a special entrance test.

MUSIC is useful for careers in:
Entertainment – groups, orchestra, bands, etc; Aerobics; Librarianship; Music Shop Sales; Speech Therapy; Disc Jockey; Folklore Studies; Composer/Arranger; Dancer; Film and Television Director; Instrument maker; Musician; National Teacher; Occupational Therapist; Physical Education; Television and Radio Production; Actor.

ACCOUNTING

Extending beyond the actual making of records, i.e. book-keeping, accounting is concerned with the use these records are put to, their analysis and interpretation. It is an excellent preparation for any business related occupation, though not essential for entry to any business college, profession training in accountancy would obviously still be a great help to students wishing to pursue any third level business related course.

ACCOUNTING is useful for careers in:
Accountancy; Auctioneering; Auditing; Banking; Book-keeping; Building Society Clerk; A vast array of Clerical Work; Commerce Teacher; Company Secretaryship, Hospital Administration; Hotel Management; Receptionist; Insurance; Market Research; Purchasing Officer; Quantity Surveyor; Sales Representative; Store Management; Taxation Consultant; Marketing; Teaching; Computer Systems; Advertising; Business Law.

BUSINESS

Business is concerned with how organisations are formed, financed and run, looking at the services involved such as banking, transport, taxation and semi-state organisations. It provides an excellent foundation for anyone contemplating a business career, though like Accounting it is not an essential subject for any course it would still be very useful.

BUSINESS is useful for careers in:
Industry; Business; Accounting; Banking; Book-keeping; Clerical Work; Commerce Teacher; Company Secretaryship; Hospital Administrator; Hotel Management; Insurance; Office Machine Operator; Purchasing Officer; Receptionist/Telephonist; Store Management; Typist; Stockbroking; Sales; Marketing; Merchandising; Customs and Exercise; Taxation; Law.

ECONOMICS

This subject covers a wide range of topics including inflation, banking, international trade, The E.U., the role of the Government in the control of the economy, competition and markets. A good preparation for entry to many third level business or journalism courses.

ECONOMIC HISTORY

A complementary subject to both the study of History and Economics, it includes such topics as growth of trade and colonies, the industrial revolution and economic interdependence.

ECONOMICS and ECONOMIC HISTORY are useful for careers in:
Administration; Accounting; Banking; Barrister; Civil Servant; Clerical Worker; Commerce Teacher; Company Secretary; Economist; Hotel Management; Insurance; Journalist; Local Government; Marketing; Personnel Officer; Politician; Public Relations Officer; Quantity Surveyor; Research (Television, Politics, etc.); Sociologist; Solicitor; Trade Union Official; Sales.

AGRICULTURAL SCIENCE

This covers the study of soils, plants and their function including farm crops and trees. Farm animals and farm buildings are also studied. It is now accepted as a laboratory science subject in all third level colleges in Ireland, though may not meet special course requirements where a specific science subject is requested.

AGRICULTURAL SCIENCE AND AGRICULTURAL ECONOMICS are useful for careers in:
Agricultural Engineering; Agricultural Inspector; Agricultural Officer; Agricultural Sales; Agricultural Science Teacher; Animal Breeder; Animal Nursing Auxiliary; Animal Trainer; Botanist; Biologist; Butter-maker and Cheese-maker; Clerk in an Agricultural Organisation, e.g. co-operatives; Conservation; Creamery Manager; Dairy Scientist; Farmer; Farrier; Food Science Technologist; Forester; Forestry Inspector; Horticulturist; Laboratory Technician; Seed Analyst; Serological Assistant; Stud Farm Employee; Trout Farmer; Veterinary Surgeon; Zoologist; Amenity Horticulture.

AGRICULTURAL ECONOMICS

This subject applies economic principles to the agricultural industry and studies the farm as a business unit, covering topics such as farm accounts, costs, planning and budgeting.

CONSTRUCTION STUDIES

Primarily relating to domestic building, broader aspects are also covered in introducing students to the knowledge and skills in construction technology, materials and practices. The course covers the historical development of buildings in addition to other relevant topics such as house purchase and mortgages. A project is also required to be submitted as part of an assessment for the Leaving Certificate.

CONSTRUCTION STUDIES is useful for careers in:

Architecture; Auctioneering; Bricklaying; Building Construction Teacher; Building Management; Carpenter; Civil and Structural Engineer and Technician; Do-it-Yourself; Electrician; Environmental Designer; Estimator; Heating and Ventilation Technician; Painter/Decorator; Plasterer; Quantity Surveyor; Site Clerk; Technical Sales; Town Planning; Housing Management; Firefighter; Insurance Claims.

ENGINEERING

This subject replaces Junior Cert. metalwork. It involves the study of a wide range of mechanical engineering processes, materials and technological applications along with the development of manipulative skills, resourcefulness and creativity. The course is divided into a Practical Section – Workshop Processes and a Theoretical Section – Materials Technology, and involves the presentation of a project as part of the Leaving Certificate Examination.

ENGINEERING is useful for careers in:

Mechanics; Aircraft Technician; Army/Air Corps Apprenticeship; Do-it-Yourself; Engineering Workshop Teacher; Fitter; Industrial Operatives; Mechanical Production; Structural and Civil Engineer and Technician; Metallurgy; Motor Mechanic; Service and Maintenance Personnel; Technical Sales; Toolmaker; Turner; Welder; Engraving; Industrial Design.

TECHNICAL DRAWING

Technical Drawing develops intellectual qualities of comprehension, analysis and problem solving as well as the skills of manipulation and dexterity and the development of overall design sensitivity.

Although It is not an essential requirement for those wishing to enter architecture or engineering course, it is generally an essential component of most technical courses.

TECHNICAL DRAWING is useful for careers in:

All Engineering and Engineering Technician careers; Aircraft Technician; Architecture and Architectural Technician; Army and Air Corps Apprenticeship; Cartographer; Construction Trades; Bricklayer, Carpenter, etc.; Engineering Trades, Fitter, Toolmaker, etc.; Industrial Designer; Maintenance and Service Personnel; Motor Mechanic; Technical Sales; Structural Design; Printing; Town Planner; Draughtsperson; Industrial Engineer.

HISTORY

Embracing the world of politics, economics, religion and philosophy, history can be a most enjoyable challenge, developing skills such as identifying main issues and the ability to select relevant information.

HISTORY is useful for careers in:

Politics; Journalism; Local Government Social Work; Sociology; Archaeology; Barrister; Civil Service; Guide; History Teacher; Law Clerk; Museum Work; Researcher; Solicitor; Trade Union Official; Prison Service; Probation Officer; Garda; Tourism; Writer; Broadcaster; Librarianship; Genealogy.

GEOGRAPHY

Concerned with the interrelationships between human activities and the physical environment, Geography includes the study of population, farming, industry, pollution, statistics, resources, landscapes and communications. For both Science and Pharmacy (TCD) it is accepted as one of the HC's in specific subjects.

GEOGRAPHY is useful for careers in:

Civil Engineering; Construction; Town Planning; Architecture; Meteorology; Surveying; Mineralogy; Agriculture; Horticulture; Auctioneering, Estate Agency; Forestry; Conservation Work; Market Research; Statistics; Archaeology; Air Traffic Controller; Anthropologist; Cartographer; Marine Officer; Courier; Development Work Abroad; Geologist; Geography Teacher; Guide; International Driver; Naval Deck Cadet; Pilot; Quantity Surveyor; Steward/Stewardess; Third Secretary in Dept. of Foreign Affairs; Tourist Office Receptionist; Transport Clerk; Travel Agency Clerk.

HOME ECONOMICS

Students can follow either a General or Scientific syllabus, the former gives a good general, theoretical and practical knowledge of nutrition, cookery, dress-making and home management, while the latter covers topics such as food constituents, physiology, microbiology, food preservation, consumerism and social issues, the family and the home. Check if the general course is acceptable in the college of your choice for entry purposes. The general course is not accepted for N.U.I. matriculation except for St. Angela's. While it is recommended for teacher training in Home Economics it is not a requirement for entry to either St. Angela's or St. Catherines. It is however a requirement for St. Catherines if you are not presenting a science subject.

HOME ECONOMICS is useful for careers in:

Baking and Confectionery; Beautician; Catering; Chef; Child Care; Consumer Adviser; Demonstrator – food, wines, etc.; Dietician; Environmental Designer; Fashion Designer; Food Science; Hairdressing; Health Inspector; Home Management; Home Economics Teacher; Hotel House-keeper and Manager; Institutional Management; Nursing; Occupational Therapist; Parenthood; Social Worker; Sewing Machinist; some artistic careers; Textile Designer; Waitress; Sales; Nursery and Pre-school Management.Sociologist; Solicitor; Trade Union Official; Sales.

PHYSICAL EDUCATION

Though not a subject for examination, this subject develops teamwork and co-operation and introduces a variety of leisure pursuits. The social interaction in participating in sports is an excellent confidence and friendship builder.

PHYSICAL EDUCATION is useful for careers in:

Recreational Management; Leisure Centres; Keep Fit and Health Studios; Teaching; Community Worker; Youth Leader; Army; Dancer; Garda; Modelling and Beauty Care; P.E. Teacher; Physiotherapy; Professional Sport: footballer, golfer, jockey, etc.; Security Officer; Youth Officer Work; Health Care; Prison Service; Journalism.

RELIGIOUS EDUCATION

Like P.E. Religious Education has not been examined at either Junior or Leaving Certificate; however, examination syllabuses are being prepared by the NCCA but as yet there is no definite date for their introduction. Religious Education helps us to grow in our understanding of society and of ourselves. It develops critical skills for examining values, morality and religion. It can raise the level of informed debate in society, in business and in the Church.

RELIGIOUS EDUCATION is useful for vocations and careers in: Religious Education, Social Work, Religious Life and Priesthood, Work with Voluntary Agencies abroad, Youth Leadership; Politics, Charity Fund Raising; Psychiatric Nursing, Religious Journalism and Publishing, Broadcasting, Archive Work and Librarianship, Church related Ministries, Philosopher, Theologian, Choirmaster or Organist.

> **The details given on these pages are not intended to be exhaustive. They merely highlight the complexity of subject requirements. All intending applicants should check with the relevant employers and admissions offices for current regulations.**

BONUS POINTS FOR SOME SUBJECTS

The majority of colleges have ceased the practice of awarding bonus points for higher level grades in certain subjects. However, the University of Limerick continue to do so for Mathematics and the DIT colleges for a small number of courses where bonus points are awarded to some relevant subjects.

Some professional bodies still offer bonus points for higher grades in Mathematics.

STUDY AND EXAMINATIONS

POINTS FROM GOALS

Score some extra points in your Leaving Certificate by having study goals.

G oals · · · · · · · · · · · · · · · *Motivation / the why of study.*

O rderly programme · · · · *Organisation and good time management.*

A dequate conditions · · · *Somewhere to study, adequate light and heat.*

L earning skills · · · · · · · · *Mnemonics to flash cards.*

S elf discipline · · · · · · · · · *10% inspiration 90% perspiration.*

STUDY:
MOTIVATION

Effective examination performance is usually the result of a planned approach to study. Although study is central to our education and despite all that we are taught at school, few students are actually given instruction on how to study. Consequently, many lack the skills required for the level of success they are capable of. But skills are not the only ingredient. The motivation to do well is by far the most important requirement.

Study is the effort to acquire knowledge. No matter how idealistic we may be about the purpose of education, realistically most of us have one thing in mind and that is passing the examinations. The knowledge that one needs to acquire is that which is tested at examinations. A prescribed syllabus is available for each subject, and as most school textbooks published in Ireland are based on this syllabus, the contents page of your books should therefore help you to gain an overall view of what needs to be done.

TIME MANAGEMENT

For each subject calculate how many topics there are. It can often be a wise decision not to study a particular topic if you have difficulty with it or simply don't like it, as most examinations have an element of choice. But don't neglect any vital areas.

Leaving about one month before the first examination for pure memory work, start by dividing what needs to be covered in each subject over the time available.

The amount of time actually spent studying is of secondary importance to the amount of information understood, organised or learned during a study period. In other words, it is the quality not the quantity of study that matters.

So, how much time should one spend studying each day and how should this be broken down? There are no hard and fast rules: the greater your powers of concentration the more efficient your study and the less time required overall on any one topic.

How do you study?

Everyone has his or her own style, if your way is working, just pick what you need from this. If you are struggling then try things this way:
- **Select a small area:** a topic, chapter, section etc.
- **Test yourself on this:** skim it for headings or look at questions. Answer it in your mind or jot down ideas or sketch answers.
- **Go through the material.** Go through it seeking to answer the questions you have on it. Pause, to ensure you do understand it. Re-phrase it, note the key points, jot down key words and do graphs, sketches or mnemonics to help your recall. Keep your mind active by asking questions and summarising.

- **Test yourself on it.** Go back to the questions you posed at the start. Hopefully you will see an increase in your knowledge and maybe indicators for further study

This should take about 30-35 minutes. This only works for long term, consistent study. If you need to do emergency study in the final few weeks or days, then this won't work so well. But, if you left it as late as that you are in trouble!

Another piece of advice worth adopting is to plan for leisure, preferably some form of sport or exercise; the fitter the body is the sharper the mind is too.

YOUR ROOM

A warm though well ventilated room, with a well lit desk and back supporting chair is to be recommended. Each study session should start with a review of the past papers - these are the key to effective study and the success at exams. This may seem like studying back to front as most students attempt to learn the material before answering questions and in doing so run the risk of learning too much or even worse, learning material which is not rele-vant. The idea is to learn only the information that is required for the exam and this involves a great deal of organisation on the part of the student.

Study therefore is simply gathering the information which could be used to answer ques-tions, leaving out less relevant information and organising it into structured answers which demonstrates your understanding of the topics.

READING

Adapt your style to the task in hand - discover the difference between skimming material to get an overall view and scanning it looking for specific information. These are areas to try to improve, particularly the technique of lifting only what is important from each page, and leaving behind what normally is the bulk of the text. Much of what is in your books is padding which helps students to understand the topics and you are not expected to be able to repro-duce all at an exam, there is simply not enough time. Remember you have a limited time to reproduce your knowledge onto the examination paper and now is the time to decide on what is relevant and what is not

MEMORY AND REVISION

Effective recall is greatly assisted when the material is meaningful to the learner, therefore it's important to understand what you are trying to learn.

Once this is achieved and the material is organised, then the hardest part is over, and the task of memorising is best left until closer to the examination.

Material which is difficult to memorise could benefit from the use of mnemonics - memory aids - e.g. NO CASH is one for recalling the chemical constituents of coal - Nitrogen, Oxygen, Carbon, Ash, Sulphur and Hydrogen.

During the revision stage, material is beginning to become very familiar but there is the danger that familiarity can lead to a false sense of security. Many fail to distinguish between the ability to recognise material and the ability to recall. The former is sufficient for multiple choice type examinations where the correct answer is given for you to recognise from among several. With recall, the answers are not supplied and a much deeper knowl-edge is required, generally in the form of an essay.

Remember that the best study method is the way you find the most effective. This takes time to discover and may take weeks of experimentation before you uncover the secrets of your own success.

EXAMINATION TECHNIQUES

Your subject teachers should explain the structure of their papers and will give guidance as to how to approach each question.

Many students overlook the fact that there is at lot writing to be done during an exam and this is best prepared for by increasing the amount of time you spend putting pen to paper as the examination draws near.

On the day of the exam you will arrive refreshed (No late night study please!). Read the paper thoroughly. Decide which questions you are answering and do an outline plan for each of the questions. Then start on the first one. Time yourself strictly on this. In general you should give three well-argued, well-developed points, supported by references and quotations or other supporting materials. Then move on to the next question and so on. Stick rigidly to timing and leave space for returning to complete an answer. If even this fails and you find yourself with lack of time in the last question(s) then jot down the relevant points in point or note form. Remember even if you write a perfect answer to one question that is still only 25% (say) of the available marks for that paper. So answer all the questions you are supposed to. If you have extra time answer more (they will have to pick your best ones). If you are stuck, answer all you can. Remember blank spaces are always wrong, so make an intelligent guess. Try everything!

After the paper, don't engage in post mortems. Steer clear of the brightest in the class or stay quiet if you are the brightest! Especially, don't panic and rearrange your CAO application in the light of your perceived performance in the exams.

Follow these hints and tips and you will be well on the way to success.

Education

Anne Byrne
Careers and Guidance Correspondent.

Read all you need to know about getting into college, course options and career opportunities.
Read Anne Byrne in The Irish Times.

For further details on our special student offers available to all second-level schools please call
1 800 798884

AUGUST • Lúnasa • 1999

THURS 26   OPEN DAY – PORTOBELLO SCHOOL – 11 am - 3 pm

FRI 27

SAT 28

SUN 29

NOTES

MON 30

TUES 31

WED 1

SEPTEMBER • Meán Fómhair • 1999

THURS 2

FRI 3

SAT 4

NOTES

SUN 5

SEPTEMBER • Meán Fómhair • 1999

MON 6

TUES 7

WED 8

THURS 9

FRI 10

SAT 11

NOTES

SUN 12

SEPTEMBER • Meán Fómhair • 1999

MON 13

Physics - Parallel Capacitors ✓

Fénin - p.236 → 235 in french ✓

English - Ou Explorations ✓

Greeks - Cortéi Phoist study / Sample Essay study / Prút next 3 ✓

Applied - '97 / '98 papers ✓

TUES 14

Sheets - Literature (french)

Business Summary p.205

Physics: Q in letter

Applied: '98 Q

Irish: Eireatai - study ✓

English: Q in copy

Maths: P.36 Q22 - 6

WED 15

English: Q 1-3 p.118

Irish: Eireatai

Maths Marked p.40

THURS 16

Irish - p 25-30 (essays) | notes - study
Maths - p. 44/50 marked
English - learn quotes
French - sheets | 100 words 4 Mon.

FRI 17

English - 3 few images
French - sheet + prev 0 - p.24/24
Irish - On trail | Reading | Poems | "Cúirt Art" | B.F - 0 |
Maths - p.50 n10

SAT 18

NOTES

General Purpose Fee - £25

SUN 19

MON 20

Irish: P.4 Q2 1-5 - [illegible]
English Q1 + 2a in Comp.
Applied Exam Q
Maths: Q on sheet

TUES 21

Maths: Q on sheet
English: Q on sheet
French: " "
Applied: Work on
Irish: Revise

WED 22

Higher Options Conference – 22nd-24th September. RDS Main Hall. Tickets Only

French: Phrases - copy
English: Q in copy
Irish: P.5 T4
Maths: Q on sheet
Music: 3- Bar melodies for next. Wed.
Applied: Work On

SEPTEMBER • Meán Fómhair • 1999

THURS 23

~~English : 2 Own Copy~~
~~Irish : P.13 TT~~
~~French : 2.63, 266 (2+3)~~
~~Amigo : Whole Day~~

FRI 24

~~French 100 words on title in copy~~
Irish: Mac an Leannáí | P.14 TT | P.12 "Mí-ádh" (mon. week)

SAT 25

SUN 26

NOTES

Get Manuscript ✓
GP. Fee ✓
Music - Wed. 4.30-6 ✓
SAT - Rem (Feis) + Piano ✓
Licence + eyesight forms. ✓

SEPTEMBER • Meán Fómhair • 1999

MON 27

TUES 28

WED 29

126

THURS 30

Irish: Condensé notes for oral

Applied: '96 Q3 a + b

English: R in copy

Maths: Revise in book

Bus: Test tomorrow / Q6 '99 — mon

French: Prose composé || sheet 1) 12 phrases (imp) ||sheet 2) Q1-4

FRI 1

French: 100 words (titles in copy)

Irish: Condense "version" Peig / Aiste

English: Summarize ch 3

Applied: Questions from prev. exams

Maths: Misc Ex 2

SAT 2

SUN 3

NOTES

Bus. Papers
Maths. Papers

MON 4

Maths: Test Tuesday / mix 2 no 10

Physics: Write up experiment

Applied: Exercise 4B + prev. exam Q

French: 100 verbs + sheets 4 Friday

English: 2 Q in copy

Irish: Notes

Business: P.222 Q2 + Q4 (see errors) p.8

TUES 5

Irish : P.186 study

English : Summary ch. 5

French : Sheets

Applied : Work On

WED 6

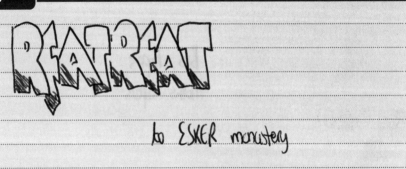

to ESKER monastery

THURS 7

French: Verbs

Maths. Test

Irish Q (A) p.15

Answers: Grant Q

Applied: Write On

FRI 8

French: 1) Prétagris 2) Lotte to punivaté

Irish: Organise Study Program / Innt / P. 32 Feirlacha Tuisceana

SAT 9

NOTES

SUN 10

MON 11

MATHS : Q in Copy ✓
APPLIED : Q on Exercise 4B ✓
FRENCH: SHEETS
IRISH : Q on

TUES 12

IRISH : P.3 BOTTOM OF PAGE.
BUSINESS : p.26 Q3

WED 13

BUSINESS: p.24 PAPERS Q.7(B) || ADD MARKETING BENEFITS 2 NOTES)
IRISH : p.3 summarize (describe)
~~MATHS: Sect Q41-45 (minix)~~
~~ENGLISH. Q in COPY~~
APPLIED. Ex. 5A
FRENCH: p.8 (FP) Sheets.

OCTOBER • Deireadh Fómhair • 1999

THURS 14

FRI 15

Irish: P3 Again

~~FRENCH: Writing (GIRL ON PHONE)~~

~~MATHS: Q7+9 p25/26~~

ENGLISH: Q in copy

APPLIED: SHEETS

SAT 16

SUN 17

NOTES

MON 18

Maths: Nothin'

Physics: Write up Experiments

Applied: Exercise 5B

French: p.288/289

Eng: Revise Hamlet.

Business: p.144 B & MP – Notes || B & MA also

Sec 3 Q.7(a) p.16 (Wed)

TUES 19

French : H1 (Verbs) (use oir) + H2

Irish: Prós (Mnré) || 16th Essay (Sum 4 BTA)

WED 20

Irish p.30 33

French p.16 Français Plus | H3 + H4 | H5 (nou)

English: Q in copy

THURS 21

Irish: p.9 DDC (B) Gébhsánn

FRI 22

Irish: 42/43 (π) || Briar || SmaT (Fin) || Leisir + Caoscuoleadh || an phrist || p.9 (A). p10. Fm

French: sheets

SAT 23

NOTES

THURS: 420-450 (singin')
TUES: 4.30-5.00

SUN 24

OCTOBER • Deireadh Fómhair • 1999

MON 25

TUES 26

WED 27

OPEN DAY – SHANNON COLLEGE OF HOTEL MANAGEMENT

OCTOBER • Deireadh Fómhair • 1999

THURS 28

FRI 29

SAT 30

SUN 31

NOTES

Third Level Education: New standard of entry (points etc.) for 1999 are now available. Check CAO website at: http://indigo.ie/~cao

MON 1

TUES 2

WED 3

APPLIED: WORK ON
IRISH: SEANCHAR / SHOT
MATHS: SHEET
FRENCH: '97 SAMPLE PAPER / ORAL PREP.

NOVEMBER • Samhain • 1999

THURS 4

Irish: p.18 Cartaí Poist
French: 5 Q in copy (100 words)
Applied: Wage Example

FRI 5

Irish: p.19 Máthair
Maths: Q. on sheet

SAT 6

SUN 7

NOTES

IEI Careers Day - Dublin (SAT 6th)
Bus 8.00am 6.00p.m.

MON 8

FRENCH: p.8 - Grammaire / p.7 - Antibruit / Aller
Applied: p.150 Q8
English: Hamlet's 2nd soliloquy (complications)
Irish: p.10 "Gasúraí"

TUES 9

French: Sheets no 5+6+7
Irish: p.27
Applied: Q10-11
English: Q on Sheet

WED 10

Applied: Q on Sheet
English: Q in copy
Irish: p.28 "Cormac Aird Ui Lorcáin"
French: p.5 Q2 Q4
Maths: Q4, 6+7 p.172-173

THURS 11   Business Show 4 Test
              French : 2 Units TV (M2 + M6)

FRI 12

Math : 1969 Q3 / 1993 Q8 / 1997 Q8
French : Module P.7 / P.10 / P.11

SAT 13

SUN 14

NOTES

NOVEMBER • Samhain • 1999

MON 15

French: (*Assessment*) Partir / français amis de la terre

Appro: Ex 6a

Music: Write up of motor

Maths: 1446 + 1445 Q3

Irish: An Banríon Ruí.

TUES 16

Irish: Irish Compose "Gráhaoidhcean" p.39, "A ógánaigh", "geibheam

French: Slides

Appro: Exercise 6B + 6C

English: Rin copy

WED 17

Irish: Summary

English: Q. in copy

Appro: 7A.

French: 10 sentences on passison in world

Maths: Exercise 3A

140

THURS 18

take out keys

Work p.1 Orémine Summary

English: Summary of today's work.

Maths: Even Q in 138

French

FRI 19

Irish - p3 Orémine

French: Sheets, Français plus

English: Essay Time: "The Peasant Plunkee's born" for Fri. next.

Maths:

SAT 20

SUN 21

NOTES

P. Exam - Fri 19th Nov @ 2.26 [Awo saved]

MON 22

Maths Nothing

Physics Write up Experiments

Applied Exercise 7B

French Nothing

Irish Free Class

English Nothing

Business Revise

TUES 23

French Summary of 3 articles / Vocabulary Study Sheet

Irish:

Applied Q9 to Exercise 7B

WED 24

OPEN DAY – ALL HALLOWS – 2.30 - 4.30 pm

French "Devoir" Prep. p.13 4 oral Sheet @ 11.15 / 1.30 Exam paper

English: Essay

Irish: stdy p.5 Oreimire

Maths Exercise 3D

Applied Exercise 7C

THURS 25 — _kish. P8 son. | P.43_

FRI 26

SAT 27

NOTES

English essay 4 Thursday:

"Pheasant Plucker's Son"

SUN 28

MON 29

TUES 30

Irish: p.53 Papers
French: Sheet, Publicity, Pouvoir/Falloir
~~English Summary~~
Maths: Exercise 4A Q1-10

WED 1

Applied = Exercise
~~English = Q in copy~~
~~Irish - Do 4 days work~~
French = Sheets + Exam Pape
Maths = Exercise 4B
~~Physics - Write up Generators.~~

DECEMBER • Nollaig • 1999

THURS 2

Irish - Gates (π)

French

FRI 3

OPEN DAY – ATHLONE I.T.

French: lettre à monique / Phrases on Jannoline + Rpes

Irish: p.65/66 Trialacha Turscéanna

SAT 4

Show in the Mall
Practice all day.

SUN 5

NOTES

MON 6

Irish   p.75/76 Gaelacha Tuisceanna
English Q: no copy
French   Sheets from magazine
Maths   Sheets of examples

TUES 7

French: Français Plus 14-15 | Comp: "le prison en bois" || SE BATTRE
Irish: p.76 / TT
Applied: Q. on diff. eqn
Maths: Sheets

WED 8

DECEMBER • Nollaig • 1999

THURS 9

FRI 10

~~FRENCH: use phrases~~ / P.10 Frus
trid: Blackboard / list "Féal"

SAT 11

SUN 12

NOTES

David
Heinen
Woz
Osc

MON 13
mussum: French

" SHARE A →
DREAM FOUNDATION "
CONCERT, WISIRELAND

SAT 18   OPERA   STARTS :

SUN 19   " JESUS   CHRIST ".

MON 20   " SUPERSTAR "

TUES 21   AND FINISHES 2DAY !

TUES 14
Who are you going to bring?
I talked to Derche about it
She said no one had asked
TBG, I said that we were all
afraid. I also told her that now
telling us not to ask her.

WED 22

WED 15 Mang - int. + Prob
She said that was because
od what happened about the
wedding. ♦ ... She said Bye.
I am going to do it NOH
After that I was slagging News

THURS 23

FRI 24

SAT 25

SUN 26

MON 27

THURS 16 mans Ver. + Prob. about his
debs partner talking to me
instead of him. He got a
bit thick. So I seriously told
him that I wanted to seek
Derche. He said I was a
sly dog because I would
not seek Therese

TUES 28

WED 29

THURS 30

FRI 31

SAT 1

FRI 17

CHRISTMAS
VAK !!!

SUN 2

MON 3

TUES 4

WED 5

But I would seek Derche.

THURS 6

ENGLISH : C₁ = 70
IRISH : C₃ = 60
MATHS : B₃ = 75
FRENCH : C₁ = 70
BUSINESS : B₃ = 75
APPLIED : C₁ = 70

FRI 7 Physics : D₃

Hey How are you? Fine! good! ANN 4 nothing

I would not shake her hand. WHY? I really don't know WHAT AR U AT? @ V.

ith no what else did she say. She likes the way u talk.
I have to stop that. I have to stop that. GROAN
Ahh fuck odd. U AR DOO! Do I really repeat
everything. Do I really repeat everything vip.

SAT 8

I like the way
I talk too. WHINER

YIP for pc.

NOTES

SUN 9

MON 10

FRENCH: p.141 Q1-11

APPLIED Applied Paper (FR WE) + TONIGHT

~~Irish~~ Notes , p.3 dréimire

TUES 11

ENGLISH: Insight into Yeats

FRENCH: p.148 Q / p.151

Irish : p.2 dréimire

APPLIED: 3.2. Exercise 8B

WED 12

THURS 13

Maths: p115 Q4, 6+8
Irish: p1 Dréimire.
Business: p.46 papers ABQ 4 next thurs.

FRI 14

SAT 15

SUN 16

MON 17

ENGLISH: ~~Q2 +3~~

MATHS: ~~Q+~~ Q1 (1,3,4) Q2 (3,4) Q3 (2,3) Q4 (1,2) Q5 (3) Q6, Q7

APPLIED: ~~Every 2nd~~ ~~Q in~~ ~~page~~ 8c

PHYSICS: ~~Do all experiments~~

IRISH: ~~Write up Seán~~

FRENCH: ~~phu~~ ~~sheets~~ ~~page 3~~ ~~x-mas exam~~

TUES 18

FRENCH Mr ~~E2(6)~~ / phrases

IRISH: '99 exam p.6 Q on Cáca Milseán

APPLIED: ~~Integ~~ on

BUSINESS: ~~App~~ 4 Thursday

MUSIC: Melodies 4 next wed. E13 4 scores

WED 19

ENGLISH: Stream of consciousness Q

BUSINESS: p.15 short questions (for next Wednesday)

IRISH: next question on "An Prúist"

FRENCH: Verbs / Cœur / Avoir (François Plus)

APPLIED: Exercise 7c work on

THURS 20
APPLIED : PAPERS FOR 2 MORROW
ENGLISH Q ON SHEET
IRISH : SUMMARY OF KAVANAGH'S MAIN POINTS
FRENCH : SENTENCES, François Plus (
MATHS : WORK ON SUM 8.0

FRI 21
FRENCH : p. 52 sheets (100 mots)
IRISH 1

SAT 22

SUN 23

NOTES
GET PAPERS (Maths, Applied, Physics)

MON 24

OUT

TUES 25

PHYSICS— LOOK AT CATHODE RAY OSCILLSCOPE
ENGLISH: EXPLORATIONS - Q2
IRISH: GRAMMAR - MOST RECENT QUESTION
MATHS: FIRST COURSE SUMS
FRENCH: WRITTEN COMPREHENSION
APPLIED: 4.A @ 4 Q's
MUSIC: HAVE IT FOR 2-MORROW!!!!

WED 26   P.18 PARED SHORT QUESTIONS!!

ENGLISH: 2 Q OFF PAPERS + QUOTES
IRISH: SEAN LE SIOMÓIN
MATHS: MARKED SUMS P. 246
FRENCH: NOTE + SUBJUNCTIVE SENTENCES
APPLIED: EXERCISE 9.B + PAST PAPER

* ABQ 4 TOMORROW *

THURS 27

Maths: Exercise 8F p.242

Irish: Searc le Diomáin || An trial

English: 1980 Q. CHOOSE QUOTES

French: FREE CLASS - finish subjunctives

Applied: Exercises WORK ON || APPLIED PAPER 4 MON - OR TUES

Physics: Write up demo || Ro. up on Box

Business: Revise

FRI 28

[1984 LC - APPLIED 4 TOMORROW] *

OPEN DAY – COLÁISTE DHÚLAIGH

School

Closed

4 Funeral

SAT 29

SUN 30

MATCH 0 0 0 0
        0 0 0 0

NOTES

Get on "air" 4 Sara

Music - Fri. (CANCEL LESSONS)

MON 31

Irish: Summarize "An Trial"
Applied: Work On
English: Quotes for Question

TUES 1

English: Q on sheet - 3 quotes from 4 poems
Irish : Summary of what we did 2day (nothing)
Maths : Q9,10,11 p.257
French: Comprehension on sheets
Applied : Work on Q21+22
Physics : write up demo

WED 2

OPEN DAYS – BRAY INSTITUTE OF FURTHER EDUCATION
– CRUMLIN CAMPUS – 12.00 - 6.00 pm

Irish:
Summary "An Trial" p.2 preimir + p.5 revise + marks Atos rahmad
Maths: Past Paper
Applied: Past Paper
French: Past Paper

THURS 3

PARENT - TEACHER

"meeting"

FRI 4

SAT 5

OPEN DAY – PORTOBELLO SCHOOL
11 am - 3 pm

NOTES

093 - 28373 → Daithí Quinn (Grinds)

SUN 6

FEBRUARY • Feabhra • 2000

MON 7
OPEN DAY – REMEMBER LIMERICK SENIOR COLLEGE OPEN DAY IS ON FEBRUARY 14th

TUES 8
OPEN DAY – MARINO COLLEGE

English : Q1,3+6 p. 200/201

Irish : Nothing

French : 90 mins ((Celtic Tiger) - 1998 Journal intime.

Applied : Test this week 1990 next Friday

Maths : hand up past paper

WED 9

Applied : Past Paper + Do sums C9-10

French : Market | 5ᵗʰ element | Celtic Tiger | Journal intime |

English : Q1,3+6 p. 209/207

Irish : Summary "an tSúil"

French : Project (not)
Irish : p3 Oissimire
English : Q1 exploration
Applied : Ex. 10B + past paper

FRI 11

French :
Irish : On scural - Summary
Maths :
Applied :
English :

SAT 12

NOTES

12 - Rumes Corrections

yes !!!

SUN 13

MON 14

French sheet / 1998 paper / 2 preis of writing
Applied it as far as possible.

English 1 opening paragraphs
Irish: Summary of "An Triail"
Maths: Questions mocher

TUES 15

Irish: Clár Am
French: Sheets
Applied 1990 from 11 Q 99 to 10
Maths: Exercise 9 C p 271
Music: Photocopi "Bohemian Rhapsody" 11 Exercise

WED 16

English: Discuss the characterisation of Shawn Keogh (Act I) ie Contrast
Maths: 1999 Q5 (a) — 1998 Q5 (a) 1997 Q5 (i,ii) 1996 Q5(ii) 1995 Q5 (i)

THURS 17
  Hist: Summary
  English: Q on "Inverted morality"
French: Sheets - "La drôle"
Applied: 1990 PAST PAPER
Physics: WRITE UP DEMO

FRI 18   ALLIANCE

Hist : Summary
Maths : 1997, 1994
English: Q in Copy
French: Journal Intime ③ + PHRASES + p.7 + p. 18/19
Applied: Q @ end of ch. 10

SAT 19

SUN 20

NOTES

MON 21

English: Q on Christi's development
Applied:
Polish: Comprehension, learn WÄME (R)
Verb: Summary "An Krail"
Applied: Lab 4: experiment

TUES 22

French: learn WÄME, p 24 faus.
English: Q in copy
Irish: Summary
Applied: Past Exam
Maths: Nothing
Music: Q on worksheet

WED 23   "Alliance !!!!! "

French: Comprehension
English: Learn Quotes
Irish: Summary "An Grail"
Applied: Exercise 11.C Q
Maths: Sheets from today

THURS 24 Irish: Summary
Maths: Free Class
French: Exam + F. Plus
English: Write up quotes (Mythry + Hamlet copy)
Physics: Revise (Grind @ 11.00 Sat.)

Connaught SF : SSC defeat St. Marys

FRI 25

SAT 26

SUN 27

NOTES

THE PARTNER !

FEBRUARY / MARCH • 2000

MON 28

French: last 2 on dutar sheet //
Applied: Exercise 11.6
Irish: Achoimre

TUES 29

Irish: Achoimre
French: Français Plus
English: Quotes
Physics: Revise + Timetable

WED 1

English: "Christy" (st, more, after) //" Ophelia + Gertrude "
Applied:

THURS 2

MOCKS

Applied

begin

Irish

"Alliance"

FRI 3

MOCKS

English paper I

Physics

SAT 4

NOTES

the PARTNER

SUN 5

MON 6

Mocks {

English paper II

French

TUES 7

MOCKS end !!

Business

Maths

WED 8

THURS 9
p.30/31 12 phrases - new sentence - FRENCH -
Applied : Ex. 12A
Learn Debate - mar

FRI 10
Cruchiúram - practice

*   *   *   *   *

DÍOSPÓIREACHT vs. Mercy

SAT 11

SUN 12

NOTES

MOCK RESULTS:
	PREDICTED	RESULT	
ENGLISH :	C₁	C₂ - 65	FRENCH : C₁ B₂ -80
IRISH :	D₁	D₁ -55	
MATHS :	C₃	C₁ -70	Total pts : 420
APPLIED :	C₃	C₁ -70	
BUSINESS :	C₁	B₂ -80	
PHYSICS :	E	D₃ -55	

MON 13

English: 2 a on Style + Browning (opening paragraph

French: [Myself | Friends | House | Family] Sheets 2 day

Irish: Revise Snat || Bring in oral copies || Bring in "Dréimire" (must recent

Music: Melodies

TUES 14

French:
Irish: Scéal | Béaltriail (study)
Maths: Mock Paper

Tráth na g Ceist

WED 15

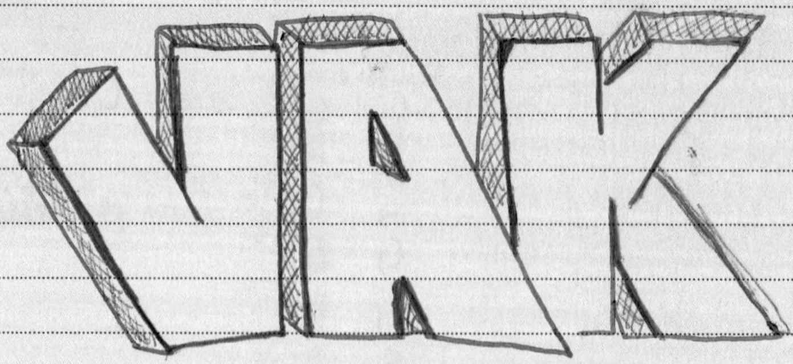

THURS 16

FRI 17

St. PADDY'S

DAY

SAT 18

NOTES

SUN 19

MON 20

TUES 21

~~French~~ sheets
~~Arcado!~~ Do Sums
English: Quiz explication

~~Music; melodies.~~

WED 22

OPEN DAY – LIBERTIES COLLEGE

French : 100 mus - sheet
~~English: No 1 in explanation~~

MARCH • Márta • 2000

THURS 23

English: Q1-3 p.194

Maths 1999 Q1 Pg I

OMS

Do Applied 1441

TRUN

Document

FRI 24

FA: What next year? What next summer?
Live in Ireland @ the moment

SAT 25

SUN 26

NOTES

(Get Music Practical)

MON 27

Business & Q3 p.14 Skeleton answer
French: Document

Appled: Bring in past exam
English Explorations Q1 + 2

TUES 28

Business: Summary
French: 100 words " Demandeurs d'asile" (Asylum seekers)

Instruments 4 Practical - 2 morrow

WED 29   ALLIANCE 1

English : Q in copy
Maths : Q1-6 on sheet
Appled : Work on - "do sums"
Physics : a 4 deadline

MUSIC

THURS 30

Business, 5 summaries
Physics: Questions
Arabic: '92 pages ✓
French: document

FRI 31

PALISADE

SAT 1

SUN 2

NOTES

Vocab: discrimination existe? notre société en induide
avoir des préjugés, marginalisé
les "ghettos" opposés de la mixité raciale attitudes
citoyens de deuxième classe. N'ou apporterons à
la famille humaine, les mêmes droits fondamentaux

APRIL • Aibreán • 2000

MON 3

Music Practical ✓
French Oral ✓
Business: AQ2 from mock
English: Style Q2

TUES 4

~~FRENCH ORAL~~
PAPER I - trialuchin tuisceanna
Béaloinn
Dréimire
English: Q3 oo shorts
Business: AQ4 other class mock
Maths: algebra 3 ya)

MUSIC PRACTICAL!!

WED 5

~~FRENCH ORAL~~
English: Comprehension - Q2
Applied: K93 Q2
Maths: ~~Sheets~~

~~FRENCH ORAL~~

174

APRIL • Aibreán • 2000

THURS 6

English: Comprehension Q5
Irish: Oral - Revise

Maths - Q4

Applied → 1992 papers
Physics → 1st 4 expts.

FRI 7   (FRENCH ORAL)

English:

Physics → 6 Q for Mon.

SAT 8   FRENCH ORALS

SUN 9

NOTES

Fri - Maloneys - Show
Tues - 9-10pm Practice
Wed - music

APRIL • Aibreán • 2000

MON 10

English : No Homework

French : Mock paper — 1st comp + writing p.66

Maths : Next few years at Q's 4+5

Applied : Work on with 1993

Physics : 6 Q in memorandum 4 tomorrow

Business : ABQ for thursday

TUES 11 ———— IRISH ORALS

English : No Homework

Maths : Next 2 years

Business : Rd. magazine

French : Comprehension

Applied : Work on.

WED 12 ———— IRISH ORALS

Applied : Finish 1993 paper / Mock 2000 + 1994 for Ecdex JNL

Business : ABQ

Physics : Work on with Questions

French : Written No.1(B) + Verbs + (B) 2 sheets

IRISH ORALS

176

THURS 13

TODAY - ORALZ

FRI 14   IRISH ORALS

SAT 15   IRISH ORALS

NOTES

SUN 16

MON 17

TUES 18

WED 19

THURS 20	WED 26
FRI 21	THURS 27
SAT 22	FRI 28
SUN 23 EASTER SUNDAY	SAT 29
MON 24	SUN 30
TUES 25	

MON 1

Still on

our

TUES 2

EASTER

WED 3

Irish: ORGANISE NOTES ② MAKE OUT REVISION PROGRAMME
French: " 25 mots - VIOLENCE ON IRISH STREETS "
English: Q4+5
Applied: FINISH PAPERS
Physics :

MAY • Bealtaine • 2000

THURS 4

Physics: Expts. / Q in Copy / Def.
Applied: 1995 Q.
French: Shitload of sheets
English: Essay
Irish: Mac an Cheannaí

FRI 5

English: Essay
Irish: Mac an Cheannaí / Organise notes
Maths: pg. 200 Q1,3,5,7.
Physics: Experiments copy.
French: Sheets

SAT 6

NOTES

SUN 7

MAY • Bealtaine • 2000

MON 8

Irish: P.2 Déimife
Maths: 1998 / 1997

French: Sheets
Physics: Q marked out
English: Essay

TUES 9

Business: p.63 Q6
French: Diary - Friend in Hospital
Irish: P.3 Déimire
Maths: 1996/1995 Q8 (option)

WED 10

English: Free ✓
Irish: Nottin' ✓
Maths: 1999/1998 Q1 Par II
Applied: Free ✓ (1997 paper for Monday)
Bus: Q1- Part 1 sec 3 mock 2hr (for Friday)
Physics: work on with Q ✓
French: comp. sheet + mobiles (frenk plw)

MAY • Bealtaine • 2000

THURS 11

Irish An Trail / mise mé féin

Maths 1997 / 1996 Par II Q1

English : Novels / bring essay

Physics : Questions / Exps.

Applied 1998 4 next week

Business :

French: Sheets + journal intime

FRI 12

Business: AB2 p.29 + p.10 short questions

French - Mock Paper - 2nd comp., Q1 to written + (1st comp.)

Irish Revise sheets / notes

Physics: Get up to date with questions

Applied: 1997 Paper - Tues (Mon)

Maths Vectors - all questions

SAT 13

SUN 14

NOTES

183

MON 15

TUES 16

Bus: ASQ p.61 4 Fri Sh. Q Thurs.
French: Campsite - Applying 4 a Job | 75 words - reaction | Sheet (fill it up).
English: Themes Act I scenes I - IV
Physics: Questions
Music: (OH "Barry" score.
Business: letter to l'EDF for Thurs

WED 17

English: Revise Quotes
Irish: Revise notes - An tOileán
Maths: Next Q4 + Q5 Pap II
Physics: Revise + Questions
French: Sheets
Business: ASQ for Fri | SQ Thurs | Break even
Applied - 1948 work on
Music: Inversions | Irish music - Q | Brian Q | Barry Q.

THURS 18 French. ~~XXXX~~ Business: A&2, break even chart. maths: Trig questions.	**THURS 25**
ALLIANCE!	
FRI 19	**FRI 26** Grad *FINISHED SCHOOL!!!*
SAT 20 / **SUN 21**	**SAT 27** / **SUN 28**
MON 22	**MON 29**
TUES 23	**TUES 30**
WED 24	**WED 31**

JUNE 2000	JULY 2000	AUGUST 2000
THURS 1	SAT 1	TUES 1
FRI 2	SUN 2	WED 2
SAT 3	MON 3	THURS 3
SUN 4	TUES 4	FRI 4
MON 5	WED 5	SAT 5
TUES 6	THURS 6	SUN 6
WED 7 *AAAAAGH! LC starts.*	FRI 7	MON 7
THURS 8	SAT 8	TUES 8
FRI 9	SUN 9	WED 9
SAT 10	MON 10	THURS 10
SUN 11	TUES 11	FRI 11
MON 12	WED 12	SAT 12
TUES 13	THURS 13	SUN 13
WED 14	FRI 14	MON 14
THURS 15	SAT 15	TUES 15
FRI 16	SUN 16	WED 16
SAT 17	MON 17	THURS 17
SUN 18	TUES 18	FRI 18
MON 19	WED 19	SAT 19
TUES 20	THURS 20	SUN 20
WED 21	FRI 21	MON 21
THURS 22	SAT 22	TUES 22
FRI 23 *WAHOO! Finished LC.*	SUN 23	WED 23
SAT 24	MON 24	THURS 24
SUN 25	TUES 25	FRI 25
MON 26	WED 26	SAT 26
TUES 27	THURS 27	SUN 27
WED 28	FRI 28	MON 28
THURS 29	SAT 29	TUES 29
FRI 30	SUN 30	WED 30
	MON 31	THURS 31 *No school tomorrow!*

186

TIME OUT

The Leaving Certificate years can be very demanding. All students should take time to rest and relax; a healthy body making for a healthy mind. Section 4 of the Yearbook provides a comprehensive guide to leisure activities and healthy living.

the
MONT CLARE
HOTEL
a special corner of Dublin

Débutantes Ball
The Night of Your Dreams

*Your Débutantes ball is an evening to be remembered forever. With the help of past Débutantes, we at **The Mont Clare Hotel** have designed a programme to ensure that your evening will be full of fond memories.*

With a choice of three five course menus, the option of dancing until 6.00a.m. and the facility to include continental breakfast, the programme allows you to design your own special evening.

***The Mont Clare Hotel** will in turn provide printed tickets, personalised menus, matchbooks, place names and beautiful floral centrepieces on each table.*

at MERRION SQUARE,
DUBLIN 2, IRELAND.
TELEPHONE: + 353 1 607 3800
FACSIMILE: +353 1 661 5663

Please contact Siobhan Fitzgerald at the Banqueting Office for further details.
Telephone: 607 3800

SPORT & LEISURE

With the high stress levels most of us are living with today, sport and exercise has become part of our daily routine. People are now turning to their leisure time as a way to destress and wind down after a days work or study.

Information on Sport

There are several ways of finding out information on clubs or sporting societies in your locality. The Department of Tourism, Sport and Recreation is a good starting point. Its Sports Activity Unit can provide a list of just about every kind of sport you can imagine. The Department is contactable at Fredrick Bldg., Dublin 2. Tel (01) 662 1444.

AFAS – the Association for Adventure Sports can provide information for the more adventurous sporting type and they are contactable at House of Sport, Long Mile Road, Dublin 12. Tel (01) 450 9845. Then again, if it's the 'great outdoors' that excites you Glenaans, is the organisation to contact. They are based at 28 Merrion Square Nth., Dublin 2. Tel (01) 661 1481/2. Glenaans specialise in sailing activities, hill walking and pony-trekking.

Other options include spending a weekend away in an outdoor pursuits centre – which will definitely give you a taste for a few of the adventure sports on offer.

What if I hate Sports?!

Not everyone wants to spend their leisure time climbing up mountains or canoeing down a river. There are plenty of organisations that cater for an array of other interests and hobbies. The National Youth Council's 'Irish Youth Directory', which is updated every two years, has detailed information on the aims, structures and programmes of numerous clubs and societies throughout the country.

For all kinds of activities, sporting and otherwise, keep your eyes on community and school noticeboards. You may even find that there are local youth organisations in your area that you didn't know existed. Also don't forget to contact your local authority office about summer projects and 'community games'.

Types of Youth groups;

1. **Irish Groups** which aim to promote the Irish language and culture.
2. **Youth Clubs** with activities centred on anything from board games to basketball, or projects in the community.
3. **Specialist Organisations** with interests in environmental issues, drama or voluntary work.

Gaisce award participants are met by the President Mary McAleese during a four day army survival course on the Wicklow mountains

Information: Gaisce - the President's Awards, State Apartments, Upper Yard, Dubln Castle, Dublin 2. Tel: 01-4758746/4758747

4. **Uniformed Associations** such as Girls' Brigade, Order of Malta Ambulance Corp or the Boy Scouts.

IRISH GROUPS
- Gael-Linn, 26 Cearnóg Mhuirfean, Baile Átha Cliath 2 (01-676 7283).
- Ógras, 6 Sráid Fhearchair, Baile Átha Cliath 2 (01-475 1487).
- Comhaltas Ceoltóirí Éireann, 32 Belgrave Sq., Monkstown, Co. Dublin (01-280 0295).
- Bord na Gaeilge, 7 Cearnog Mhuirfean, Baile Átha Cliath 2 (01-676 3222).
- Comhchoiste Náisiúnta na gColáistí Samhraidh, Aras na Comhdhála, 46 Sr. Cill Dara, Baile Átha Cliath (01-679 4780), (agus An Cumann Scoil-Dhrámaíochta).

YOUTH CLUBS/ORGANISATIONS AND SUPPORT GROUPS
- Community and Youth Information Centre, 4 Sackville Place, Dublin 1. (01-8745284).
- National Youth Federation, 20 Lr Dominic St., Dublin 7 (01-8729933).
- National Youth Council of Ireland, 3 Montague St., Dublin 2 (01-4784122).
- Chomhairle Le Leas Óige, 70 Morehampton Road, Dublin 4 (01-668 3198).
- Catholic Youth Council, Arran Quay, Dublin 7 (01-872 5055).
- Irish Youth Foundation, 1 Renault House, Kylemore Road, Dublin 10 (01-6261090).
- Church of Ireland Youth Council, The Old School House, 30 Phibsboro Road, Dublin 7, Tel: (01-830 0299.

SPECIALIST GROUPS
- Foróige, The National Youth Developmental Organisation, Irish Farm Centre, Bluebell, Dublin 12 (01-450 1166).
- An Óige, 61 Mountjoy St., Dublin 1 (01-830 4555).
- Interculture Ireland, 10a Lr. Camden Street, Dublin 2. (01-478 2046)
- National Association of Youth Drama, 34 Upr. Gardiner Street, Dublin 1 (01-8781301).
- Voluntary Service International, 30 Mountjoy Sq., Dublin 1 (01-855 1011).

UNIFORMED GROUPS
- Boys Brigade, The Scots Centre, 1 Lr. Abbey Street, Dublin 1, Tel: (01-874 5278).
- Catholic Boy Scouts of Ireland, 19 Herbert Place, Dublin 2 (01-676 1598).
- Catholic Guides of Ireland, 12 Clanwilliam Tce., Grand Canal Quay, Dublin 2 (01-661 9566).
- Girls Brigade, 5 Upr Sherrard Street, Dublin 1 (01-836 5488).
- Irish Girl Guides, 27 Pembroke Park, Dublin 4 (01-668 3898).
- Irish Red Cross Society, 16 Merrion Square, Dublin 2 (01-676 5135).
- Order of Malta, Ambulance Corps, St. John's House, 32 Clyde Road, Dublin 4 (01-668 4891).
- The St. John Ambulance Brigade of Ireland, 29 Upr. Leeson St., Dublin 4 (01-668 8077).
- The Scout Association of Ireland, 22 Nassau Street, Dublin 2 (01-671 1244).

190

TRAVEL

Travelling and seeing the world is a great way to broaden your horizons and meet new and interesting people. Many Irish students are now finding it hard to resist the lure of summer month's abroad, earning next years keep. May and June signal the beginning of the mass exodus to pastures greener and definitely warmer!

If travelling to Thailand isn't for you this year, don't take a back seat. It is never too early to invest in student travel concession cards. USIT is the place to go to get your ISIC – International Student Identity Card with 'travel-save' stamp or the under 26's EYC – European Youth Card. Although these may initially set you back they are invaluable whilst travelling in or outside Ireland. Not only do they supply numerous discounts, they are also a recognised form of student ID

If you are planning to head off for the summer months, a bit of planning is advised;

• Start early in the year. Ask yourself questions such as; Which country? Do I need a work permit? Is there much accommodation? USIT or your travel agent should be able to advise you or if necessary contact the relevant embassy – addresses are available from the Department of Foreign Affairs, 80 St. Stephen's Green, Dublin 2. Tel (01) 478 0822.

• Money, money, money… as usual finances must come into the equation. If you are interested in travelling to a far off destination, maybe you are going to need to take out a student loan. If you do so, will you be able to make enough money to pay this off? Remember things like rent – don't underestimate how cheap it is to live at home! You will need to bring enough money to put a deposit on a flat and pay the first month's rental. Perhaps, consider a job in the hotel industry, which provides room and board.

• Do you know anyone who has worked abroad? One of the best things you can do is seek advice from friends and family who have worked away. Also check up on your family tree! Are there any long lost relatives living in the country you are travelling to? You never know you may hit gold!

• When considering what country to travel to, always consider unique places. If everyone is going to Long Island, why don't you go to Hawaii or Alaska? Places that aren't saturated with Irish students will have more work and more accommodation to choose from.

FURTHER INFORMATION

• **Action Group for Irish Youth, AG IY,** London Voluntary Sector Resource Centre, 356 Holloway Road, London N 7 6PA. Tel: 0044-171-700 8137.
• **Aer Lingus** – bookings can be made at any of their offices by calling in person. Telephone bookings can only be accepted at (01-844 4777).
• **British Rail,** 123 Lr. Baggot Street, Dublin (01-661 2866) 10.00am – 12 noon Mon-Fri.
• **Bus Átha Cliath** (Dublin Bus) (01-873 4222).
• **Bus Éireann** (Provincial Service) (01-836 6111)
• **Funtrek,** 32 Bachelor's Walk, Dublin 1 (01-873 363).
• **Iarnród Éireann** (Rail) (01-836 63333);
• **Irish Chaplaincy in Britain,** St Mellitus' Church, Tollington Park, London N4 3AG, Tel: 0044-171-2631 477.
• **Irish Ferries,** 2-4 Merrion Row, Dublin 2 (01-6610511); Ferry Tours, 2-4 Merrion Row, Dublin 2 (01-661 0533); 9 Bridge Street, Cork (021-504333).
• **Léargas** – Avoca House, 189 Parnell St., Dublin 1 (01-873 1411).
• **Ryanair,** Head Office, Dublin Airport (01-844 4400); reservations (01-677 4422).
• **Stena Sealink Line,** 15 Westmoreland St., Dublin 2. (01-280 8844; Rosslare (053-33115; Cork 021-272965; Limerick (061-316259)· Larne (08-0574-273 616).
• **USIT,** 19 Acton Quay, Dublin 2 (01-079 8833).

EOLAS DON ÓGRA

YOUTH
INFORMATION

Youth Information Centres (YICS) provide a free confidential information service to young people and those who work with them on a wide variety of subjects.

The atmosphere in Youth Information Centres is warm and informal.

If You Want To.....

• Make the most of your spare time

• Travel and see the world

• Check out third level and other vocational training courses

• Find a job

• Become involved in youth work

• Know more about your rights and entitlements

• Find a flat

• Or just have someone to talk to in a difficult situation

... your local Youth Information Centre is a good place to start.

The national network of Youth Information Centres is funded by the Youth Affairs Section of the Department of Education & Science.

Website
www.youthinformation.ie

YOUTH INFORMATION CENTRES

CLARE
Ennis YIC, Carmody St. Tel. (065) 682 4137

CORK
Cork YIC, 11/12 Marlboro St. Tel. (021) 27 01 87
West Cork YIC, North Main St., Bandon. Tel. (023) 4 40 09

DONEGAL
Donegal YIC, Upper Main St. Tel. (073) 2 30 29
Letterkenny YIC, Lr. Main St. Tel. (074) 2 96 40

DUBLIN
Blanchardstown YIC, Main St. Tel. (01) 821 2077
Clondalkin YIC, Monastery Rd. Tel. (01) 459 4666
Dun Laoghaire YIC, Marine Rd. Tel. (01) 280 9363
Tallaght YIC, Main Rd. Tel. (01) 451 6322
Dublin Corporation operates the Community & Youth Information Centre at Sackville Place, Dublin 1 Tel. (01) 878 6844

GALWAY
Ballinasloe YIC, Society St. Tel. (0905) 4 41 44
Galway YIC, St. Augustine St. Tel. (091) 56 24 34

KERRY
Killarney YIC, 72 New St. Tel. (064) 3 17 48
Listowel YIC, Church St. Tel. (068) 2 15 44
Tralee YIC, Denny St. Tel. (066) 712 1674

KILDARE
Naas YIC, Basin St. Tel. (045) 89 78 93

KILKENNY
Kilkenny YIC, New St. Tel. (056) 6 12 00

LIMERICK
Limerick YIC, 35 O'Connell St. Tel. (061) 41 69 63

ROSCOMMON
Roscommon YIC, Castle St. Tel. (0903) 2 53 95

SLIGO
Sligo YIC, 5A Market St. Tel. (071) 4 41 50

TIPPERARY
Carrick on Suir YIC, New St. Tel. (051) 64 19 46
Clonmel YIC, 12 Upr. Irishtown. Tel. (052) 2 55 18
Thurles YIC, Croke St. Tel. (0504) 2 37 42
Tipperary YIC, O'Brien St. Tel. (062) 5 26 04

WATERFORD
Dungarvan YIC, St. Augustine's St. Tel. (058) 4 16 98
Waterford YIC, 130 The Quay. Tel. (051) 87 73 28

WEXFORD
'Youth Info', South Main St. Tel. (053) 2 32 62

WICKLOW
Bray YIC, Florence Rd. Tel. (01) 282 8324

When times are tough and the teenage blues are getting you down, don't despair, there is always help at hand. Being a teenager and dealing with all kinds of physical as well as emotional issues can be a very confusing time. Regardless of what you may think though, you are not the first and certainly won't be the last person to struggle through it.

Never be too proud to turn to your Mam or Dad or even a good friend. For most of us just talking about our problem and getting it off our chest is the main thing. Sometimes you may have a problem which you feel extends beyond these people or is possibly too sensitive to confide to your parents about. In these cases approaching the school guidance counsellor can be your first step to seeking help. They can provide you with names and phone numbers of the relevant support agencies.

Printed below is a list of national agenices should you prefer to seek the help yourself.

INFORMATION
Citizens Information Centres
There are over eighty centres throughout the country, providing information on a variety of topics including: social welfare entitlements, benefits, taxation, local or other information. Check the Golden Pages for one near you or contact the National Social Services Board (NSSB), Hume House, Dublin 4 (01-605900)..

Youth Information Centres

Youth Information Centres provide young people with free information on all subjects of interest to them e.g. careers, education, training, employment matters, health and welfare services, leisure activities, sport and travel.
See page 192 for a list of Centres or contact the Youth Information Resource Unit, Hawkins House (Floor 11), Hawkins Street, Dublin 2. Tel: 01-873 4700.
Internet: http://www.youthinformation.ie

AIDS/SEXUALLY TRANSMITTED DISEASES

- **Aids Helpline** (01-8724277) Mon–Fri 7–9pm Sat 3–5pm – provides non-judgmental, non-directive confidential telephone counselling service.
- **DUBLIN AIDS ALLIANCE**
  53 Parnell Sq. West, Dublin 1.
  Tel. 01-8733799.
  Monday – Friday 10am – 5.30pm

- **AIDS HELP WEST – Education, Support and Helpline:** (Mon-Fri 9.30am-5.30pm) (091-566266).
- **CORK AIDS ALLIANCE GROUP** – 16 Peter Street, Cork. (021) 275837. *Helpline:* (021) 276676
- **LIMERICK RED RIBBON PROJECT** – *Helpline:* 94 Henry Street, Limerick (Mon & Fri 9.30am-5.30pm) (061) 316661.
- **S.T.D. Clinics** for the treatment of sexually transmitted diseases operate at the following hospitals: Mater Dublin *(Male Wed & Thurs 5-7pm, Female Tues & Thur 4-7pm, 3-4pm)* (01-8301122); James St., Dublin (Mon 9.45am-11.30am, Tues & Thurs 1.30pm-3.30pm (01-4535245/4537941); Victoria Cork (Fri 9.30am-11.30am) (021-964333) (Mon 5.30pm-7pm, Wed 10am-12 noon; Regional Limerick (061-301111); Regional Waterford — Ardkeen (051-302000).
- **Merchants' Quay Project** – offers advice to drug users affected by AIDS. Contact: Sean Cassin, 4 Merchants' Quay, Dublin 2 (01-6790044; Mon–Fri 10am–4.30pm, Closed 1pm-2pm).
- **Baggot Street Clinic** – a statutory body providing information and advice on all aspects of HIV. Contact Dr. Mary Scully, (DIR), HIV Services for E.H. Board, 19 Haddington Road, Dublin 4 (01-6602149/6602271). Drop in Time Tues (2-5pm) Wed & Thurs (5-7pm).
- **CAIRDE** – Support group for people affected by AIDS. 25 Mary's Abbey, off Capel Street, Dublin 7. (01-8730006).

ALCOHOL/DRUGS/ SUBSTANCE ABUSE

- **Drugs Awareness Programme,** Catholic Social Service Conference, The Red House, Clonliffe College, Dublin 3 (01-8375103) – educational, counselling and referral services, including Youth to Youth which employs young people to teach other young people to say No to drugs.
- **Narcotics Anonymous,** P.O. Box 1368, Sheriff St., Dublin 1 – recovering drug addicts support groups (01-8300944).
- **Mater Dei Counselling Centre,** Mater Dei Institute, Clonliffe Road, Dublin 3 (01-8371892). Counselling centre for adolescents and their families, with a special interest in substance abuse.

- **Coolmine Therapeutic Community,** Induction Centre, 19 Lord Edward Street, Dublin 2 (01-6794822). Drug-free therapeutic community for the rehabilitation of drug/alcohol addicts.
- **Rutland Centre Ltd.,** Knocklyon House, Knocklyon Road, Dublin 16 (01-4946358/4946761). A residential centre for the professional treatment of alcoholism, other drug dependancies and compulsive gambling.
- **Al-Anon Information Centre,** 5 Capel Street, Dublin 1 (01-8732699). Al-Anon and ALATEEN are support groups for relatives and friends of alcoholics. Alateen groups are in every county in Ireland and details are available about ALATEEN groups from Al-Anon.
- **Alcoholics Anonymous,** 109 South Circular Road, Dublin 8. (01-4538998, after hours call 6795967).
- **Drug Treatment Centre,** 30–31 Pearse St., Dublin 2 (01-6771122).

COUNSELLING DISTRESS/DEPRESSION

- **The Samaritans,** 112 Marlborough St., Dublin 1 – provide a 24-hour confidential telephone service to those in distress. Dublin (01-8727700); Cork (021-271323); Galway (091-61222); Limerick (061-412111); Waterford (051-72114); Ennis (065-29777); Sligo (071-42011); Tralee (066-22566); Athlone (0902-73133); Newbridge (045-435299).
- **Aware** – a voluntary organisation whose aims are to assist those whose lives are directly affected by depression. Address: Aware Administration Office: 147 Phibsboro Road, Dublin 7 (01-8308449) – a list of support groups throughout the country available on request. Helpline (01-6791711).
- **Bereavement Counselling Service,** (01-6767727) Non-denominational and free. Call for a list of countrywide services.

EMIGRATION

- **Emigrants Advice Centre,** 1A Cathedral St., Dublin 1 (01-8732844) for list of similar centres nationwide.
- **Irish Advice Centre,** 55 Fulham Palace Road, Hammersmith, London W6 8AU. Tel.: 081-741-0466 (from Ireland 0044-181-741-0466).
- **IECE,** Irish Episcopal Commission for Emigrants, 57 Parnell Square West, Dublin 1. (01-8723655)

FINANCE

- **F.I.S.C. (Financial Information Services Centres),** 87/89 Pembroke Road, Ballsbridge, Dublin 4 (01-6682044) – confidential, free financial advice to people who can't afford the services of accountants. There are 16 centres in Dublin and also ones at Bray, Cavan, Cork, Louth, Limerick, Newbridge and Wexford.

HEALTH

- **Irish Cancer Society,** 5 Northumberland Road, Dublin 4 (01-6681855).
- **Asthma Society,** 15 Eden Quay, Dublin 1 (01-8788511).
- **Irish Epilepsy Association,** 249 Crumlin Road, Dublin 12 (01-4557500/4554133).
- **Coeliac Society of Ireland,** Carmichael House, North Brunswick St. Dublin 7. Recorded List of contacts or office open Monday (01-8721471).

HOUSING

- **Threshold,** 19 Mary's Abbey, Dublin 7 (01-8726311); 8 Fr. Matthew Quay, Cork (021-271250); Ozanam House, St. Augustine Street, Galway (091-563080) – advises on a whole range of housing problems.

- **Focus Point,** 14a Eustace St., Dublin 2 (01-6712555) (emergency numbers). Advice centre on homelessness. Focus Point have a very useful package called "Leaving Home"
- **Simon Community,** 119 Capel Street, Dublin 1, (01-8720188); Cork (021-300970); Dundalk (042-39583); Galway (589415).

LAW

- **Gárda Síochána.** As well as your local Garda station which provides a range of services there is also the Garda Public Relations, Phoenix Park, Dublin 8 (01-6771156); Juvenile Liaison Officer (JLO) Scheme and the Garda Drugs Unit, both at Harcourt Sq., Dublin 2 (01-4755555).
- **Legal Aid Board,** St. Stephens Green, Dublin 2. A state-funded organisation which provides the services of solicitors to persons of modest means at little cost. It does not apply to criminal cases. Contact 01-6615811 for a full list of nationwide centres.
- **Free Legal Advice Centres** – provide advice on legal problems. To find out your nearest centre contact FLAC, 49 South William St., Dublin 2 (01-6794239) or your local Citizens Information Centre.

PREGNANCY/ADOPTION/ FAMILY PLANNING

- **Pact** – Protestant Adoption Society and Single Parent Counselling Service, 15 Belgrave Road, Rathmines, Dublin 6. (01-4976788).
- **CÚNAMH,** formerly known as **(CPRSI),** 30 South Anne St., Dublin 2 (01-6779664) – services for unmarried mothers and their children.
- **Life,** 29–30 Dame St., Dublin 2 (01-6798989) – voluntary and non-denominational association offering pregnancy testing and confidential counselling and assistance with accommodation, medical issues, Social Welfare entitlements and adoption. Mon–Sat (12–2pm) and Tues & Thurs (7–9pm) – offers free pregnancy testing and confidential counselling.
- **Cura** – a confidential referral/information/ counselling service for pregnant girls, established by the Catholic Bishops. 30 South Anne St., Dublin 2 (01-6710598); Kilkenny (056-22739); Cork (021-277544); Waterford (051-76452); Limerick (061-318207); Galway (091-62558); Sligo (071-43659); Dundalk (042-37533); Letterkenny (074-23037); Athlone (0902-78833); Ennis (065-29905); Wexford (053-22255); Tralee (066-27355).
- **Cherish,** 2 Lr. Pembroke St., Dublin 2 (01-6629212) – a non-denominational organisation providing, counselling, information and advice to single women before and after pregnancy and to single parent families.

- **Gingerbread Ireland,** 29 Dame St., Dublin 2 (01-6710291). A self-help organisation for one-parent families.
- **Irish Family Planning Association,** 16 Lower O'Connell Street, Dublin 1. (01-8780366).
- **Irish Family Planning Association Clinics,** 5/7 Cathal Brugha Street, Dublin 1 (01-8727276/8727363).

RAPE/SEXUAL ABUSE

- **Rape Crisis Centres,** 70 Lr. Leeson St., Dublin 2 (1800 778888) after hours and weekends call 6614564. Centres also in Clonmel (1800 340340); Cork (021-5055577); Galway (091-564983); Limerick (061-311511); Waterford (051-73362);
- **Childline c/o ISPCC,** 20 Molesworth St, Dublin 2. Freefone (1-800-666666).

INFORMATION

- **Community Information Centres.** There are over 70 centres throughout the country providing information on topics such as *health, social welfare, housing, local organisations* and *social services.* A full list of CIC's is available from the National Social Service Board, Hume House, Dublin 4 (6059000).
- **Youth, Community and Information Centre,** Sackville Place, Dublin 1 (behind Clery's) (01-8786844) – information on most topics of concern to young people; confidential legal advice; regular exhibitions.

OTHERS

- **Association for Children and Adults with Learning Disabilities,** Suffolk Chambers, Suffolk St., Dublin 2 (6790276).
- **National Rehabilitation Board (NRB),** Head Office, 25 Clyde Road, Dublin 4 (01-6684181) and branches throughout the country. Government agency providing service for disabled persons.
- **Employment Equality Agency,** 36 Upper Mount Street, Dublin 2.
- **Gambler's Anonymous,** Carmichael House, North Brunswick Street, Dublin 7 (01-8721133).

NATIONAL TRAINING & DEVELOPMENT INSTITUTE

COOLAMBER NATIONAL TRAINING COLLEGE

Vocational training for students with special needs including learning difficulties, epilepsy, depression and other similar conditions.

Courses	Duration	Certification
Professional Cookery	2 yrs.	City & Guilds
Hotel Accommodation Multi Skills	2 yrs.	City & Guilds
Agriculture	2 yrs.	Teagasc
Horticulture	2 yrs.	Teagasc

On site accommodation available.

* No fees apply * Statutory benefits retained * Weekly training allowance paid
* Materials and equipment supplied
* Extra supports provided in Personal Development,
Work Experience and job-seeking skills

EUROPEAN COMMUNITY
European Social Fund

✂ -

For more information on these or any NTDI course complete the coupon and return to: John O'Connor, NTDI, Coolamber National Training College, Lisryan, Co. Longford. Tel: (043) 85159. Fax: (043) 85203.

Name: _____

Address:_____

_____

Daytime telephone number: _____

SYCD 4/99

FURTHER EDUCATION & TRAINING

Pass and Honours students are catered for in this section's comprehensive coverage of apprenticeships, Post-Leaving Cert. courses and Third Level Education,

There is much variety and flexibility in courses nowadays e.g. many PLCs and apprenticeships afford graduates the prospect of transferring to other colleges and universities.

Photo shows Orla Keane from Shannon Aerospace who has just completed her apprenticeship with the company. Orla is a past pupil of Ard Scoil Mhuire, Corbally, Limerick.

YOUTH TRAINING & EMPLOYMENT SCHEMES

Improve your employment prospects

UNEMPLOYMENT BY LEVEL OF EDUCATION

No Qualifications	Junior Certificate	Leaving Certificate
48.5%	16.3%	3.6%

The figures above, taken from the most recent annual school leaver's survey, dramatically illustrate how you can increase your employment prospects by staying in school or on a training course for an extra few years.

There has been a tremendous growth in the number of youth training and employment schemes. They are all positive attempts by government and other concerned agencies to improve people's employment prospects by giving them skills and training and by encouraging those who have the initiative and maturity to become self employed.

In this special "Student Yearbook" supplement we have identified the schemes available, provided a summary of each and offered you an address or phone number for further contact.

- Read this section in conjunction with the P.L.C. Cert, and FÁS training courses listed in the Yearbook. Having some type of skill in addition to school certificates will improve your prospects of success.

- Some of the schemes are intended for community organisations. If there are youth groups, community councils or parish committees in your locality concerned about employment, bring their attention to the existence of the various schemes outlined in this supplement.

YOUTHREACH

Young people who leave school without any qualification or with only basic Junior Certificate standard very often fail to get a job.

YOUTHREACH is a special initiative sponsored by the Departments of Education and Enterprise & Employment to give early school leavers a second chance.

YOUTHREACH is intended for young people who are typically at least six months in the labour market, are aged between 15 and 18 years, have left the school system without formal qualification or vocational training, who are not catered for within the traditional educational or training provision, and have not secured full time employment. The aim of YOUTHREACH is to provide participants with the knowledge, skills and attitudes required to successfully make the transition to work and adult life.

YOUTHREACH is a guarantee of at least two years training, work experience and temporary employment for early school leavers. It essentially involves an integrated response by education, training and community agencies to the problems which young people experience, and which result in their opting out of school early, and subsequently failing to secure a foothold in the labour market.

> **"If you are an early school-leaver or have friends who have left school early, you or your friends should contact your local FÁS Employment Services Office."**

YOUTHREACH is available in more than 120 FÁS and VEC funded centres throughout the country. Trainees receive regular FÁS allowances and a National Certificate on successfully completing their training.

Further information from your local Fás Office or YOUTHREACH National Co-Ordinator, C.D.U., Sundrive Road, Crumlin, Dublin 12.

V.T.O.S.

The Government has approved funding for extra places on the Vocational Training Opportunities Scheme (VTOS), which is open to unemployed adults. It proposes is to make attendance at such courses compulsory for long-term unemployed people under 21 years of age if they wish to retain their full dole allowances.

At present the VTOS is available mainly in vocational schools, but it is expected that other schools will be able to offer it in the future. The participants follow different programmes – some take Leaving Certificate subjects or other vocational training courses which would allow them to go back into the jobs market with new skills. They are paid an allowance by the VECs equivalent to their unemployment assistance.

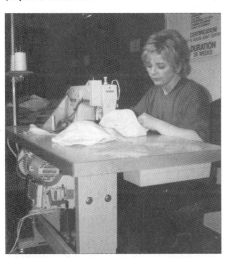

COMMUNITY EMPLOYMENT

Community Employment is designed to provide temporary community based employment for unemployed people, whilst carrying out beneficial work for the community and improving the quality of life in communities. Examples of Community Employment projects include, arts, heritage, cultural, tourism, sports and environment. Workers are employed for an average of 39 hours per fortnight and receive personal development and training.

Information from, your local FÁS Employment Services Office.

COMMUNITY TRAINING WORKSHOPS

These workshops are aimed at out-of-school people most in need of basic vocational training and are managed by representative community committees.

They play a major role in the implementation of YOUTH REACH.

COMMUNITY TRAINING PROGRAMME

This programme provides training for unemployed persons who are registered for employment with the FÁS Employment Services Office.

Training is on local projects which will result in improved community amenities/services.

For information on project vacancies contact your local FÁS Office.

TEAGASC CERTIFICATE IN FARMING

Over 800 farms act as hosts each year for young farmers who wish to take the "Green Cert." (See Agriculture category).

The Certificate course incorporates formal course work, projects and work experience. The scheme is levy funded. Details from Teagasc head office or any local Teagasc office.

CERTS BASIC SKILLS
TRAINING PROGRAMME

The good news from this course was that a very high percentage of the participants were placed in permanent jobs. A basic skills training in bar service, cookery, food service, housekeeping and porterage was provided for those who took part. It is levy funded and you may get information from CERT House, Amiens Street, Dublin 1. (01-8556555).

ADDRESSES

CERT House, Amiens Street, Dublin 1. (01-8556555).

Dept. of Employment & Enterprise, Kildare Street, Dublin 2. (6614444).

FÁS Employment Services. See addresses and phone numbers at the back of this section).

IDA (renamed FORBAIRT to encourage local industries. IDA (Ireland) will continue to encourage international investment), Wilton Park House, WIlton Place, Dublin 2 (01-6034000).

Teagasc, 19 Sandymount Ave., Dublin 4 (01-6688188).

REGISTER WITH FÁS

Information on Youth Training and Employment Schemes is available in your local FÁS Employment Services Office. These are listed under FÁS Employment Service Offices elsewhere in this Directory.

The Standards-Based Apprenticeship is a system which was developed as a result of the agreement in 1991 (in the programme for Economic and Social Progress) between employers and trade unions on the need for a new approach to apprenticeship.

What is an Apprenticeship?
Apprenticeship is a method by which a person works for an employer in a chosen occupation and learns the necessary skills, knowledge and attitudes to become a qualified craftsperson.

What is the Standards-Based Apprenticeship?
As the name suggests the apprenticeship system is standards-based. This means you will undergo specific tests and assessments to ensure you achieve certain pre-set standards of skill and competence during the course of your apprenticeship.

Apprenticeship comprises on-the-job training with your employer and off-the-job training normally in a FÁS Training Centre or Educational College.

You also receive an apprentice wage/training allowance.

On successful completion of apprenticeship, you will receive a National Craft Certificate, recognised in Ireland as well as in other European Union countries and non European Union countries. This will allow you to follow a craftsperson's career in your chosen occupation.

Also you will be able to make use of the access provided by the National Craft Certificate to further training and education.

How to become an apprentice under the Standards-Based Apprenticeship?
1. Boys and girls who have reached the age of 16 years and who have, as a minimum, obtained grade D in any five subjects in the Junior Certificate are eligible for apprenticeship. Career prospects for women in craft trades have increased considerably. FÁS actively encourages females to apply for apprenticeships including offering a bursary to employers.

2. You may obtain an apprenticeship by:
   (a) Studying job advertisements in the local and national press. Many of the larger organisations such as EBS, the Army, Iarnód Éireann and Aer Lingus advertise their apprenticeship vacancies through these outlets.

   (b) Registering with your local FÁS Employment Services Office, who will put you in touch with employers seeking apprentices.

FÁS APPRENTICESHIP SCHEME

During your apprenticeship you will be required to follow a specific course of training and undergo a series of assessments to confirm that you've reached the required standards.

Apprenticeship consists of 7 phases of training both on-the-job with your employer and off-the-job in a FÁS Training Centre or Educational College, as shown below.

	Phase 1	Phase 2	Phase 3	Phase 4	Phase 5	Phase 6	Phase 7

ON-THE-JOB with Employer

OFF-THE-JOB in FÁS or Educational College

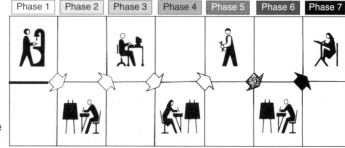

(C) Applying directly to local firms for an apprenticeship. Prepare your Curriculum Vitae and bring it with you when visiting the company in which you are interested (refer to the Golden Pages for a listing of companies). This approach is especially important as the competition for places in (a) and (b) is considerable.

(d) Consult with the guidance counsellor or school principal as some employers recruit through local schools.

Before taking up employment young people and their parents should satisfy themselves that the prospective employers will fulfil the obligation to register the apprentice with FÁS, to give good training including off-the-job training release. Within two weeks of taking up employment the apprentice should be registered as an apprentice with FÁS.

Welcome to WATIS

The WATIS system offers you the following possibilities:

Vacancies: Retrieve information on Vacancies

Courses: Retrieve information on Training Courses

Check out all Fás courses and vacancies on the new **WATIS** system http://www.fas.ie

STANDARDS BASED APPRENTICESHIP APPLIES TO THE FOLLOWING TRADES

FURNITURE
Wood Machinist; Cabinet Maker;

CONSTRUCTION
Plasterer; Brick/Stone Layer;
Painter/Decorator*; Construction Plant Fitter*;
Plumber; Electrician*; Carpenter/Joiner
Floor/Wall Tiler

ENGINEERING
Sheet Metal Worker; Refrigeration
Craftsperson*; Aircraft Mechanic*; Metal
Fabricator; Toolmaker; Instrumentation
Craftsperson*; Fitter*

MOTOR
Vehicle Body Repair*; Agricultural Mechanic*;
Heavy Vehicle Mechanic*; Motor Mechanic*.

PRINTING
Carton Maker*; Originator*; Bookbinder*;
Printer*.

* A person wishing to become an apprentice in one of the above trades marked * must pass a colour vision test approved by FAS.

CONTACT YOUR LOCAL FÁS EMPLOYMENT SERVICES OFFICE OR TRAINING CENTRE FOR INFORMATION.

FÁS COURSES

Hairdressing, electronics, computers, and sales are just some of the different courses available in FÁS Training Centres. The list of courses below gives a general overview of the range of FÁS courses offered at Training Centres. Specific courses may be deleted or alternative new courses added to this list from time to time. Many FÁS Training Centres offer evening courses to clients who are not in a position to attend during normal working hours. A modest fee is charged. Contact your local Training Centre for details.

A

Access Network Technician
Accounts – Coputerised & Business Admin.
Accounting – Technician
Advanced Computer Application
Advanced Desktop Publishing
Advanced Desktop Publishing
Aeronautical Skills
Aircraft Maintenance
Alarm Installation

B

Basic Computer Literacy
Basic Computer Skills
Beautician
Boatbuilding – CYTP
Book-Keeping – Computerised
Bridging Foundation
Bridging Programme
Business & Office Administration
Business & Office Technology
Business & Office Technology
Business Accounting
Business Administration
Business Administration – Traineeship
Business Administration – Processing
Business Administration
Business Administration and Management Skills
Business Appraisal
Business Appraisal Training Programme

C

CAD Computer Aided Engineering & Draughting
CAD/CAM/CNC
CNC/CAD
C.N.C. Machine Tool Operatives
Career Development (18-25)
Child Care
Child Care Worker
Clerical Skills
Clerical Skills Updating
Community Care Practice Specialising in Disability Studies
Computer Aided Design
Computer Aided Design – Construction
Computer Aided Draughting & Design
Computer Aided Engineering

Computer Aided Engineering, Milling & Turning
Computer Applications – Basic
Computer Applications – Contracted Training
Computer Applications
Computer Applications – Advanced
Computer Applications & Programming – Traineeship
Computer Applications Telesales P/T
Computer Applications Windows
Computer Applications via Multi Media
Computer Business Skills
Computer Network Management & Maintenance
Computer Skills – Introduction
Computer Technology/Basic 35mm Photography
Computer Technology & Industrial automation
Computer & Video Skills – CYTP
Computerised Business skills
Computerised Office Procedures
Computerised Office Skills
Computerised Office Systems
Computers - Introduction
Computer Programming
Computing & Information Technology
Construction Operatives
Construction Plant Operating
Construction Skills
Construction Multi-skills Athlone
Construction plant Operating
Construction Skills
Construction/Stone Building

D

Data Communications
Desk Top Publishing
Digital Media
Domestic Appliance Servicing
Donegal Ancestry Computer Course
Draughting
Draughting – Building Services
Draughting – CAD
Draughting – Traineeship

E

Electronics
Electronics & Computing Systems
Electronic Assembly
Electronic Mechanical Service Engineer
Electronic Office
Electronic Office Systems Maintenance

Electronic Servicing
Electronic Servicing – Foundation
Electronics – Industrial
Engineering – Multi Skills
Engineering Production Operatives
Engineering Skills
Enterprise & Business Skills
Equestrian

F

Fashion – Cutting and Technical Skills
Freight Forwarding – Traineeship
Food Technology
Fork Truck Driving
Fork Truck

G

General Engineering for Operatives
Glasnevin Heritage
Glass Reinforced Plastics
Graphics & Desktop Publishing

H

Hairdressing
Heavy Goods Vehicle
Horticulture

I

Industrial Automation
Industrial Automation Mantenance
Industrial Automation – Traineeship
Industrial Electronics
Industrial Sewing
Information Technology
Injection Moulding Setters
Injection Moulding Technician
Instrumentation
Insurance Broker – Traineeship
Interior Design
Internet Service Support
Introductory Electronics
Introduction to Office & Computer Skills x 2
Irish Hardy Nursery Stock Association – Traineeship

J

Jet Technology – Traineeship
Jewlery Production Skills
Jobs Club

K

Keyboard/Computer Skills

Visit FÁS website at http://www.fas.ie
for information on:

Services to Job-Seekers	Services to Business	Services to Community	FÁS Allowances	Job Vacancies

Announcement!

FÁS Target Irish Living Abroad in Jobs Awareness Campaign

Sites Index

A - B - C - D - E - F - G - H - I - J - K - L - M - N - O - P - Q - R - S - T - U - V - W - X - Y - Z

FÁS - Training & Employment Authority (Ireland)
P.O. Box 456, 27-33 Upper Baggot Street, Dublin 4. Ireland
Telephone: 353 1 6070500   Fax: 353 1 6070600

L

Light Production Assembly
Logistics & Distribution Traineeship

M

Machine Tool Operating
Machine Tool Operating – Traineeship
Manual Arc Gas Operating
Marketing for Travel & Tourism Programme
Material Management Training Traineeship
Media Techniques
Micro Computer Maintenance
Maintenance – Automated Factory Control Systems
Motorcycle Mechanic
Multi-Media Production
Multi-Skills for LTU – Contracted Training

O

Office Procedures
Office Technology Applications
Open Door

P

PC Maintenance & Networks
Pharmacy Sales

Practice Firm (Start your own Business)
Pre-Apprenticeship
Precision Engineering – Traineeship
Preparatory Training
Production Skills

Q

Quality Assurance

R

Resource Based Learning
Retail Sales
Retail Sales – Traineeship
Return to Work

S

Sales Assistant
Sales & Marketing
Sales & Marketing – Traineeship
Sales Assistant – Traineeship
Sales Training & Marketing
Sales Representative
Security Officer
Sewing Machine Operating
Sewing Machinist
Sign Writing
Skills Foundation
Software Engineering
Software Support

Stores & Stock Control
Stores Material Control
Supervisory Management

T

Tele-Marketing Skills

V

Video Production

W

Warehousing, Transportation & Distribution
Web Page Design
Welding
Welding – Basic
Welding – Advanced
Welding – Advanced Pipe
Welding and Fabrication – Traineeship
Welding & Fabrication
Welding, Fabrication & Glasswork
Welding – Manual Arc and Gas
Wood Finishing C & G
Word Processing/Business Administration

OPPORTUNITIES 2000
Attend Ireland's biggest careers exhibition organised by FÁS in early February in the RDS, Dublin.

203

FÁS OFFICES AND TRAINING CENTRES

FÁS Head Office: 27/33 Upper Baggot Street, Dublin 4
Phone: 01-6070500   Fax: 01-6070600

FÁS provides its services on a regional and local basis. FÁS is divided into 10 regions as outlined below.

Regions	Regional Offices	Phone Number	Fax Number
DUBLIN NORTH (Dublin 1, 2, 3, 4, (50% 5, 7, 8, (80%) 9, 11, 13, 15, 17)	FÁS Regional Office Baldoyle Industrial Estate Baldoyle, Dublin 14	(01) 8167400	(01) 8167401
DUBLIN SOUTH & WICKLOW (Dublin 6, 14, 16, 18 and part of 4. Borough of Dun Laoghaire/Rathdrum All of Wicklow)	FÁS Regional Office Wyattville Road Loughlinstown Co. Dublin	(01) 2043600	(01) 2821168
DUBLIN WEST AND KILDARE (Dublin 10, 12, 20, 22, 24 and part of 8. All of Co. Kildare)	FÁS Regional Office Ballyfermot Hill Ballyfermot, Dublin 10	(01) 6055900	(01) 6055960
MIDLANDS (Laois, Longford, Offaly, Roscommon, Westmeath)	FÁS Regional Office Barrycastle Athlone Co. Westmeath	(0902) 74481	(0902) 74795
MID-WEST (Clare, Limerick, Tipperary North)	FÁS Regional Office Industrial Estate Raheen, Limerick	(061) 487900	(061) 301992
NORTH EAST (Cavan, Louth, Meath, Monaghan)	FÁS Regional Office Industrial Estate Coes Road Dundalk, Co. Louth	(042) 9355700	(042) 9355777
NORTH WEST (Donegal, Leitrim, Sligo)	FÁS Regional Office Ballytivan Sligo	(071) 61121	(071) 69506
SOUTH EAST (Carlow, Kilkenny, Tiperary South, Waterford, Wexford)	FÁS Regional Office Industrial Park Cork Road Waterford	(051) 301500	(051) 301512
SOUTH WEST (Cork, Kerry)	FÁS Regional Office Rossa Avenue Bishopstown, Cork	(021) 856200	(021) 544291
WEST (Galway, Mayo)	FÁS Regional Office Island House Cathedral Square, Galway	(091) 567165	(091) 562718

N.B. There are 57 FÁS Employment Offices and 20 Training Centres nationwide for personal callers.

Coláiste Dhúlaigh

Open Day - Friday 28th January 2000

• Advertising • Animation • Architecture • Art • Business • CAD • Communications •
• Computer Science • Electronics • Engineering • European Languages and Computer Applications •
• Graphic Design • Interior Design • International Teleservices • Journalism • Leisure • Marketing •
• Media • Medical Laboratory Science • Multimedia • Outdoor Adventure Management • Secretarial •
• Social Studies • Software Systems for Business • Theatre • Tourism •

PLC COURSES

Barryscourt Road, Dublin 17 Telephone: 847 4399 Fax: 847 4294
Email: info@cdc.cdvec.ie Web: www.colaistedhulaigh.cdvec.ie

PLC Courses are assisted by the European Social Fund   City of Dublin Vocational Education Committee

Crumlin College
Pearse College
St. Kevin's College

POST LEAVING CERTIFICATE AND FURTHER EDUCATION COURSES 1999/2000

Crumlin College, Crumlin Road, Dublin 12
Phone: 454 0662 Fax: 453 8855 E=mail: enrol@crumlin-college.cdvec.ie

- Computer Programming, Computer Networks & Software Systems
- Computer Applications, Advanced Computer Applications
- Accounting & Computer Applications, Accounting Technician
- Secretarial & Computers, Secretarial & Reception
- International Teleservices, Tourism, Reception & Office Skills

- Business Administration with Languages
- Fashion Buying & Merchandising, Visual Merchandising
- Advertising & Graphic Design, Design in Multimedia Computing
- Hotel, Catering & Tourism, Floristry & Interior landscaping
- Sports Therapy, Beauty Therapy
- Hairdressing & Cosmetic Studies
- Selling & Sales Management

Pearse College, Clogher Road, Dublin 12
Phone: 453 6661 Fax: 454 1060 E=mail: information@pearse.cdvec.ie

- Amenity Horticulture
- Architectural Draughting
- Bar Management/Business Studies
- Back to Your Future/Computer Work Skills
- Diploma in International Business & Computer Studies
- Holistic Health Studies

- Languages for Tourism & Business
- Media Production Skills
- Retail Management & Business Studies
- Eco Business Skills/The Green Entrepreneur
- Tobar na nOidhreachta/Heritage, Business & Computer Skills

St. Kevin's College, Clogher Road, Dublin 12
Phone: 453 6397 Fax: 473 0868 E=mail: info@stkevins.cdvec.ie

- Adventure Leadership Skills
- Adventure Sports Diploma
- Laboratory Science
- Food Science (Dietetics Link)
- Quality Assurance
- Media Production Diploma

- Photography
- Applied Art & Design
- Electronic & Mechanical Engineering
- Apprenticeship Foundation (Building or Engineering Trades)

CRUMLIN CAMPUS OPEN DAY: Wednesday, 2nd February 2000 (12-6 pm)

ENROLMENT & REGISTRATION:
Applications for all Courses can be made directly to the Admissions Office in all three Colleges from **March–September 2000**

City of Dublin Vocational Education Committee

POST LEAVING CERTIFICATE COURSES [PLCs]

Race horse trainer or receptionist?

Whether you want to be a racehorse trainer or a receptionist there is probably a PLC for you. A recent survey indicated that 80% of PLC graduates got employment and others were offered college places without having the necessary points.
This section of Student Yearbook has produced Ireland's most comprehensive cross reference grid on PLC'S. The grid follows the classification system used in our table of contents, so you can compare both when using either section. It will provide you with an idea of the range of courses available and their career path.

Your Personal Checklist for a PLC

Here are ten things to ask when you find a PLC that sounds like it might interest you...

1. Is the course running this year and is it planned to run it next year?
2. What level of award is given and by whom?
3. Do any IT's give points for the course, or are there links with colleges or industry?
4. Where have graduates of this course found work or gone for further study?
5. What is the closing date for applications?
6. Are there any special entry requirements: interview, portfolio, audition, fitness test, sports reference etc.?
7. What are the costs involved: course, equipment, materials, outings etc.?
8. Where will the work experience take place?
9. Have they a list of accommodation available locally?
10. Is the course eligible for a grant and how and where do you apply?

BRAY INSTITUTE OF FURTHER EDUCATION

POST LEAVING CERTIFICATE COURSES 1999/2000

DEPT. OF SECRETARIAL STUDIES

- **S1** Court Reporter/Stenography/Realtime Reporting
- **S2** Advanced Secretarial Course (for the Executive Personal Assistant)
- **S3** Teacher's Diploma in Typewriting
- **S4** Secretarial and European Studies with Modern Languages – (Italian, Spanish, German, French)
- **S5** Legal Secretary
- **S6** Secretarial Studies & Information Technology
- **S7** Medical Secretary

DEPT. OF TELESERVICES

- **T1** International Teleservices with Modern Languages – 2 year Advanced Cert.
- **T2** English Language Teleservices/Call centre Operations

DEPT. OF INFORMATION TECHNOLOGY

- **N1** Information Technology – Computer Applications
- **N2** Programming & Systems Support 2 year Advanced Cert. (Level 3)

DEPT. OF APPLIED SCIENCE

- **C1** Computer Aided Design
- **C2** Advanced Computer Aided Design
- **C3** Engineering and Computer Aided Design
- **C4** Electronics and Computer Aided Design

DEPT. OF MEDIA AND DRAMA STUDIES

- **M1** Performing Arts – Drama
- **M2** T.V. and Video Production
- **M3** Sound Engineering and Electronics
- **M4** Photography and Journalism

DEPT. OF ARTS AND CERAMICS

- **A1** Art Portfolio Preparation
- **A2** Art/Ceramic Portfolio Preparation
- **A3** Ceramic Craft Design

DEPT. OF DESIGN

- **D1** Computerised Graphic Design
- **D2** Advanced Computerised Graphic Design
- **D3** Fashion Design and Portfolio Preparation
- **D4** Advanced Fashion Design
- **D5** Interior Design — Rhodec Assoc. Dip
- **D6** Interior Design – Rhodec Int. Dip
- **D7** Furniture Design & Cabinet Making
- **D8** Craft Design

DEPT. OF TOURISM AND LEISURE

- **L1** Tourism, Reception & Reservation Studies
- **L2** Tourism and Enterprise Development
- **L3** Sport and Recreation Studies
- **L4** Sport and Leisure Management
- **L5** Business & Tourism Studies

DEPT. OF COMMUNITY AND HEALTH CARE

- **H1** Pre Nursing Studies
- **H2** Childcare Studies
- **H3** Community and Social Care
- **H4** Community and Health Care
- **H5** NNEB Dip. in Child Care
- **H6** Holistic Health Studies
- **H7** Nurses Aide
- **H8** Animal Care

DEPT. OF BUS.STUDIES & MGMT. SYSTEMS

- **J1** Business Studies & Computer Systems
- **J2** Diploma in Internat. Trade & Marketing
- **J3** Marketing & Business Administration
- **J4** Accounting Technician
- **J5** Computers, Work Skills & Teleservices (for adults)

REPEAT LEAVING CERTIFICATE

- **R1** Choice of 17 subjects at Higher Level

DEGREE PROGRAMMES

B.A. or B.Sc. (Honours) Open University Degrees in Social Science, Social Science with Psychology Social Science with Social policy Social Science with health and social Care

---

Co. Wicklow Vocational Education Committee

ALL COURSES CERTIFIED BY N.C.V.A. AND RELEVANT PROFESSIONAL BODIES

Enquiries and Application Forms: BRAY SENIOR COLLEGE, NOVARA AVENUE, BRAY, CO. WICKLOW.

TEL: (01) 286 6233   (01) 282 9668   (01) 282 8721

Assisted by the European Social Fund

What are PLCs?

Post Leaving Certificate Courses are full time courses that last one or two years. They are a mixture of hands on practical vocational skills and work experience. They give qualifications in themselves and can lead on to further qualification and training.

Where are they run?

They are run in large Secondary, Vocational or Community schools throughout the country. Many of the schools run only PLCs and have a national and international reputation for their courses.

What areas do they cover?

PLCs cover a huge variety of areas, from Acting to Veterinary Nursing, from Accounting to Visual Studies. While some of these lead directly to qualifications for employment many do not and there has been a huge duplication of courses without any regard as to whether there are jobs in these areas or whether a PLC would be a sufficient qualification.

You can break it down as follows:

- Direct Qualifications for Employment: Once you have this qualification you are all set to get your job. Examples are Secretarial, Childcare, Hotel and Catering, Nursery Nursing, Montessori and Telesales.

- Indirect Qualifications for Employment: These courses don't give you the actual qualifications you need to get working; they get you started in the right direction. Many people don't finish these courses because they start work or begin an apprenticeship while doing them. Examples are Engineering, Construction Studies, Hairdressing and Cosmetic Studies.

- Direct Qualifications for Further Study: These are courses that prepare you directly for undertaking further study provided you meet the requirements. Examples are Portfolio Preparation for Art Colleges, Pre-Nursing Studies or Health Science, Preliminary Engineering Studies and Information Technology. In these courses you get a good introduction to what is involved in the courses you are considering and can discover without the longer term commitment whether these courses are for you or not.

- Indirect Qualifications for Further Study or Work: These courses give you an idea and appreciation of what work and study would be like in a particular area. But you will need a lot more determination, work, study and effort to get work and to succeed in these areas. Examples are Journalism, Broadcasting, Popular Music Performance, Acting, Public Relations and Soccer.

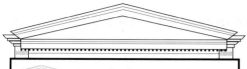

THE ABC OF PLCs

- Below is a check list of PLCs available country-wide. For more detailed information you should contact the individual colleges for details of closing dates, special entry requirements, course content and availability. You could also contact the Vocational Education Committee (VEC) of the relevant counties.

- The headings used follow the career categories used earlier in the Yearbook and are general e.g. "Hotel" covers courses like the Catering course in Athy Senior College, Kildare. While "Computers" appears under a separate heading below they also form part of various other courses e.g. Business Studies and Engineering.

- In addition to these courses there are many other Secretarial and Computer courses available in local schools.

- All PLCs offered are open to applicants nationwide.

COURSE / COLLEGE	Ballsbridge College, Dublin 4 (01-6684806)	Ballyfermot Senior College, D. 10 (01-6269421)	Kylemore College, (01-6265901)	St. Kevin's College, Clogher Rd., D. 12 (01-4536397)	Coláiste Dhulaigh, Dublin 5 (01-8474399)	Crumlin College, Dublin 12 (01-4540662)	Finglas (Coláiste Íde), Dublin 11 (01-8342333)	Inchicore Vocational School, Dublin 8 (01-4535358)	St. Peters, Killester, Dublin 5 (01-8336990)	Liberties Vocational School, Dublin 8 (01-4540082)	Marino College, D. 3 (01-8334201)	Pearse College, Dublin 12 (01-4536661)	Rathmines Senior College, Dublin 6 (01-4975334)	Ringsend Technical Institute, Dublin 4 (01-6684498)	Whitehall (Plunket College), D. 9 (01-8371689)	Whitehall House Senior College (01-8376011)	Deansrath College (01-4574114)	Dundrum College (01-2982340)
COUNTY	Dublin City	Dublin City	Dublin City	Dublin City	Dublin City	Dublin City	Dublin City	Dublin City	Dublin City	Dublin City	Dublin City	Dublin City	Dublin City	Dublin City	Dublin City	Dublin City	Co. Dublin	Co. Dublin
Animals/Horticulture							●		●				●		●			●
Art/Design/Crafts/Portfolio		●		●	●	●	●	●							●			●
Computers/Information Technology	●	●		●	●	●	●	●		●			●	●	●	●	●	●
Constr./Trades/Professional (e.g. Architecture/Auctioneering)	●			●	●		●						●		●			●
Engineering/Electronics		●	●	●	●		●		●					●	●			●
Entertainment/Leisure/Culture/Sport			●	●	●	●	●	●		●	●							●
Fashion/Beauty Care/Hairdressing						●	●											
Hotel/Catering/Tourism		●		●	●	●	●		●	●	●					●	●	●
Media/Print Management/Communications		●		●	●						●	●	●	●		●		
Medical/Nursing/Health Science		●		●		●		●	●		●	●				●		
Office/Business/Secretarial/Accounts	●	●		●	●	●	●	●	●		●	●	●			●	●	●
Sales/Marketing/Advertising/P.R./Teleservices	●	●		●	●	●						●	●			●		
Science/Environmental			●	●		●	●	●	●					●				
Security/Legal							●				●		●	●	●			
Social/Community/Childcare		●			●		●	●	●								●	●
Transport/Vehicle Maintenance			●			●		●							●			

210

CONTINUED ON P. 214

Dun Laoghaire Inst. of Further Education (01-2809676)	Co. Dublin
St. Tiernans Community School (01-2953224)	Co. Dublin
Stillorgan Senior College (01-2880704)	Co. Dublin
Collinstown Park Community College (01-4572300)	Co. Dublin
Grange Community College (01-8471422)	Co. Dublin
Greendale Community College (01-8322735)	Co. Dublin
Riversdale Community College (01-8201488)	Co. Dublin
College of Commerce, Dundrum (01-2985412)	Co. Dublin
Greenhills College (01-4507779)	Co. Dublin
Muinebheag Vocational School (0503-21335)	Co. Carlow
Hacketstown Vocational School (0508-71198)	Co. Carlow
Carlow Vocational School (0503-31187)	Co. Carlow
College of Further Studies (049-32633)	Co. Cavan
Ennis Community College (065-29432)	Co. Clare
Cobh Vocational School (021-811325)	Co. Cork
Cork College of Commerce (021-270777)	Cork City
MacSwiney Community College (021-397740)	Cork City
Midleton, St. Colmans (021-631696)	Co. Cork
St. John's Central College, (021-276410)	Cork City
Scoil Stiofain Naofa, (021-961020)	Cork City
Ballyshannon Vocational School (072-51276)	Co. Donegal
Letterkenny Vocational School (074-21047)	Co. Donegal
Athenry Vocational School (091-44159)	Co. Galway
Community College, Móinín na gCiseach (091-755464)	Co. Galway
Fr. Griffin Road, Vocational School (091-581342)	Co. Galway
St. Michael's Ballinasloe (0905-42165)	Co. Galway
Killarney Community College (064-32164)	Co. Kerry
Listowel Community College (068-21023)	Co. Kerry
Tralee Community College (066-712174)	Co. Kerry
Killorglin Community College	Co. Kerry
St. Conleths, Newbridge (045-431417)	Co. Kildare
St. Patricks College Naas (045-897885)	Co. Kildare
Kildare College of Further Studies (045-52187)	Co. Kildare
Grennan College, Thomastown (056-24112)	Co. Kilkenny
Ormond College (056-22108)	Co. Kilkenny
Abbeyleix Further Education Centre	Co. Laois
Mountmellick F.E.C.	Co. Laois

Post Leaving
Courses for 1999/2000

- Personal Satisfaction and Development: These courses don't necessarily lead towards any job or area of study, but instead focus on personal growth and development. Examples are Skills and Personal Competency, General Studies, Local History or Psychology. These can all help to promote personal growth and development and lead on to work, further study or greater happiness.

What qualifications do you get?
The courses offer a variety of awards. The most common and one that is most recognised in Ireland is the NCVA (National Council for Vocational Awards). Normally a PLC student will get a Level 2 award.

Who recognises them?
This depends on the areas of study and the level of qualifications you have achieved. NCVA qualifications are recognised throughout Ireland. Other qualifications are recognised by the differing bodies that regulate the areas concerned. If you have any doubts about the qualifications and courses on offer, talk to the college or someone who would employ people in that area of work.

NCVA
NCVA, the National Council for Vocational Awards, plays an important role in certifying courses. The Council helps streamline the awards system and bring them in line with international developments. Normally P.L.C. students will get a LEVEL 2 award. An award at National Vocational Certificate Level 2 is made to a candidate who reaches required standard in a minimum of 8 modules, as follows:

5 Vocational modules (including mandatory and elective modules)

2 General Studies Module (one of which must be Communications)

1 Preparation for Work Work Experience module.

Candidates who reach the required standard in one or more modules, but who do not meet the criteria for an award will qualify for an NCVA Record of Achievement. Thus, a candidate may accumulate credits towards an award over time.

Modules are graded as:

Pass	50% – 64%
Merit	65% – 9%
Distinction	80% – 100%

Awards will be granted in the following areas:

1. Art, Craft and Design
2. Business and Administration
3. Science, Technology and Natural Resources.
4. Services, Leisure and Tourism.
5. Communications, Performing Arts and General Studies.

LIBERTIES

COLLEGE

The College in the City

General course areas

- Performance
- Counselling
- Media Production
- Tourism
- Art-Craft-Design
- Childcare
- Social Studies
- Community Care
- Montessori Education
- Nursery Nursing

Open Day
22nd March
2000
1-5pm

LIBERTIES COLLEGE
Opposite St. Patrick's Cathedral and
close to the City Centre

Admissions, Liberties College,
Bull Alley Street, Dublin 8
Tel; 01 454 0044, Fax; 01 454 6348
E-mail; office@liberties.cdvec.ie

213

THE ABC OF PLCS

- Below is a check list of PLCs available country-wide. For more detailed information you should contact the individual colleges for details of closing dates, special entry requirements, course content and availability. You could also contact the Vocational Education Committee (VEC) of the relevant counties.

- The headings used follow the career categories used earlier in the Yearbook and are general e.g. "Animal" covers courses like the Equestrian course in Dunshaughlin Community College, Meath. While "Computers" appears under a separate heading below they also form part of various other courses e.g. Business Studies and Engineering.

- In addition to these courses there are many other Secretarial and Computer courses available in local schools.

- All PLC's offered are open to applicants nationwide.

COLLEGE	Heywood Community School (0502-33333)	Portlaoise Vocational School (0502-21480)	Vocational School, Drumshambo (078-41085)	Cappaghmore Voc. Sch. (061-381272)	Croom (061-397700)	Drumcollogher Community College (063-83121)	Limerick Senior College (061-414344)	Newcastle West Vocational School (069-62205)	Cappamore Voc. School (061-38172)	Lanesboro Comm. College (043-21139)	Longford Vocational School (043-45455)	Ardscoil Padraig, Granard (043-86209)	VS Ballymahon (0902-32211)	Drogheda College of Further Education (041-37105)	Dundalk O'Fiaich College (042-31398)	Ballina Moyne College (096-21472)	Castlebar College of Further Education (094-23134)
COUNTY	Co. Laois	Co. Laois	Co. Leitrim	Co. Limerick	Co. Limerick	Co. Limerick	Co. Limerick	Co. Limerick	Co. Limerick	Co. Longford	Co. Longford	Co. Longford	Co. Longford	Co. Louth	Co. Louth	Co. Mayo	Co. Mayo
Animals/Horticulture	●	●	●		●	●											
Art/Design/Crafts/Portfolio		●					●	●						●	●	●	
Computers/Information Technology	●	●					●			●	●	●	●	●	●	●	●
Construction/Trades/Professional (e.g. Architecture)		●		●		●								●			
Engineering/Electronics		●									●			●	●		
Entertainment/Leisure/Culture/Sport		●	●		●												
Fashion/Beauty Care/Hairdressing		●					●		●								
Hotel/Catering/Tourism		●					●							●	●	●	
Media/Print Management/Communications																	
Medical/Nursing/Health Science	●				●		●							●	●		
Office/Business/Secretarial/Accounts	●	●	●	●			●	●	●	●	●	●	●	●	●	●	●
Sales/Marketing/Advertising/P.R./Teleservices		●					●							●	●		
Science/Environmental							●										
Security/Legal		●															
Social/Community/Childcare	●	●		●	●		●		●							●	●
Transport/Vehicle Maintenance														●			

County	Institution	1	2	3	4	5	6	7	8	9	10	11	12	13
Co. Mayo	Crossmolina Vocational School (096-31236)			•	•			•		•				
Co. Mayo	St. Louis Community School, Kiltimagh (094-81228)													
Co. Mayo	Westport Vocational School (098-25241)	•	•	•			•	•	•		•			
Co. Mayo	Belmullet St. Brendan's (097-81437)			•										
Co. Mayo	Navan Community College (046-28915)			•				•		•				
Co. Meath	Nobber Vocational School (046-52177)						•		•					
Co. Monaghan	M.I.F.E.T. (047-84900)	•	•	•		•	•	•	•	•	•			•
Co. Monaghan	Castleblaney (042-40066)	•	•									•		
Co. Offaly	Edenderry Oaklands College (0405-31573)													
Co. Offaly	St. Rynagh's, Banagher			•										
Co. Roscommon	Roscommon Vocational School (0903-26670)												•	
Co. Sligo	Municipal Tech. Inst., Ballinode (071-45480)				•									
Co. Tipperary	Cappawhite Vocational School (062-75225)	•									•			•
Co. Tipperary	Carrick-on-Suir Vocational School (051-40131)		•	•	•			•		•	•	•		•
Co. Tipperary	Clonmel, Central Technical Institute (052-21450)	•	•											
Co. Tipperary	Thurles Vocational School (0504-21734)													•
Co. Tipperary	St. Joseph's, Newport (061-378262)	•												
Co. Tipperary	St. Sheelan, Templemore (0504-31922)		•											
Co. Tipperary	St. Albes, Tipperary Town (062-51905)			•	•			•			•			•
Co. Tipperary	Scoil Ruain, Killenaule. (052-56332)			•	•			•			•			•
Co. Tipperary	Coláiste Dun Iascaigh, Cahir (052- 42905)		•	•		•								
Co. Waterford	Central Technical Institute (051-874053)	•	•		•	•	•	•	•	•	•	•	•	
Co. Waterford	Dungarvan Technical College (058-41184)					•								
Co. Westmeath	Athlone Community College (0902-72640)	•			•		•	•						
Co. Westmeath	Castle Pollard Vocational School (044-61163)				•		•							
Co. Westmeath	Killucan Vocational School (044-74107)				•	•	•							
Co. Westmeath	Moate Vocational School (0902-81178)				•									
Co. Westmeath	Mullingar Vocational School (044-40786)	•	•					•	•	•	•			•
Co. Westmeath	St. Josephs College, Athlone (0902-92383)									•				
Co. Wexford	Adamstown Vocational School (054-40525)			•			•		•	•	•		•	
Co. Wexford	Enniscorthy Vocational College (054-34185)	•		•	•	•	•	•		•	•	•		•
Co. Wexford	Gorey Community School (055-21000)													
Co. Wexford	New Ross Vocational School (051-21278)													
Co. Wicklow	Arklow Community College (0402-32149)		•			•		•	•	•	•	•		•
Co. Wicklow	Bray, Senior College (01-2866233)	•												
Co. Wicklow	Carnew Vocational School (055-26378)	•	•									•	•	
Co. Wicklow	Abbey Community College, Wicklow (0404-647567)									•	•			

INCHICORE COLLEGE OF FURTHER EDUCATION

CDVEC

EMMET ROAD, DUBLIN 8

The Centre for Post Leaving
Continuing Second Chance VTOS
and Further Education

PATHWAYS TO HIGHER EDUCATION

In September 1998 over eighty students from Inchicore continued onto Universities in Ireland and Great Britain to complete degree programmes. Many students were given time credit (up to two years) in some cases for the two years spent at Inchicore.

M.Sc. (Distance Learning)
SOCIOLOGY OF SPORTS
& SPORTS MANAGEMENT
(Awarded by University of Leicester)

Students with NCVA Level 2 Certificates qualify for admissions to all institutes of Technology in Ireland through the Links Programme.

Some Institutes of Technology in Ireland offer credit of one or two years for graduates with an appropriate HND.

further details

Telephone: 4535358 - 4533330

Fax: 4545494

e-mail: enquiries@inchicore.cdvec.ie
or from your Guidance Counsellor

Opportunities for Unemployed People

Post-Leaving Certificate

If you are 21 years of age or over and have been on unemployment register for six months you may continue to draw social welfare benefits while you attend a course.

COURSES AVAILABLE

SESSION 1999/2000

Post-Leaving Certificate Courses

Leisure & Recreation Management
Higher National Diploma BTEC HND
Leisure & Recreation - Sports Coaching Awards/Golf Management
Leisure & Recreation - Sport & Disability Studies BTEC HND
Child Care/Nursery Nurse - Diploma NNEB
Child Care - Pre-Nursing
Child Care - Montessori
Social Studies - Higher National Diploma BTEC HND
Care of the Elderly in the Community
Pre-Accountancy - Accounting Technician BTEC HND
Administration & Legal Studies BTEC HND
Computer Studies/Computer Application (HND Option)
Tourism - Higher National Diploma BTEC HND
Modern Languages with Business Skills
Theatre Studies - Performance (Acting or Dance)
Theatre Studies - Directing
Theatre Studies - Stage Craft, Lighting & Sound Production, Set Construction
Arts Administration
Laboratory Techniques & Technical Studies
Skill & Personal Competency
Art & Design
Display
Costume Wardrobe & Construction
Insurance
Computer Science Technology

All Courses offer NCVA Level 2 Awards

ENTRY REQUIREMENTS

1. Irish Leaving Certificate - 5 passes.
2. Mature Students, i.e., 20 years of age and older, who do not possess the number of passes in the Leaving Certificate
3. Others who satisfy the Course Director that he/she will benefit from the course.

MONAGHAN INSTITUTE OF FURTHER EDUCATION & TRAINING

PLC COURSES - 1999/2000

(assisted by the European Social Fund)

1. BUSINESS ADMINISTRATION
(NCVA, Level 2)
2. SECRETARIAL (NCVA, Level 2)
3. LEGAL SECRETARIAL (NCVA, Level 2)
4. INTERNATIONAL TELESERVICES
(NCVA, Level 3)
5. CALL CENTRE OPERATIONS
(NCVA, Level 2)
6. NURSING STUDIES Full & Part-time
(NCVA, Level 2)
7. NURSERY NURSING
(NNEB Diploma, Level 3)
8. CHILDCARE Full & Part-time
(NCVA, Level 2)
9. COMMUNITY CARE Full & Part-time
(NCVA, Level 2)
10. INFORMATION TECHNOLOGY
(NCVA, Level 2)
11. INFORMATION PROCESSING
(NCVA, Level 2)
12. NETWORKS & SOFTWARE SYSTEMS
(NCVA, Level 3)
13. HOTEL AND CATERING
(CERT/NCVA, Level 2)
14. SPORT & RECREATION
(NCVA, Level 2)
15. LEISURE & TOURISM
(BTEC GNVQ, Level 3)
16. TOURISM (CERT/NCVA, Level 2)
17. OUTDOOR RECREATION
(NCVA, Level 2)
18. ART, CRAFT & DESIGN (NCVA, Level 2)
19. PERFORMING ARTS (NCVA, Level 2)
20. MEDIA PRODUCTION (NCVA, Level 2)
21. FURNITURE DESIGN (NCVA, Level 2)

Apply:
**Director, Monaghan Institute of Further
Education & Training,
Armagh Road, MONAGHAN.**
Tel: (047) 84900 / 81021 / 81833
Fax: (047) 81564 / 83080 / 82787

**MIFET IS A CO. MONAGHAN
VEC INITIATIVE FOR THE
THIRD MILLENNIUM**

Can you go on for further study?

Some courses prepare you directly for further study (Art, Nursing, Engineering etc.) while other courses have links with Institutes of Technology or the Dublin Institute of Technology. The DIT has a formal link with the colleges of the City of Dublin VEC. In the form of enhanced points for those who have done a relevant PLC here a distinction will get you 60 additional points, a merit 50, a credit 40 and a pass 30.

There are less formal links with many of the Institutes of Technology depending on the relevance of the PLC to the area you wish to study. Contact the college offering the PLC, the NCVA or the Institute of Technology offering the follow on course for details.

Many PLC courses also have links with UK colleges and universities and it may well be possible to transfer on to a degree level course there.

What are the costs? Are there any grants?

There are no fees for PLC courses other than registration. Students on PLC courses will be eligible for grants subject to means testing.

Check with your Local Authority or VEC for further details.

How do I apply?

At present there is no centralised applications procedure for PLC's like the CAO, so you must apply to each college individually. There is no standard closing date either, so you must check with the college concerned. Some courses fill up quickly and early application is advisable; others only start filling up in September. Some colleges will interview all applications and ask for portfolios, auditions or records of achievement and references in sport depending on the course applied for.

The best advice is to check early with the colleges that offer the courses you are interested in.

Where can I find out more?

Start by looking at the detailed listings in this article. Contact the colleges of your choice and ask them to send prospectuses.

Your local VEC (Vocational Education Committee - they run most of the Community Colleges and Vocational Schools) will have details of courses offered in your area (see index).

The Qualifax computer programme lists all the PLCs available and you can search it for the particular areas you are interested in. Finally, of course, you have the "fount of all wicdom" in your Guidance Counsellor.

Going Places...

...get your PLC prospectus from Coláiste Íde at 834 2333

or contact your Guidance Counsellor

School of Art & Fashion
- Portfolio Preparation in Art & Design
- Art & Design II
- Fashion & Textile Design

School of Business Studies
- Accounting Technician
- Certificate in Materials Management
- Diploma in International Trade
- Human Resource Management
- Secretarial & Computer Studies

School of Catering
- Delicatessen Management
- Hotel, Catering & Tourism (cert)
- Hotel & Catering (cert)

School of Computing
- Computers Applications
- Computer Management
- Information Technology - Programming
- Computer Programming

School of Sports
- Association Football
- Sports & Leisure

School of Technology & Science
- Architectural Technology & CAD
- Electronic and Electrical Technology
- Pharmaceutical Technician

School of Teleservices & Tourism
- Teleservices
- Travel Agents Certificate - ABTA
- Travel & Tourism - IATA/UFTAA

COLÁISTE ÍDE
COLLEGE OF FURTHER EDUCATION

**Coláiste Íde Senior College Cardiffsbridge Road,
Finglas West, Dublin 11.
Tel: 834 2333 - 834 2450 Fax: 834 7242**

Limerick Senior College student, Irene Caulfield (left), worked in a museum called MuseumsDore in Cloppenbury, Germany. Pictured here, working on the museum's own newspaper, Irene explains how her 17 weeks work placement "was both a challenging and positive experience" for her. Irene was given the opportunity to work in every area of the museum, from administrative work in the office to carrying out guided tours.

THIRD LEVEL EDUCATION

OVER ONE THIRD OF STUDENTS DROP OUT OF COLLEGES

Thirty seven per cent of students at several of the Institutes of Technology dropped out during or at the end of their first year, a new study has found.

The survey was carried out through a questionnaire of students who had enrolled for the first time in 1996-97. It found the main reasons for dropping out were

1. Low Leaving Certificate exam grades;
2. Unclear career aspirations;
3. Lack of information on courses and career options;
4. Choosing unsuitable courses;
5. Difficulties with some or all all of the subjects taken;
6. Financial and work-related problems.

Specific problems included the amount of part-time work the students did. Nearly two-thirds of those who dropped out were working over 11 hours per week, compared to under half of those who completed first year.

Almost half the students who left said the main reason was that they had chosen the wrong course and wanted to follow a different career.

Few adults expect the average school leaver to be absolutely certain about their college or course choice. As can be seen from the study, pupils do change their minds. It is very difficult for a seventeen or eighteen year old to know with certainty that they will like or be suitable for a course.

However, there are certain steps which one can take to help to clarify such decisions thus making good choices more likely.

Anthony Creevy
All Hallows graduate

Twenty-six years old Anthony Creevy is currently pursuing two careers - one in teaching, the other in politics.

After his Leaving Cert in The Donahies Community College in Donaghmede in Dublin in 1990, Anthony started a degree in Applied Science at Kevin St, but left after a month. He then enrolled for a certificate in Social Studies at Coláiste Dhulaigh, Coolock, which he really enjoyed.

There were elements of theology on the course, so he decided to take it further with a BA in Theology and Psychology at All Hallows College in Drumcondra.

"I had a great time there," he says. "At the time it was in transition from being a seminary to an institute of education. The lecturers were really enthusiastic and classes were small - there were only about 150 pupils in the whole college."

With a Higher Diploma in Education now under his belt as well, Anthony teaches Civic, Social and Political Education, Religion and History at St Kevin's Community College in Clondalkin.

In 1997, he was co-opted on to Dublin Corporation for the Democratic Left party. He ran in the general election of that year, but was unsuccessful. Success finally came his way in 1999 when he won a seat for the Labour Party on Dublin Corporation.

Anthony sees his future in politics. "I really enjoy teaching, but I may not do it forever."

CAO APPLICATION 5 SUCCESSFUL STAGES

Do not be put off by what appears to be a difficult CAO application process. Read the CAO literature and listen to your guidance counsellor. Start by reducing the process to the 5 easy stages explained in this section of the yearbook.

Stage 1 ⮕ *BEFORE YOU APPLY*

Stage 2 ⮕ *THE APPLICATION*

Stage 3 ⮕ *ACKNOWLEDGEMENT OF OFFER*

Stage 4 ⮕ *CHANGE OF MIND*

Stage 5 ⮕ *OFFERS AND ACCEPTANCE OF PLACES*

CAO ON THE WEB

Students can now apply to the CAO on-line. For further information contact NCTE

- By telephone at: 1850 70 40 40
- EMail: cao@ncte.ie
- Internet: http://www.ncte.ie
- CAO webpage: http://indigo.ie/~cao

Check it out particularly for points update.
Final points will be available late October on this site.

American College Dublin

American College Dublin

Our commitment to your Education

- ✔ Recognised degrees with 10 week internship programme
- ✔ Small class groups
- ✔ An enjoyable and challenging experience
- ✔ Practical skills
- ✔ An opportunity to meet people of different nationalities
- ✔ Best of Irish and American educational practice

American College Dublin offers the following validated degrees:

BA in Behavioural Science
Sociology

BA in Psychology (Honours) •
BA in International Tourism

BA in International Business
Management • Marketing

BA in Liberal Arts
English • History • International Relations

National Certificate in Humanities

Applications should be made directly to the College. If you would like a copy of our Prospectus or require further information please contact:

American College Dublin
2 Merrion Square
Dublin 2, Ireland
Tel: +353 1 676 8939
Fax: +353 1 661 4981
Email: degree@amcd.ie
Web: www.amcd.ie

STAGE 1
BEFORE YOU APPLY

You may not fill in your choices for third level courses until December or January of your Leaving Cert. year but the decision process has to begin long before that.

You will have narrowed the careers you favour to one or two areas which seem to match your interests and abilities. The next step is to translate the general career area(s) into a list of courses. Here is a simple guide to help you do this:

- The most important material is contained in the **CAO Handbook**. It is essential that you read it carefully.

- Read the faculty booklets and prospectuses *thoroughly*. Check internet sites.

- Check **QUALIFAX** the most comprehensive computer programme available on Third Level Education.

- Attend *open days / lectures.* Make sure you speak to the college or faculty representatives. Don't be shy! You will find them very helpful and encouraging.

- Talk to *college or university students*. Your school may be able to arrange a meeting with a past pupil.

- Read current newspaper articles on careers e.g. the Education and Living Supplement every Tuesday in the Irish Times.

- Speak to your *guidance counsellor* and those adults who are familiar with relevant and up to date information. Beware of twenty year old anecdotes or hearsay! Colleges have changed enormously since the family sage attended.

- Where possible acquire *relevant work experience* no matter how short the period of time.

- For information on each courses' job prospects read the college's **CAREERS AND APPOINTMENTS** annual report. Your guidance counsellor will have a copy.

Take particular care in choosing specific career oriented courses e.g. medicine or architecture. If in doubt consider:

1. A general course with wide options e.g. Arts or Business Studies.

2. **Defer** (postpone) for a year. Check college policy on this as they vary considerably.

3. A **Post Leaving Cert. Course** especially one with related skills or work experience. Apart from helping you clarify your choice you may also have the benefit of a transfer to an IT with less points than other applicants.

STUDENT YEARBOOK POINTS CALCULATOR

The **Points System** is a crude but fair method of allocating college places *(currently under review)*.
To help you be realistic about your college prospects fill in the charts below. Choose courses in your order of preference.

DEGREE LIST SECTION

	COURSE CODE	COURSE TITLE	POINTS 1999	SPECIFIC REQUIREMENTS
1	GT350	Information Technology		
2	LM051	Computer Systems		
3	LM083	Information Techn. + Comm		
4	LM059	Computer Systems w/French		
5				
6				
7				
8				
9				
10				

DIPLOMA/CERT SECTION

	COURSE CODE	COURSE TITLE	POINTS 1999	SPECIFIC REQUIREMENTS
1				
2				
3				
4				
5				
6				
7				
8				
9				
10				

POINTS SYSTEM FOR YEAR 2000 ENTRY

% Band	Leaving Certificate Grades	Points Scale for Leaving Certificate Higher Level Paper	Points Scale for Leaving Certificate Ordinary Level Paper
90-100	A1	100	60
85-89	A2	90	50
80-84	B1	85	45
75-79	B2	80	40
70-74	B3	75	35
65-69	C1	70	30
60-64	C2	65	25
55-59	C3	60	20
50-54	D1	55	15
45-49	D2	50	10
40-44	D3	45	5

Note: Six subjects only from one sitting of the Leaving Cert. for calculating points total.

University of Limerick awards bonus points for Honours Mathematics. Bonus points also apply to DIT Course FT221 (see Prospectus).
In the case of certain subjects, e.g. Home Economics (General), Alternative Ordinary Level Mathematics, Foundation Level Mathematics or Foundation Level Irish, some HEIs may not award the points shown above. If in any doubt, check with the Admissions Office of the appropriate HEIs.

L.C.V.P. Link Modules:
Institutes of Technology (with the exception of Dublin Institute of Technology) award points as set out below for results in Leaving Certificate Vocational Programme Link Modules, in place of a sixth Leaving Certificate subject.

Result	I.T. Points	University/DIT Points
Distinction	70	50
Merit	50	40
Pass	30	30

Other institutions may award points for Link Modules, but any queries about this should be addressed to the Admissions Office of the appropriate institution(s).

A Department of Education commission is currently reviewing the points scheme. Details of the Commission's findings will be sent to all schools.

IN THE CHART BELOW GIVE A REALISTIC PREDICTION OF YOUR LEAVING CERTIFICATE RESULTS.

	SUBJECT	LEVEL	GRADE	POINTS
1	ENGLISH	H	C1 ✓	70 ✓
2	IRISH	H	C3	60
3	MATHS	H	C1 ✓	70 ✓
4	PHYSICS	H	D1	55
5	APPLIED MATHS	H	C3 ✓	60 ✓
6	BUSINESS	H	B2 ✓	80 ✓
7	FRENCH	H	B3 ✓	75 ✓
8	MUSIC	H	A2 ✓	90 ✓

Total points from your 6 best
Leaving Cert. results in box **445**

Class Leaving Cert   Date 8ᵗʰ Nov. 1999

Name Jonathan Kirby

225

STAGE 2 *THE APPLICATION*

CAO Applications:
No applicant should attempt to complete the Form without first doing three things:

1. Examine carefully the appropriate HEI literature about the courses available, entry requirements, course content, restrictions, etc. There may be many optional subjects available within an HEI.

   (Contact the appropriate institution admissions office if unclear about any points in the HEI literature.)

2. Find out whether fees are payable for the course. The "Free Fee Scheme" may not apply to all courses/applicants.

3. Examine carefully the contents of the CAO Handbook.

Completing application (pages 1 and 2 of Form):
Pages 1 and 2 of the Form are self-explanatory and will normally be sufficient for Republic of Ireland schoolleavers who form the vast majority of the applicants and who are presenting one or more of the examinations named on page 1. (Results of those examinations are obtained by CAO direct from the examining authorities).

Pages 3 and 4 of the Form are designed to cater for applicants whose applications fall into one or more of the special categories mentioned in page 3 of the Form.

CAO Order of Preference:
It is MOST IMPORTANT to state course choices in view of genuine preference and/or career plans. IT IS A MISTAKE to base your choices on your present expectation of examination performance. There is no need to fear that a statement of your genuine order of preference will militate against you. If you are not successful in your first choice this will have no effect on your chances of obtaining a place in one of your lower preferences.

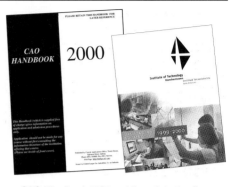

CAO Handbook 2000 and the relevant college prospectuses – essential reading for all students applying to third level colleges.

THE CAO JOINT APPLICATION SYSTEM
The majority of third level courses available to school leavers can be found in colleges which operate under the CAO system. Applications to these are processed through a central office, using a single application form. A total of 20 courses may be chosen from the entire range in the CAO system, 10 from the Degree list and 10 from the Diploma/Certificate list. In both case, courses are listed in order of preference.

Application packs which include a detailed handbook are available in schools from September or from the –

CAO at Tower House, Eglinton St., Galway. Tel: (091) 509800 Fax: (091) 562344

ENTRY REQUIREMENTS

- **Minimum**
  All colleges set down minimum requirements often called matriculation requirements, for entry to their courses. These normally include passing certain subjects and achieving specific grades. In most cases these specify requirements in English and Mathematics. However in addition, all constituent and recognised colleges of the N.U.I. require applicants to have passed Irish and a further language from their matriculation programme. There are exemptions but these are few, e.g. for those born outside Ireland or students applying to NCAD may now present Art instead of the third language.

- **Specific Course Requirements**
  In addition to minimum entry requirements college faculties and courses require specific grades in subjects that they feel most relevant to their particular course (see Subject Matters section) .

- **Points System**
  Where demand exceeds the number of places on a course, most colleges operate a points system which is described later on in this Directory. This system is under review by a special government commission.

- **Aptitude /Other Selection Tests**
  A small number of courses require applicants to take an aptitude test, audition or interview. Art courses in particular normally require the submission of a "portfolio" of work.

CAO APPLICATION DATES & FEES:

	Fee	Closing Date
EU Applicants (Normal Fee)	£18.90 (€24)	1 Feb 2000
EU Applicants (Late Fee)	£37.80 (€48)	1 May 2000
Non-EU Applicants (Normal Fee)	£37.80 (€48)	15 Dec. 1999
Non-EU Applicants (Late Fee)	£56.70 (€72)	1 May 2000
Change of Mind Closing Date		1 July 2000

RESTRICTED APPLICATION COURSES

The courses now listed are those for which there are early assessment procedures – usually around March or April. Check very carefully the list of Restricted-Application Courses.

WARNING: The right is reserved not to consider an application for a Restricted-Application Course unless it has been mentioned by the applicant in an application received in CAO not later than 1st February 2000.

DEGREES

AD001	Art and Design Education
AH001	Theology and Philosophy
CE001	Primary Teacher Training (Church of Irl. Coll of Ed.)
CK103	Music
CK104	Arts with Music
CR121	Music
DC211	Music Performance
DN011	Music
FT101	Architecture
FT544	Interior and Furniture Design
FT545	Design - Visual Communication
FT546	Fine Art
FT601	Music
LM072	Industrial Design
MD401	Religion, Education and Music
MH103	Music
SN001	Commerce
TR001	(Subject Options Music and Drama Studies only),
TR002	Music
TR009	Music Education
TR025	Drama &Theatre Studies
WD027	Music

DIPLOMA/CERTS

AL020	Design (Communications)
BC001	Art and Design
BC002	Art and Ceramics
CR094	Nautical Science
CR095	Marine Engineering
CR201	Art - Fine Art
CR202	Design - Ceramic Products
DL002	Commercial Photography
DL008	Art
DL009	Communication Design A
DL010	Communication Film/TV B.
DL011	Communication Animation C.
DL012	TV and Video Production
DT102	Architectural Technology
DT515	Design - Display
DT516	Design - Presentation
DT517	Media Production
DT602	Music Teaching
DT603	Speech and Drams Studies
DT604	Music Foundation
GA015	Furniture Design and Manufacture
GA017	Art and Design
LC001	Art and Design
PT404	Social Care
SG231	Art
SN101	Business Studies
WD018	Social Care

FORMAL ACKNOWLEDGEMENT WITH CAO APPLICATION NUMBER

1. After submitting your application, you will receive from CAO a formal acknowledgement.
   This will take the form of a Statement of Course Choices. This will show your CAO Application Number as well as the Course Choices which have been recorded for you.
   It is very important that you check the Course Choices immediately to ensure that they are absolutely correct. Any errors must be reported to CAO without delay.
   You should, where possible, use your Application Number in any subsequent correspondence.

2. Persons submitting completed applications by 1st February will receive the Statement of Course Choices by 15th March at the latest (Late Applicants by 1st June).

3. **If the Statement has not arrived by 15th March (1st June for Late Applications), write to CAO immediately.**

SUBSEQUENT CONFIRMATION OF APPLICATION RECORD

1. Before the end of May, each applicant will be sent a Statement of Application Record as a final acknowledgement to enable her to verify that all information has been recorded accurately.

2. **If this Statement has not arrived by 15th June, write to CAO immediately.**

CAO FORM

Page One
Application Form 2000
(Complete in BLOCK LETTERS.)

N.B. Read the CAO Handbook carefully before completing this Form.
Tá leagan Gaeilge den fhoirm seo ar fáil.

SURNAME MARTY

OTHER NAME(S) JONATHAN

TITLE (if desired) MR **Sex (F or M)** M **Date of Birth (ddmmyyyy)**

Day	Mth	.Year
0 9	0 9	1 9 8 2

COUNTRY OF BIRTH REPUBLIC OF IRELAND **NATIONALITY** IRISH

PERMANENT HOME ADDRESS
POLLINORE, COROFIN, CUMMER
TUAM, CO. GALWAY
ÉIRE **Tel. No.** 093-41498

ADDRESS FOR CORRESPONDENCE (if different) (Note:Only one address may be shown here)
AS ABOVE
Contact Tel. No. 093-41498

Name and address of second-level school(s) and years attended
ST. JARLATH'S COLLEGE
TUAM, CO. GALWAY
ÉIRE

	From:	To:
	1 9 9 5	2 0 0 0

If taking 2000 Leaving Cert., enter Exam. Number here.
Tick (✓) if Number not yet supplied to you.

Leaving Cert.
00 | ✓

If taking 2000 NCVA Level 2, enter Exam. Number here.
Tick (✓) if Number not yet supplied to you.

NCVA Level 2
00

Leaving Cert. exams 1983 - 1999 ——>

Year	Exam. No.	Year	Exam. No.	Year	Exam. No.

I have read the regulations described in the CAO Handbook 2000 and in the CAO Application Form 2000 and I agree to be bound by them. I affirm that the particulars given in this application are true and complete.

Signed (for pages 1 & 2) *Jonathan Murphy* **Date** 6-12-99

Check [ ] Office Use Only

228

Application may be made for up to ten **DEGREE** courses and up to ten **DIPLOMA/CERT** courses by completing the appropriate section(s) below.

In both cases, courses should be entered in order of preference.

All of the higher education courses in the CAO system are categorised as either **DEGREE** or **DIPLOMA/CERT**.

Take special care NOT to mix DEGREE courses and DIPLOMA/CERT courses.

DEGREE SECTION		**DIPLOMA/CERT SECTION**	

Pref.	Course Code	Pref.	Course Code
1		1	
2		2	
3		3	
4		4	
5		5	
6		6	
7		7	
8		8	
9		9	
10		10	

NOTE:

There are restrictions on the introduction of certain courses into an application for the first time after 1st February 2000. See Handbook pages 2 & 3 - 'Restricted-Application Courses'. In addition, individual higher education institutions may impose restrictions on certain categories of applicant if applying after 1st February. See Handbook page 5.

Is any Special Category, mentioned on page 3 of this Form, applicable in your case ?
Write 'Yes' or 'No' in the box on the right.

The application is incomplete unless you write 'Yes' or 'No' in this box.

In the case of Category E, failure to disclose the appropriate information
may result in the cancellation of the application.
Checks are made to ensure that this information has not been omitted.

STAGE 4 *CHANGE OF MIND*

Change of Mind in respect of course choices (Closing date 1st July 2000):

In May applicants will receive a Change of Mind Form with the Statement of Application Record. This form may then be used to register a change of course choices, if desired up to 1st July 2000.

Any such change will be acknowledged by the issue of a further Statement of Course Choices.

Subject to the exceptions and restrictions mentioned below, course choices may be changed (without fee) as often as desired up to 5:15 pm on the 1st July 2000.

DEGREES and DIPLOMA/CERTS are treated sep-arately from each other; e.g. a change of DEGREE course choices will not affect DIPLOMA/CERT choices.

The submission of a Change of Mind Form cancels and supersedes the previous course choices. However, DEGREE and DIPLOMA/CERT choices are considered to be completely separate from each other for this purpose.

The right is reserved not to consider applications for the Restricted-Application Courses introduced via a Change of Mind for the first time after 1st February (see restricted list).

STAGE 5 *OFFER AND ACCEPTANCE OF PLACE*

General

Decisions on applications are normally taken in August and September following receipt of the results of the annual school-leaving examinations.

In the cases of a very few applicants, mainly mature and Non-EU applicants, decisions may be taken at an earlier date.

Normally, however, applicants should not expect to have decisions before August.

All offers of places will be sent by post.

Examination Results

During August, CAO receives, direct from the examination authorities, the results of the Leaving Certificate and GCE Northern Ireland examinations.

Round Zero

In early August there may be an issue of a small number of offers of places which go to certain categories of applicants who are not awaiting current-year examination results.

Round One

Issue of the main body of offers takes place as soon as possible after Leaving Certificate Examination results become available and normally occurs towards the end of August.

At the same time as first round offers of places are issued to successful applicants notices are sent to those who do not receive any offer.

Round Two

A second round of offers will be issued, usually in early September, to fill any remaining vacancies.

After Round Two

Thereafter, offers will be issued as necessary until the end of October to fill any vacancies which may arise.

Offer Procedures:
General

The procedures for acceptance of an offer are very simple and very clear. They are designed to ensure fair treatment for ALL applicants.

Offers will be issued independently in respect of DEGREES and DIPLOMA/CERTS so that some applicants may receive two offers of places simultaneously.

Formal Offers

An applicant who is being admitted will be sent a formal offer of a place by post together with the necessary instructions as to how to proceed. Applicants must comply in full with all instructions set out in the offer notice.

Lapse of Offers

The offer will lapse unless accepted within a specified period- i.e. unless Part C of the offer notice is received in CAO by 5:15 p.m. on the Reply Date set out in the Offer Notice.

If the course being accepted requires payment of a deposit, Part C of the Offer Notice should be stamped by a bank to indicate that this has been paid. If no payment is required there is no need to go to a bank.

More than one acceptance

Persons receiving more than one offer may make successive acceptances but an acceptance automatically cancels and supersedes any previous acceptance(s) - an applicant may have only one current acceptance in the entire CAO system.

Offer of highest preference

Each applicant will be offered a place in the highest of her course preferences to which she is entitled (if any).

This will be done, independently, in respect of DEGREE choices and DIPLOMA/CERT choices.

Exclusion from lower preferences

IMPORTANT: When an applicant has been offered a place in one of her course preferences, she is excluded from further consideration for any course which is lower in her order of preference than the one in which she has been offered a place.

This means that while an applicant may subsequently move upwards in her order of preference (if places become available due to withdrawals) she will not be considered for a place in a course which is a lower preference than that already offered. *(Cont. on page 232)*

GETTING A QUALIFICATION

Many students are pleasantly surprised to discover that they can train for practically any job or profession at the highest level with relatively low points from the Leaving Certificate. It may take a few years extra but you can arrive at exactly the same destination as your classmates who score higher grades simply by taking a different route. The fancy word for this is progression.

Below we demonstrate how this progression works. Most Institute of Technology certificate level courses lead on to the option of an extra year for diploma level. An increasing number of diploma course holders have the option of proceeding to degree level. Please read this in conjunction with the qualification's column in the CAO listing of this section of the Yearbook

Institute of Technology	National Certificate	National Diploma	Degree
Athlone	Plastics Engineering	✓	✓
Carlow	Business Studies	✓	✓
Cork	Computing	✓	✓
Dublin	Civil Engineering	✓	✓
Dundalk	Construction Studies	✓	✓
Tralee	Information Technology	✓	✓

✓ denotes course available at this level.

LEVELS

Consideration should be given to the level of award at which to aim initially.

Primary Degree

This is the highest award that a school leaver can apply for and normally takes three to four years to complete, though many professional courses such as architecture and medicine take longer. The minimum entry requirements vary slightly from college to college, with most requiring two HC's. However, actual entry standards are determined by the standard of applicants and the number of places available and as a consequence, areas where the number of places are extremely limited tend to require a very high standard for entry.

National Diploma

A National Diploma normally takes three years to complete and many are ab initio courses where the completion of a National Certificate is not a prerequisite. Others are add-on Diplomas for students who have completed a National Certificate. Five OD's is the normal minimum entry requirement.

National Certificate

These are awarded after two years and many holders continue their studies by taking a National Diploma or transferring to a Degree Course. This ladder of opportunity opens up possibilities which would otherwise be closed if results of school leaving examinations were considered alone.

PART-TIME/EVENING/CORRESPONDENCE COURSES

Though minimum age requirements may initially make these unavailable to you, many colleges offer evening programmes which lead to the award of degrees, diplomas, etc. Correspondence courses such as that offered by the Open University and DCU's Distance Education Programme afford opportunities to those who cannot attend full-time education. The National Association for Adult Education (AONTAS) have produced an excellent guide outlining the opportunities available through part-time study – "The Opportunity Guide to Qualifications Part-Time Courses in Ireland" (Wolfhound Press).

Later offers for higher preference

An applicant who is being offered a place in a course which is not her first preference may subsequently be offered a place in a course of higher preference if such a place becomes available.

This applies whether or not the earlier offer has been accepted by the applicant. It is NOT necessary to accept an offer in order to be considered for a higher preference if it becomes available later.

Non-acceptance of subsequent offers

Having accepted an offer of a place, an applicant is not obliged to accept a subsequent offer. She may retain the original offer simply by ignoring the subsequent one.

Enquiries at Offer Stage:

Persons making enquiries to CAO at the offer stage should present their queries in concise written form, quoting their Application Number. Every applicant will receive an inquiry form for this purpose.

Deferred entry:

1. An applicant who receives an offer of a place and who wishes to defer taking up the place for one year must seek the agreement of the appropriate HEI. Such agreement is not guaranteed and is totally at the discretion of the appropriate HEI.
2. In general, the position of the various HEIs is as set out below. However, applicants who may wish to defer an offer of a place are strongly urged to check direct, and well in advance, with the Admissions Office of the appropriate HEIs about the conditions under which deferred entry might be granted.
3. Except for National College of Art & Design and Dun Laoghaire Institute of Art, Design & Technology, all HEIs will consider applications for deferred entry.
4. Applications for deferred entry will NOT be considered in respect of the following courses:
   Institute of Technology, Tralee: TL101
   University College Dublin (NUI): DN022.
5. In the following courses, application for deferred entry will be considered ONLY IN EXCEPTIONAL CIRCUMSTANCES :
   Royal College of Surgeons: All courses.
   University College Cork (NUI): CK701, CK702.

Deferral Procedure:

If the HEI has confirmed that it operates deferred entry to the course in question, on receipt of an Offer Notice:

1. Do **NOT** accept the offer in the manner shown on the Offer Notice. Do **NOT** make any payment.
2. Write **IMMEDIATELY** to the Admissions Office of the appropriate HEI, setting out the reason(s) for the request. Mark **"DEFERRED ENTRY"** clearly on the envelope
3. Part C of the Offer Notice **must** be attached to the letter.
4. The letter **must** arrive in the Admissions Office **at least two days** before the "Reply Date" shown on the Offer Notice.
5. The HEI will communicate the decision to the applicant. If the deferral is not granted, the offer may still be accepted for the current year.
6. In order to take up the deferred place, the applicant must reapply through CAO in the succeeding year, **placing the deferred course as the only preference on the Application Form.**

All communications about deferral must go to Admissions Offices and **NOT** to CAO.

Making sense of the symbols

The symbols attached to the points on the following pages mean:

*   Not all on this points score were offered places

**   Matriculated candidates are considered but admission is on the basis of performance in the music test and interview

***   Applicants are ranked as for other courses but the final decision depends on performance in interview.

†   Test or interview, etc.

††   Specific entry requirements, interview and portfolio.

†††   Specific entry requirements and interview.

AQA   All qualified applicants.

~   Admissions is based solely on the results of the RCSI entrance examination.

ATHLONE INSTITUTE OF TECHNOLOGY

DEGREES

*Apply by inserting the Codes below
in the Degree Section of the Application Form.*

Code	Minimum points '98	Title (NOT to be entered on Application Form)
AL030	250	Engineering (Polymer Engineering)
AL031		Computer and Software Engineering
AL032		Polymer Technology

DIPLOMAS/CERTIFICATES

*Apply by inserting the Codes below
in the Diploma/Certificate Section of the Application Form.*

Code	Minimum points '98	Title (NOT to be entered on Application Form)	
AL001	165	Business Studies	CT + DP + DG
AL003	210	Office Information Systems	CT + DP + DG
AL006	355	Applied Social Studies in Social Care	CT + DP + DG
AL007	170	Front Office Administration	CT + DP + DG
AL009	120	Plastics Engineering	CT + DP + DG
AL010	130	Mechanical Engineering	CT + DP
AL011	250	Electronics and Computer Engineering	CT + DP + DG
AL012	180	Electronic Engineering	CT + DP + DG
AL013	145	Civil Engineering	CT + DP
AL015	160	Construction Studies	CT + DP
AL016	145	Science (Applied Biology)	CT + DP + DG
AL017		Science (Applied Chemistry)	CT + DP + DG
AL023	AQA	Accounting Technician (Two-year course)	+ DP + DG
AL008	160	Hotel and Catering Supervision (Three-year course)	CT + DP + DG
AL014	AQA	Mineral Engineering	DP
AL018	220	Hotel and Catering Management	DP + DG
AL019	270	Professional Accounting	DP + DG
AL020	590	Design (Communications) (Restricted)	DP
AL022	290	Computing	DP
AL024		Engineering - Mechatronics	DP
AL025		Equine Studies	CT

OFF-CAMPUS COURSES - 1ST YEAR ONLY

Code		Title (NOT to be entered on Application Form)	Qualification
AL002	AQA	Business Studies - Cavan College of Further Studies, Cavan.	CT + DP + DG
AL004	AQA	Office Information Systems - Cavan College of Further Studies, Cavan.	CT + DP + DG
AL005	AQA	Office Information Systems - Greendale College of Further Education, Kilbarrack, Dublin 5.	CT + DP + DG

> *The " Qualification " column indicates, in bold , the initial qualification awarded, together with follow-on opportunities, if any are available, and which may be in the same or a related discipline. Follow-on opportunities may also be available in another institution. You MUST consult the institution literature.*
>
> *CT = Certificate;   DP = Diploma;   DG = Degree.*
>
> *CT courses are 2 years long and DP courses are 3 years long (in total), unless indicated otherwise.*

BURREN COLLEGE OF ART

DIPLOMAS/CERTIFICATES

Code	Minimum points '98	Title (NOT to be entered on Application Form)	
BC001		Art and Design (Restricted)	CT

CARLOW COLLEGE, CARLOW

DEGREES

Code	Minimum points '98	Title (NOT to be entered on Application Form)
PC410		Humanities

DIPLOMAS/CERTIFICATES

Code	Minimum points '98	Title (NOT to be entered on Application Form)	
PC402	AQA	Humanities (in Philosophical and Theological Studies)	DP + DG
PC404	280	Social Care (Restricted)	CT + DP

INSTITUTE OF TECHNOLOGY, CARLOW

DEGREES

Code	Minimum points '98	Title (NOT to be entered on Application Form)
CW046	330*	Computer Networking

DIPLOMAS/CERTIFICATES

Code	Minimum points '98	Title (NOT to be entered on Application Form)	
CW001	415	Science - Applied Physiology and Health Science	CT
CW002	205	Science - Applied Physics	CT + DP + DG
CW005	180	Engineering - Mechanical	CT + DP + DG
CW006	200	Engineering - Electronic	CT
CW007	200	Engineering - Civil	CT + DP
CW008	200	Construction Studies	CT + DP
CW009	240	Construction Studies (Architectural Graphics)	CT + DP
CW011	255	Business Studies	CT + DP + DG
CW012	260	Business Studies (Office Information Systems)	CT + DP + DG
CW019	250	Computing (with Options in Computer Applications & Commercial Programming)	CT + DP + DG
CW020	230	Computing (Networking and Optical Communications)	CT + DP + DG
CW021	200	Science (Environmental Monitoring and Instrumentation)	CT
CW022	200	Science - Applied Biology or Applied Chemistry	CT + DP+ DG
CW023	230	Business Studies (Accounting & Business Information Systems)	CT
CW024	190	Engineering - Electronics & Computer Engineering	CT + DP
CW025	190	Engineering - Electronics & Communications Systems	CT + DP

Code	Points	Title	Requirements
CW129	180	Engineering - Electro-Mechanical	CT
CW015	265	Design - Industrial	DP + DG
CW027	200	Business Studies (International Business and French)	DP
CW028	250	Business Studies (International Business and German)	DP
CW029	250	Business Studies - Office Information Systems and German	DP
CW038	220	Business Studies - Office Information Systems and French	DP
CW044	220	Computing with French	DP + DG
CW045	220	Computing with German	DP + DG
CW097		Process Control & Instrumentation	DP
CW099	210	Accounting & Management Studies	DP

CORK INSTITUTE OF TECHNOLOGY

DEGREES

Code	Minimum points '98	Title (NOT to be entered on Application Form)
CR105	420	Chemical & Process Engineering
CR106	345	Computer Applications
CR107	380	Electronic Engineering
CR108	390	Mechanical Engineering
CR115		Software Development with German
CR116	400	Software Development for Computer Networking

CORK SCHOOL OF MUSIC

Code	Minimum points '98	Title (NOT to be entered on Application Form)
CR121	340	Music (Restricted)

DIPLOMAS/CERTIFICATES

Code	Minimum points '98	Title (NOT to be entered on Application Form)	Requirements
CR001	275	Applied Physics & Instrumentation	CT + DP + DG
CR006	280	Applied Biology	CT + DP + DG
CR007	250	Applied Chemistry	CT + DP + DG
CR016	345	Computing	CT + DP + DG
CR021	335	Business Studies	CT + DP + DG
CR022	315	Business Studies (Office Information Systems)	CT + DP + DG
CR023	244	Business Studies (Advanced Certificate in Accounting)	CT + DP + DG
CR031	370	Applied Social Studies (Social Care)	CT + DP + DG
CR032	350	Business Studies (Recreation & Leisure)	CT + DP + DG
CR036	340	Technology in Print Media Communications	CT + DP
CR041	360	Business Studies (Tourism)	CT + DP + DG
CR042	275	Business Studies (Hotel & Catering Supervision)	CT + DP
CR046	200	Automobile Technology	CT + DP
CR051	305	Engineering (Civil)	CT + DP + DG
CR052	240	Construction Studies	CT + DP
CR053		Construction (Interior Architectural Technology)	CT
CR061	245	Engineering (Electronic)	CT + DP + DG
CR062	265	Engineering (Electrical)	CT + DP
CR071	220	Engineering (Mechanical)	CT + DP + DG
CR072	230	Engineering (Building & Industrial Services)	CT + DP
CR085	455	Medical Laboratory Science	CT + DG
CR090	345	Construction Studies (Architectural Technology)	DP
CR094	205	Science (Nautical Science) (Restricted)	DP
CR095	215*	Engineering (Marine) (Restricted)	DP

Code	Minimum points '98	Title (NOT to be entered on Application Form)	
CR201	575	Art - Fine Art (Restricted)	DP + DG
CR202	400	Design - Ceramic Products (Restricted)	DP + DG

UNIVERSITY COLLEGE CORK (NUI)

DEGREES

Code	Minimum points '98	Title (NOT to be entered on Application Form)
CK101	380*	Arts - Three year degree programme, with the following first year subjects: Applied Mathematics, Archaeology, Celtic Civilisation, Computer Science, Economics, English, French, Gaeilge/Irish, Geography, German, Greek, Greek and Roman Civilisation, History, Italian, Latin, An Léann Dúchais, Mathematical Studies, Mathematics, Philosophy, Sociology, Spanish, Studies in Music, Studies in Psychology.
CK102	415*	Social Science - Three year degree programme.
CK103	AQA	Music - Four year degree programme. (Restricted - see page 2)
CK104	415	Arts with Music - Three year degree programme. (Restricted - see page 2)
CK105		European Studies - Four year degree programme, where the third year is spent abroad.
CK106	505	Applied Psychology - Three year honours degree programme.
CK107	390	Language and Cultural Studies - French - Four year degree programme where the third year is spent abroad.
CK108	320	Language and Cultural Studies - German - Four year degree programme where the third year is spent abroad.
CK109	315	Language and Cultural Studies - Italian - Four year degree programme where the third year is spent abroad.
CK110	370	Language and Cultural Studies - Spanish - Four year degree programme where the third year is spent abroad.
CK111	410	Early Childhood Studies - Three year degree programme.
CK201	435*	Commerce
CK202	430*	Accounting
CK203	475*	Business Information Systems
CK204	440*	Finance
CK205	480	Commerce (European) - with French
CK206	435*	Commerce (European) - with German
CK207	AQA	Commerce (European) - with Italian
CK208	345	Commerce (European) - with Spanish
CK209	405	Commerce (European) - with Irish
CK210		Government and Public Policy
CK301	480*	Law
CK302	495*	Law and French
CK303	445*	Law and German
CK304		Law and Irish
CK401	400*	Computer Science - leading to degrees in the following subject areas: Computer Science or Multimedia Technology and Software Engineering or Computer Science and Economics or Computer Science and Mathematics or Computer Science and Statistics.
CK402	415	Biological and Chemical Sciences - leading to degrees in the following subject areas: Applied Ecology, Applied Psychology, Biochemistry, Biomedical Sciences, Chemistry, Chemistry of Pharmaceutical Compounds, Neuroscience, Microbiology, Physiology, Plant and Microbial Biotechnology, Plant Science, Zoology.
CK403	375	Chemical/Mathematical/Physical Sciences - leading to degrees in the following subject areas: Chemistry, Geography, Geology, Physics, Applied Mathematics, Mathematics and Statistics.

National College of Ireland
Sandford Road, Ranelagh
Dublin 6, Ireland

Tel: +353 1 406 0500 / 0501
Fax: +353 1 497 2200
email: info@ncirl.ie
Website: www.ncirl.ie

National
College *of*
Ireland

*The college for a
learning society*

National College of Ireland
offers the following

FULL-TIME DAY COURSES
2000 - 2001

- **BA in Accounting and Human Resource Management (CAO Code NC001)**

- **BA in European Business Studies and Languages (CAO Code NC002)**

- **BSc in Software Systems (CAO Code NC003)**

- **National Certificate in Business Studies (Industrial Relations/ Human Resource Management) (CAO Code NC101)**

- **National Certificate in Computing (Applications & Support) (CAO Code NC102)**

NCI full-time day courses are offered through the CAO system and are eligible for Free Fees and for grants under the Higher Education Grants Scheme.

NCI is offering up to 10% of places on the above courses to students who live in designated Area Based Partnership areas. Separate CAO codes apply.

For further information please contact the Admissions Office at National College of Ireland. Ph: (01) 406 0585.

Located in Ranelagh and 40 off-campus centres around Ireland, The National College of Ireland (formerly NCIR) provides high-quality, third-level education programmes for today's knowledge-based society. Guided by the principles of access, opportunity and excellence, NCI's programmes represent a ladder of opportunity by which individuals can access the kind of education that best suits their situation and aspirations. NCI's virtual campus, incorporating innovative technology, delivers student-centred learning within the classroom and through distance education.

CK404	345	Earth Sciences - leading to degrees in the following subject areas: Applied Ecology, Earth Science, Geography, Geology, Plant Science and Zoology.
CK501	385*	Food Business
CK502	400	Food Science
CK503	350	Food Technology
CK504	445*	Nutritional Sciences
CK601	AQA	Food Process Engineering
CK602	445	Civil & Environmental Engineering
CK603	490	Electrical Engineering and Microelectronics
CK701	545	Medicine
CK702	525*	Dentistry

ALL HALLOWS COLLEGE, DUBLIN

DEGREES

Code	Minimum points '98	Title (NOT to be entered on Application Form)
AH001	240	Theology and Philosophy (Theology with English, or Theology with Philosophy, or Theology with Psychology, or Theology with Spirituality) (Restricted)

AMERICAN COLLEGE, DUBLIN

DEGREES

Code	Minimum points '98	Title (NOT to be entered on Application Form)
AC110	215	Liberal Arts with omnibus entries to English, History and International Relations
AC120	235	International Business with omnibus entries to International Marketing and International Management
AC130	210	International Tourism
AC141		Psychology (Honours)
AC142		Sociology

Code	Minimum points '98	Title (NOT to be entered on Application Form)		
AC100	AQA	Humanities	CT	+ DG

CHURCH OF IRELAND

College of Education, Dublin 6

DEGREES

Code	Minimum points '98	Title (NOT to be entered on Application Form)
CF001	400	B. Ed. (Restricted)

COLÁISTE MHUIRE MARINO

Griffith Avenue, Dublin 9

DEGREES

Code	Minimum points '98	Title (NOT to be entered on Application Form)
CM001	460*	B. Ed.
CM002	420*	B. Ed. - Gaeltacht Applicants

DUBLIN BUSINESS SCHOOL

DEGREES

Code	Minimum points '98	Title (NOT to be entered on Application Form)
DB512		Business Studies
		Second Year Branches: Languages, Finance, Information Systems
DB521		Accountancy and Finance
DB531		Marketing

DIPLOMAS/CERTIFICATES

Code	Minimum points '98	Title (NOT to be entered on Application Form)	
DB522		Business Studies (Accounting)	CT + DG
DB533		Business Studies (Marketing)	CT + DG
DB542		Business Studies (Computer Applications)	CT + DG

DUBLIN CITY UNIVERSITY

DEGREES

Code	Minimum points '98	Title (NOT to be entered on Application Form)
DC111	425	Business Studies
DC112	470	European Business (French)
DC113	440	European Business (German)
DC114	420	European Business (Spanish)
DC115	435	Accounting and Finance
DC116		European Business (Transatlantic Studies)
DC118	415	Airgeadas, Ríomhaireacht agus Fiontraíocht
DC121	420	Computer Applications
DC122	450	Applied Computational Linguistics
DC125	410	Mathematical Sciences
DC126	515	Financial and Actuarial Mathematics
DC131	475	Communication Studies
DC132	465	Journalism
DC133		Multimedia
DC141	460	International Marketing & Languages (French/German)
DC142	475	International Marketing & Languages (French/Spanish)
DC143	445	International Marketing & Languages (German/Spanish)
DC144	385	International Marketing & Languages (Japanese)
DC146	500	International Business & Languages (French/German)
DC147	495	International Business & Languages (French/Spanish)
DC148	470	International Business & Languages (German/Spanish)
DC149	425	International Business & Languages (Japanese)
DC151	420	Applied Languages (French/German)
DC152	410	Applied Languages (French/Spanish)

DC153	375	Applied Languages (German/Spanish)
DC154	375	Applied Languages (Japanese with French,German or Spanish)
DC161	400	Analytical Science
DC162	380	Pure and Applied Chemistry
DC163	380	Chemistry with French
DC164	360	Chemistry with German
DC171	330	Applied Physics
DC172	350	Physics with French
DC173	385	Physics with German
DC181	385	Biotechnology
DC191	380	Electronic Engineering
DC192	370	Telecommunications Engineering
DC193	385	Mechatronics Engineering
DC194	425	Bachelor's/Master's in Electronic Systems
DC195		Computer-aided Mechanical and Manufacturing Engineering
DC196		Manufacturing Engineering with Business Studies
DC197		Medical Mechanical Engineering
DC198		Mechanical and Manufacturing Engineering (undenominated entry; second-year branches: Computer-aided Mechanical and Manufacturing Engineering; Manufacturing Engineering with Business Studies; Medical Mechanical Engineering)
DC201		Common Entry into Science
DC202		Sport Science and Health
DC203		Science Education
DC211		Music Performance at Royal Irish Academy of Music (Restricted)

DUBLIN INSTITUTE OF TECHNOLOGY

DEGREES

Code	Minimum points '98	Title (NOT to be entered on Application Form)
FT101	566†	Architecture (Restricted)
FT110	395	Property Economics (Valuation Surveying)
FT111	385	Construction Economics and Management (Quantity Surveying)
FT112		Geomatics
FT125	325	Engineering Common 1st Year - Options: Mechanical, Manufacturing, Building Services, Structural.
FT128		Transport Technology
FT130		Printing Management
FT221	330	Electrical/Electronic Engineering Common 1st & 2nd Year - Options: Electrical Power Systems, Control Systems, Communication Systems, Computer Engineering.
FT222	325	Applied Sciences Common 1st Year - Options: Chemistry and Physics, Chemistry and Mathematics, Food Science and Food Technology, Mathematics and Physics, Physics and Physics Technology.
FT223	500*	Human Nutrition and Dietetics
FT224	520*	Optometry
FT225		Applied Sciences/Computing Common 1st Year - Options: Computer Science and Mathematics, Computer Science and Physics, Computer Science and Software Engineering, Computer Science and Chemistry.
FT255	435	International Business and Languages (French)
FT256	405	International Business and Languages (German)
FT257	355	International Business and Languages (Spanish)
FT259	390	Photography
FT281		Computer Engineering
FT351	405	Business Studies
FT352	470*	Communications - Film and Broadcasting
FT353	445*	Communications - Journalism
FT354	390	Information Systems Development
FT401	355*	Hospitality (Hotel and Catering) Management

DUBLIN INSTITUTE *of* TECHNOLOGY

Institiúid Teicneolaíochta Bhaile Átha Cliath

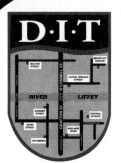

TAKE THE ROUTE THAT LEADS PLACES

Located in the heart of Dublin city with centres north and south of the River Liffey, the DIT offers ready access to extensive cultural and leisure amenities.

With a student population of 22,000 students and a range of course opportunities to suit your needs at Certificate, Diploma, Degree and Post graduate levels, DIT is the place to be.

DIT has over 80 courses in areas such as:

- **Applied and Paramedical Sciences**
- **Architecture**
- **Art and Design**
- **Building and Surveying**
- **Business**
- **Catering**
- **Communications**
- **Computing**
- **Printing**

- **Engineering (various specialisations)**
- **Food Science**
- **Hotel Management**
- **Information Technology**
- **Languages**
- **Marketing**
- **Music**
- **Social Studies**
- **Tourism**

For further information, please contact:

**DIT Admissions Office,
30 Upper Pembroke Street,
Dublin 2.
Tel. (01) 402 3445.
Fax: (01) 402 3392.**

FT402	395	Tourism Marketing	
FT403		Culinary Arts	
FT404	360	Leisure Management	
FT471	400	Social Care	
FT472	350	Early Childhood Care & Education	
FT491	405	Environmental Health	
FT541	390	Marketing	
FT542	375*	Administration and Marketing	
FT543	355	Retail Management	
FT544	905*	Design - Interior+Furniture (Restricted)	
FT545	935†	Design - Visual Communication (Restricted)	
FT546	855†	Fine Art (Restricted)	
FT601	325†	Music (Restricted)	

DIPLOMAS/CERTIFICATES

Code	Minimum points '98	Title (NOT to be entered on Application Form)	
DT102	475*	Architectural Technology (Restricted)	DP
DT114	330	Construction Technology	CT + DP + DG
DT116	360*	Auctioneering Valuation and Estate Agency	CT + DP + DG
DT120	300	Preliminary Engineering	
DT126	290	Civil Engineering Technician	CT + DP + DG
DT127	230	Building Services Engineering Technician	CT + DP + DG
DT128	295	Mechanical Engineering Technician	CT + DP + DG
DT150	210	Transport Engineering/Management	CT + DP
DT171	185	Buildings Maintenance Technician	CT
DT200	AQA	Bakery Technology and Management	DP
DT214	425	Medical Laboratory Sciences	CT + DG
DT231	280	Electrical & Control Engineering Technician	DP + DG

**All College
Hallows**
DUBLIN·IRELAND

Course Listing 1999/2000

All Hallows College

Grace Park Road, Drumcondra, Dublin 9. Tel: 01-837 3745
Fax: 01-837 7642 email: info@allhallows.ie

Bachelor of Arts in Theology & Philosophy
*with option to take: Philosophy, Psychology, Spirituality
or English Literature as a subsidiary subject from second year*

Graduate Diploma in Humanities: Holistic Development
A formation for Pastoral Leadership (One year)

Master of Arts (Mode B) in Pastoral Leadership
*(Course Work and Dissertation)
One year full-time/two years part-time/ACCS scheme*

Master of Arts (Mode A) in Pastoral Studies
(Research and Major Thesis)

For further information on entry requirements and fees
please call or write to the Registrar or visit our
web-site at http://www.allhallows.ie

DT244	190	Electrical and Electronic Draughting	CT
DT266	355	Computer Science	DP + DG
DT273	300	Applied Science	DP + DG
DT284	AQA	Industrial Electronic Systems	CT + DP
DT287	320	Applied Electronics	DP + DG
DT289	255	Electronics Technician	CT
DT306	185	Transport Management	CT
DT315	345*	Business Studies	CT + DP + DG
DT402	305	Hotel and Catering Management	DP + DG
DT410	370	Travel and Tourism	CT
DT440	215	Hotel and Catering Supervision	CT
DT444	170	Culinary Arts (Professional Chef)	CT
DT493	275	Food Technology	CT + DP
DT496	AQA	Food Quality Assurance (Horticulture)	CT + DP
DT497	325	Environmental Resources Management	DP
DT498	300	Health Care Technology	CT + DP
DT503	350*	Marketing	CT + DP + DG
DT515	775†	Design - Display (Restricted)	CT
DT516	770†	Design - Presentation (Restricted)	CT
DT517		Media Production (Restricted)	CT
DT521	295*	Business Studies - Management	CT + DP + DG
DT522	275*	Business Studies - Retail Marketing	CT + DP + DG
DT523	230	Business Studies – Proprietorship	CT + DP + DG
DT525	250	Business Studies – Security	CT + DP + DG
DT531	AQA	Business Studies - Meat Management	CT
DT541	210	Business Studies - Bar Management	CT + DP
DT602	380†	Music Teaching (Restricted)	DP
DT603	320†	Speech and Drama Studies (Restricted)	DP
DT604	AQA†	Music Foundation (Restricted)	

DUN LAOGHAIRE INSTITUTE of ART, DESIGN & TECHNOLOGY

DIPLOMAS/CERTIFICATES

Code	Minimum points '98	Title (NOT to be entered on Application Form)	
DL002	600††	Technology - Commercial Photography (Restricted)	CT + DP
DL012	785††	T.V. & Video Production (Restricted)	CT
DL121		Audio Visual Media Technology	CT
DL008	735*††	Art (Restricted)	DP + DG
DL009	820*††	Design - Communication : Design A (Restricted)	DP + DG
DL010	870*††	Design - Communication : Film/Video B (Restricted)	DP + DG
DL011	665††	Design - Communication : Animation C (Restricted)	DP
DL131	115	Computing - Multimedia Programming	DP
DL231	105	Business Studies (Entrepreneurship)	DP
DL232		Business Studies (Electronic Commerce Systems)	DP

FROEBEL COLLEGE,

Sion Hill, Blackrock, Co Dublin

DEGREES

Code	Minimum points '98	Title (NOT to be entered on Application Form)	
FR001	455*	B. Ed.	
FR002	425	B. Ed. - Gaeltacht Applicants	

GRIFFITH COLLEGE DUBLIN

DEGREES

Code	Minimum points '98	Title (NOT to be entered on Application Form)	
GC400		Business Studies (with work experience) Omnibus entry: (Marketing, Human Resource Management, Finance, Computing, Industry Option)	
GC401		Accounting & Finance	
GC430		Computing Science (with work experience)	
GC450		Journalism & Media Communications	

DIPLOMAS/CERTIFICATES

Code	Minimum points '98	Title (NOT to be entered on Application Form)	
GC415		Legal Studies	DP + DG
GC416		Business Studies	CT + DG
GC440		Computing	CT + DG
GC465		Journalism & Media Studies	DP + DG
GC490		Interior Architecture	DP

INSTITUTE OF TECHNOLOGY, BLANCHARDSTOWN

DIPLOMAS/CERTIFICATES

Code	Minimum points '98	Title (NOT to be entered on Application Form)	
BN001		Electronics and Computer Engineering	CT
BN002		Computing (Information Technology)	CT
BN003		Business Studies	CT
BN004		Business Studies, Information Technology and French	DP
BN005		Business Studies, Information Technology and German	DP
BN006		Business Studies, Information Technology and Spanish	DP

INSTITUTE OF TECHNOLOGY, TALLAGHT

DIPLOMAS/CERTIFICATES

Code	Minimum points '98	Title (NOT to be entered on Application Form)	
TA002	350	Computing (Information Technology)	CT + DP + DG
TA003	240	Science (Applied Biology or Applied Chemistry or Instrumentation and Applied Physics)	CT + DP + DG
TA004	265	Engineering (Electronics)	CT + DP + DG
TA005	225	Engineering (Mechanical)	CT + DP + DG
TA101	300	Business Studies (Accounting)	CT + DP + DG
TA102	320	Business Studies (Business Administration)	CT + DP + DG
TA103	330	Business Studies (Marketing & Languages)	CT + DP + DG
TA104	430	Audio/Visual Communications	CT + DP
TA105	260	Applied Languages	CT
TA106	260	Applied Language for Communication and Administration	CT
TA107	300	Languages with Heritage Studies	CT

LSB COLLEGE, DUBLIN

DEGREES

Code	Minimum points '98	Title (NOT to be entered on Application Form)
LS101	AQA	Anthropology
LS201	AQA	Arts (General) - Three first year subjects from Anthropology, Art History, Economics, French or German, Literature and Drama, Philosophy, Politics, Psychoanalysis.
LS202	AQA	Arts (Psychology)
LS203		Arts (Sociology)
LS301	AQA	Psychoanalytic Studies
LS401	AQA	Business (Computing)
LS501		Business (Marketing)
LS502		Business (Psychology)
LS601	AQA	Tourism (Language)
LS602		Tourism (Marketing)

DIPLOMAS/CERTIFICATES

Code	Minimum points '98	Title (NOT to be entered on Application Form)	
LS211		Arts in Cultural Studies (One Year Course)	CT + DG
LS421	AQA	Information Technology/Computing	CT + DG
LS422	AQA	Business Studies (Office Information Systems)	CT + DG
LS521	AQA	Business Studies	CT + DG

LIMERICK INSTITUTE OF TECHNOLOGY
INSTITIÚID TEICNEOLAÍOCHTA LUIMNIGH

The Limerick Institute of Technology is a multi-location campus in the City of Limerick, capital of the Mid-West Region. The Institute traces its origins back to 1852 when the Athenaeum Society started a School of Fine Arts & Crafts in Limerick.

Today, the Institute continues to provide courses at Post-Graduate, Masters, Degree, Diploma/Certificate, Professional, Higher Technological and Craft levels. The disciplines covered in Art & Design are Painting, Printmaking, Sculpture, Graphics, Ceramics, Fashion Design and Art Teacher Training. At the Moylish Park campus, courses are provided in Business Studies, Marketing, Electronics, Electro-Mechanical Systems, Telecommunications, Radar, Computing, Chemistry, Biology, Environmental & Analytical Science, Construction Studies, Civil Engineering, Site Management, Architectural Technology, Chartered Surveying, Mechanical & Motor Engineering, in addition to a range of courses for CERT and Craft apprentices.

For full details, please write to the
Admission Office, Limerick Institute of Technology, Moylish Park, Limerick
or telephone: (061) 208208 Fax: (061) 208209 email: mcadm@lit.ie

MATER DEI INSTITUTE OF EDUCATION

DEGREES

Code	Minimum points '98	Title (NOT to be entered on Application Form)
MD201	385	Religion, Education and English
MD301	380	Religion, Education and History
MD401	350†	Religion, Education and Music (Restricted)

MILLTOWN INSTITUTE of THEOLOGY and PHILOSOPHY

DEGREES

Code	Minimum points '98	Title (NOT to be entered on Application Form)
PT011	320	Philosophy
PT012	320	Theological and Philosophical Studies
PT013	320	Philosophy and Theology

NATIONAL COLLEGE OF ART AND DESIGN

DEGREES

Code	Minimum points '98	Title (NOT to be entered on Application Form)
AD001	††	Art and Design Education (Restricted) Industrial Design (Apply for LM072) - (Restricted)

NATIONAL COLLEGE OF IRELAND (NCI)

DEGREES

Code	Minimum points '98	Title (NOT to be entered on Application Form)
NC001	353	Accounting and Human Resource Management
NC011	285	Accounting and Human Resource Management - Area Based Partnership Applicants
NC002	360	European Business and Languages
NC012		European Business and Languages - Area Based Partnership
NC003		Software Systems
NC013		Software Systems - Area Based Partnership

DIPLOMAS/CERTIFICATES

Code	Minimum points '98	Title (NOT to be entered on Application Form)	
NC101	310	Business Studies (Industrial Relations/Human Resource Management)	CT + DP + DG
NC201	235	Business Studies (Industrial Relations/Human Resource Management) - Area Based Partnership	CT + DP + DG

NC102	175	Computing in Applications and Support	CT + DP + DG
NC202		Computing in Applications and Support - Area Based Partnership	CT + DP + DG

PORTOBELLO COLLEGE, DUBLIN

DEGREES

Code	Minimum points '98	Title (NOT to be entered on Application Form)
PB251	285	Accounting and Finance
PB252	250	Business Information Management
PB253	250	Business Studies
PB254	255	Marketing
PB255	250	Human Resource Management (with work experience)

DIPLOMAS/CERTIFICATES

Code	Minimum points '98	Title (NOT to be entered on Application Form)	
PB202	AQA	Computing	CT + DG
PB203	120	Business Studies	CT + DG
PB204		Business Studies (Accounting and Financial Services)	CT + DG
PB205		Business Studies (Computer Applications)	CT + DG
PB206		Business Studies (Marketing)	CT + DG

Athlone Institute of Technology
Institiúid Teicneolaíochta Bhaile Átha Luain

Entry 1999
DEGREE/PROFESSIONAL COURSES

- BEng Polymer Engineering (AL030)*
- BSc Polymer Technology
- BSc Toxicology**
- BSc Applied Chemistry**
- BSc Computer & Software Engineering*
- Bachelor of Business Studies**
- BA Accounting and Finance**
- BBS Tourism and Hospitality Management**
- BA Healthcare Management**
- BEng Software Engineering**
- MSc Software Engineering**

- MSc Toxicology**
- CIMA Chartered Institute of Management Accountants**
- ACCA Chartered Association of Certified Accountants**
- CPA Institute of Certified Public Accountants**
- Graduate Diploma in Computing**
- Graduate Diploma in Production and Operations Management**
- Graduate Diploma in Highway Technology***

Full Range of National Certificate and National Diploma courses in Business, Science, Engineering, Social Studies and Design.

*Entry through CAO
**Check Prospectus for appropriate Certificate/Diploma/Degree required for entry
*** Distance Learning

Further Information: Admissions Office, Athlone Institute of Technology, Athlone
Tel: 0902-24400 Fax: 0902-24417

ROYAL COLLEGE OF SURGEONS in IRELAND

DEGREES

Code	Minimum points '98	Title (NOT to be entered on Application Form)
RC001	535	Medicine without Scholarships
RC002	~	Medicine with RCSI Scholarships
RC003	580*	Medicine with Leaving Certificate Examination Scholarships
RC004		Physiotherapy

ST CATHERINE'S COLLEGE,

Sion Hill, Co Dublin

DEGREES

Code	Minimum points '98	Title (NOT to be entered on Application Form)
CS001	435*	B. Ed. (Home Economics)

ST PATRICK'S COLLEGE,

Drumcondra, Dublin 9

DEGREES

Code	Minimum points '98	Title (NOT to be entered on Application Form)
PD101	470*	B. Ed.
PD102	430	B. Ed. - Gaeltacht Applicants
PD103	405	B. A. in Humanities

TRINITY COLLEGE DUBLIN

DEGREES

Code	Minimum points '98	Title (NOT to be entered on Application Form)
TR001	Note 1	Two-subject Moderatorship (Restricted application for subjects Music and Drama Studies)
TR002	400**	Music (Restricted)
TR003	450	History
TR004	540	Law
TR005	430	Philosophy
TR006	525	Psychology
TR007	500*	Clinical Speech and Language Studies
TR008	310	Biblical and Theological Studies
TR009	330	Music Education (Restricted)
TR010	405	Computer Science, Linguistics and German
TR011	455	Computer Science, Linguistics and French
TR012	520	History and Political Science
TR013	430	Computer Science, Linguistics and Irish.
TR014	500	Philosophy & Political Science

TR018	570*	Law and French.
TR019	540	Law and German
TR021	450	Classics
TR022	355	Early and Modern Irish
TR023	475	English Studies
TR024	490	European Studies
TR025	450***	Drama and Theatre Studies (Restricted)
TR026	405	Germanic Languages
TR031	485	Mathematics
TR032	420	Engineering (including civil, structural and environmental, mechanical and manufacturing, electronic, computer, electronic/computer (joint programme))
TR033	455	Computer Science
TR034	490*	Management Science and Information Systems Studies
TR035	530*	Theoretical Physics
TR036	285	Computer Science (Evening Lectures)
TR037	310	Information and Communications Technology
TR051	560	Medicine
TR052	535	Dental Science
TR053	530	Physiotherapy
TR054	495*	Occupational Therapy
TR055	520	Therapeutic Radiography
TR071	445	Science (includes Biochemistry, Botany, Chemistry, Environmental Sciences, Genetics, Geography, Geology, Microbiology, Physics, Physiology, Science of Materials, Zoology)
TR072	550	Pharmacy
TR073	535	Human Genetics
TR074	375	Computational Chemistry/Computational Physics
TR075		Medicinal Chemistry
TR081	465	Business, Economic and Social Studies (includes Business Studies, Economics, Political Science, Sociology)
TR083	460	Sociology and Social Policy
TR084	485	Social Studies (Social Work)

THE MILLTOWN INSTITUTE
of Theology and Philosophy

BA Degree in Philosophy (PT011) (3 years)
Critical Exploration of Human Life, Society and Major Ideas of the Great Phiolosophers

BA Degree in Theological & Philosophical Studies (PT012) (4 years)
Introduction to Philosophy and the Human Sciences (Year 1)
Theory and Practical Application of Theology (Years 2-4)
Placements in Schools, Hospitals and Social Work Situations

BA Degree in Philosophy & Theology (PT013) (4 years)
(2 years Philosophy: 2 years Theology)
Develop Skills in Critical Thinking: Explore Major Ideas of the Great Philosophers
What Christians Believe and Why: Explore Issues of Life and Faith

Enquiries: Admissions Office, The Milltown Institute, Milltown Park, Dublin 6.
Tel: (01) 269 8388 Fax (01) 269 2528
Website: http://www.milltown-institute.ie Email: info@milltown-institute.ie

TR085   525   Business Studies and French
TR086   475*   Business Studies and German
TR087   410   Business Studies and Russian
TR088   370   Business Studies and Chinese

Note 1:   Applicants for TR001 (Two-subject Moderatorship) must NOT enter TR001 on the Application Form. Instead, they should enter the letters TR followed by a Subject-Option Code taken from the grid below to indicate a choice of a combination of two subjects. For example, TR259 indicates an application for English/German. The entry on the Application Form, therefore, would be TR259 as the Course Code. The absence of a Code in a grid position means that the corresponding combination of subjects is not permitted. The Two-subject Moderatorship course may appear more than once in an application provided different subject-combinations are mentioned.

SUBJECT OPTION CODES FOR THE TR001 (TWO-SUBJECT MODERATORSHIP) COURSE

Please ignore this section unless you are applying for TR001

(Use a ruler as an aid in selecting codes from this page)

	AH	BT	CC	DR	EI	EC	EN	FR	GG	GE	GK	HS	AR	MI	IT	LT	MT	MU	PH	PS	RU	SC	SP
AH	-	102	-	-	-	-	106	107	-	-	110	112	113	-	115	116	-	-	-	-	121	-	123
BT	102	-	133	-	156	-	136	137	-	139	140	142	143	144	-	146	-	-	149	150	151	152	153
CC	-	133	-	185	-	-	166	167	-	-	170	172	173	174	175	176	-	-	179	-	181	-	183
DR	-	-	185	-	-	-	276	306	-	366	395	-	485	515	545	575	-	635	-	-	725	755	785
EI	-	156	-	-	-	-	-	-	-	-	-	456	486	-	-	576	-	-	-	-	-	-	-
EC	-	-	-	-	-	-	-	-	198	199	-	202	-	-	-	-	207	-	209	210	211	212	213
EN	106	136	166	276	-	-	-	257	-	259	260	262	263	264	265	266	267	268	269	270	271	272	273
FR	107	137	167	306	-	257	-	-	-	289	-	292	293	294	295	296	297	298	299	300	301	302	303
GG	-	-	-	-	198	-	-	-	-	-	-	322	-	-	-	-	327	-	329	330	-	332	-
GE	-	139	-	366	-	199	259	289	-	-	-	352	353	354	355	-	357	-	359	-	361	362	363
GK	110	140	170	395	-	-	260	-	-	-	-	382	-	-	-	385	-	-	389	-	391	-	393
HS	112	142	172	-	456	202	262	292	322	352	382	-	443	444	445	446	-	448	449	-	451	452	453
AR	113	143	173	485	486	-	263	293	-	353	-	443	-	-	475	476	-	478	479	-	-	482	483
MI	-	144	174	515	-	-	264	294	-	354	-	444	-	-	505	506	-	508	509	-	511	512	513
IT	115	-	175	545	-	-	265	295	-	355	385	445	475	505	-	536	-	-	539	540	541	542	543
LT	116	146	176	575	576	-	266	296	-	-	385	446	476	506	536	-	567	-	569	-	571	-	573
MT	-	-	-	-	-	207	267	297	327	357	-	-	-	-	-	567	-	598	599	600	-	-	-
MU	-	-	-	635	-	-	268	298	-	-	-	448	478	508	-	-	598	-	629	630	-	-	-
PH	-	149	179	-	-	209	269	299	329	359	389	449	479	509	539	569	599	629	-	660	661	662	-
PS	-	150	-	-	-	210	270	300	330	-	-	-	-	-	540	-	600	630	660	-	-	692	-
RU	121	151	181	725	-	211	271	301	-	361	391	451	-	511	541	571	-	-	661	-	-	-	723
SC	-	152	-	755	-	212	272	302	332	362	-	452	482	512	542	-	-	-	662	692	-	-	753
SP	123	153	183	785	-	213	273	303	-	363	393	453	483	513	543	573	-	-	-	-	723	753	-

AH   Ancient History and Archaeology   GE   German   MU   Music
BT   Biblical & Theological Studies   GK   Greek   PH   Philosophy
CC   Classical Civilisation   HS   History   PS   Psychology
DR   Drama Studies   AR   History of Art   RU   Russian
EI   Early Irish   MI   Modern Irish   SC   Sociology
EC   Economics   IT   Italian   SP   Spanish
EN   English   LT   Latin
FR   French   MT   Mathematical Sciences
GG   Geography

UNIVERSITY COLLEGE DUBLIN (NUI), DUBLIN

DEGREES

Code	Minimum points '98	Title (NOT to be entered on Application Form)
DN001	495*	Architecture
DN002	540*	Medicine
DN003	430	Engineering
		Omnibus entry. Second year branches: Agricultural & Food, Chemical, Civil, Electrical, Electronic, Mechanical

251

DN004	500	Radiography
DN005	545	Veterinary Medicine
DN006	525*	Physiotherapy
DN007	420	Social Science
		Two subject degree in Social Policy and/or Sociology. The second subject can also be: Archaeology; Economics; Geography; Information Studies; Politics
DN008	395*	Science
		Omnibus entry. Degree subjects: Biochemistry, Botany, Cell & Molecular Biology, Chemistry, Computer Science, Environmental Biology, Environmental Geo-Chemistry, Experimental Physics, Genetics, Geology, Geophysical Science, Industrial Microbiology, Mathematics, Mathematical Physics, Pharmacology, Physiology, Plant Genetic Engineering, Psychology, Statistics, Zoology
DN009	495	Law (BCL)
DN010	370	Agricultural Science
		Omnibus entry. Degree options: (1) Animal & Crop Production; (2) Animal Science; (3) Agribusiness & Rural Development; (4) Agricultural & Environmental Science; (5) Food Science; (6) Engineering Technology; (7) Commercial Horticulture; (8) Landscape Horticulture; (9) Forestry
DN011	AQA†	Music (BMus) (Restricted)
DN012	385*	Arts
		First year subjects (no two subjects may be taken from the same section and not more than two subjects with asterisks may be chosen):
		A. Arabic, Economics*, Greek & Roman Civilisation, History of Art, Linguistics
		B. Greek, History*, Music, Statistics, Welsh
		C. Early Irish, German, Hebrew, Information Studies*, Latin, Mathematics (H), Mathematical Studies, Spanish
		D. Archaeology, English*, Politics*
		E. Irish, Italian, Philosophy, Sociology*
		F. Celtic Civilisation, French, Geography*, Mathematical Physics, Psychology
DN014	410*	Commerce (International) – with Modern Irish
DN015	440*	Commerce
		Omnibus entry. Majors in: Accounting, Banking & Finance, Business & Industrial Systems, Business Management & International Business, Human Resource Management, Management Information Systems, Marketing
DN016	465*	Commerce (International) – with German
DN017	525*	Commerce (International) – with French
DN018	445*	Commerce (International) – with Spanish
DN019	445*	Commerce (International) – with Italian
DN020	530*	Actuarial and Financial Studies
DN021	445	Business and Legal Studies
DN022	AQA	Arts (Modular Evening Course)
		Foundation level subjects available (one subject may be selected from either or both groups):
		Group P: Economics, English, Linguistics, Spanish.
		Group Q: Drama Studies, German, History, Irish, Mathematical Studies.
DN026	460*	Economics & Finance
DN029		Law with French Law (BCL)
DN030	445*	Computer Science
DN031	470	Theoretical Physics
DN032		Mathematical Science
DN040		Food Science
DN041		Landscape Horticulture
DN050		BA (Computer Science) + 2 Arts subjects from Groups A,B,C, and F under DN012
DN051		Economics
DN052		History
DN053		Philosophy
DN054		Psychology
DN057		BA (International – French)
DN058		BA (International – German)
DN059		BA (International – Spanish)

DUNDALK INSTITUTE OF TECHNOLOGY

DEGREES

Code	Minimum points '98	Title (NOT to be entered on Application Form)
DK104	335	Accounting and Finance

DIPLOMAS/CERTIFICATES

Code	Minimum points '98	Title (NOT to be entered on Application Form)	
DK002	110	Electronics	CT + DP + DG
DK003	270	Computing (Software Development)	CT + DP + DG
DK054		Computing (Applications and Support)	CT + DP
DK005	145	Business Studies (Management and Administrative Studies)	CT + DP + DG
DK006	200	Business Studies (Marketing with Language)	CT + DP + DG
DK007	200	Office Information Systems (Information Technology)	CT + DP + DG
DK107	200	Office Information Systems (Language)	CT + DP + DG
DK207	200	Office Information Systems (Public Relations)	CT + DP + DG
DK008	AQA	Civil Engineering	CT + DP
DK009	AQA	Construction Studies	CT + DP + DG
DK010	AQA	Manufacturing Engineering	CT + DP + DG
DK011	AQA	Mechanical Engineering	CT + DP + DG
DK012	AQA	Biology	CT + DP
DK050	AQA	Food Science	CT + DP
DK051	AQA	Chemistry	CT
DK053	AQA	Environmental Science	CT + DP
DK001	AQA	Electronics (Product Development)	DP + DG
DK052		Applied Cultural Studies	DP
DK152	165	Applied Cultural Studies (French)	DP
DK252	AQA	Applied Cultural Studies (German)	DP
DK103	250	Computing (Software Development - French)	DP + DG
DK203	250	Computing (Software Development - German)	DP + DG
DK154	205	Computing (Applications and Support - French)	DP
DK254	205	Computing (Applications and Support - German)	DP

GALWAY-MAYO INSTITUTE OF TECHNOLOGY

DEGREES

AT GALWAY

Code	Minimum points '98	Title (NOT to be entered on Application Form)
GA019	320	Hotel and Catering Management
GA020	290	Manufacturing Technology
GA042	335	Construction Management
GA044		Gnó agus Cumarsáid

DIPLOMAS/CERTIFICATES

AT GALWAY

Code	Minimum points '98	Title (NOT to be entered on Application Form)	
GA002	340	Business Studies	CT + DP + DG
GA004	250	Business Studies in Agri-Business	CT + DP + DG
GA005	325	Business Studies in Office Information Systems	CT + DP + DG
GA017	400	Art and Design (Restricted see page 2)	DP + DG
GA036	420	Film and Television	DP +DG

GA041	295	Heritage Studies	DP + DG
GA018	265	Hotel & Catering Management	DP + DG
GA021	120	Hotel Accommodation and Languages	CT + DP + DG
GA009	300	Civil Engineering	CT + DP
GA010	275	Construction Studies	CT + DP + DG
GA040	285	Forest Management	DP
GA016	325	Property Valuation and Estate Agency	DP + DG
GA011	290	Electronic Engineering	CT + DP + DG
GA012	200	Industrial Engineering	CT + DP + DG
GA013	255	Mechanical Engineering	CT + DP + DG
GA045		Medical Device Engineering	CT + DP + DG
GA006		Science	CT + DP + DG
GA030	205	Aquaculture	CT + DP + DG
GA031		Biology	CT + DP
GA032		Chemical & Pharmaceutical Sciences	CT + DP + DG
GA033		Physics & Instrumentation	CT + DP + DG
GA034		Applied Microbiology/Biochemistry	CT + DP + DG
GA014		Medical Laboratory Science	CT
GA037		Computing in Business Applications	CT + DP + DG
GA038		Computing in Software Development	DP + DG

AT CASTLEBAR

DIPLOMAS/CERTIFICATES

Code	Minimum points '98	Title (NOT to be entered on Application Form)	
GA160	100	Business Studies	CT + DP + DG
GA169		Business Studies in Computer Applications	CT + DP + DG
GA167	250	Tourism and Languages	DP + DG
GA166	300	Outdoor Education and Leisure	DP
GA168	150	Rural Heritage	DP + DG
GA161	AQA	Construction Studies	CT + DP + DG
GA162	260	Computing in PC Programming	CT + DP + DG
GA163	100	Electronic Engineering	CT + DP + DG

AT LETTERFRACK

DIPLOMAS/CERTIFICATES

Code	Minimum points '98	Title (NOT to be entered on Application Form)		
GA015	835	Furniture Design and Manufacture (Restricted)	CT	+ DG
GA043	305	Furniture Production	CT	+ DG

NATIONAL UNIVERSITY of IRELAND, GALWAY

DEGREES

Code	Minimum points '98	Title (NOT to be entered on Application Form)
GY101	390	Arts

A combination of four First Year subjects is available, with certain restrictions, taking only one subject from any group.
Group 1. Greek, History, Mathematics, Mathematical Studies
Group 2 English, Legal Science, Information Technology ✔
Group 3. Classical Civilisation, Geography/Tíreolaíocht, German

Group 4. Archaeology, Economics, Latin
Group 5. Psychology, Sociological & Political Studies, Welsh
Group 6. French, Applied Mathematics, Mathematical Physics,Philosophy
Group 7. Irish, Italian, Spanish

Code	Points	Title
GY102	330	Arts (Economic and Social Studies) at St. Angela's College, Sligo
GY103	360*	Arts (Public and Social Policy)
GY201	395*	Commerce
		Specialisms are available in the following: Accounting, Economics, Human Resource Management, Management Information Systems, Marketing, Operations/Logistics, and Italian.
GY202	455	Commerce (International) with French
GY203	415	Commerce (International) with German
GY204	375	Commerce (International) with Spanish
GY250	465*	Corporate Law
		Law subjects combined with core Commerce subjects. Language (French, German, Spanish) is optional
GY251		Bachelor of Civil Law (B.C.L.)
GY301	360	Science
		Degree subjects: Anatomy, Applied Mathematics, Applied Mathematics and Physics, Applied Physics and Electronics, Biochemistry, Botany, Chemistry, Computational Science, Experimental Physics, Geology, Mathematics, Mathematical Physics, Mathematical Science, Microbiology, Physiology, Zoology.
GY302	335	Applied Physics and Electronics or Experimental Physics
GY303	510*	Biomedical Science
GY304	490*	Biotechnology
GY305	315	Chemistry and Applied Chemistry
GY306	370	Computing Studies/Mathematical Science
GY307	370*	Earth Sciences
GY308	445	Environmental Science
GY309	435	Financial Mathematics and Economics
GY310	390	Marine Science
GY350	440	Information Technology
GY401	440*	Engineering (Undenominated)
		Second year branches: Civil, Electronic, Industrial Engineering and Information Systems, Mechanical, Electronic and Computer Engineering, Biomedical Engineering, Environmental Engineering.
GY402	410*	Civil Engineering
GY403	405	Electronic Engineering
GY404	380	Industrial Engineering & Information Systems
GY405	400*	Mechanical Engineering
GY406	425	Electronic and Computer Engineering
GY407	340	Management Engineering with Language
GY408		Biomedical Engineering
GY409		Environmental Engineering
GY501	540*	Medicine

LETTERKENNY INSTITUTE OF TECHNOLOGY

DIPLOMAS/CERTIFICATES

Code	Minimum points '98	Title (NOT to be entered on Application Form)	
LY002	AQA	Institute of Accounting Technicians of Ireland	CT
LY003	120	Business Studies	CT + DP + DG
LY004	155	Business Studies (Office Information Systems)	CT + DP + DG
LY018	160	Business Studies (Office Information Systems and Languages)	CT + DP
LY005	AQA	Córais Eolais Oifige	CT + DP + DG
LY006	100	Legal Studies	CT + DG
LY008	AQA	Civil Engineering	CT + DP

LY009	115	Construction Studies	CT + DP
LY010	AQA	Electronics	CT + DP
LY039	125	Electronics and Computer Engineering	CT + DP
LY011	AQA	Mechanical Engineering	CT + DP
LY012	205	Computing	CT + DP + DG
LY001	110	Aquatic Science	CT + DP
LY013	105	Science - Applied Biology	CT + DP
LY014	AQA	Science - Applied Chemistry	CT + DP
LY007	AQA	Business Studies/Languages & European Studies	DP + DG
LY015	350	Design, Graphics	DP
LY016	310	Design, Industrial Design	DP
LY017	100	Food Science	DP

LIMERICK INSTITUTE OF TECHNOLOGY

DEGREES

Code	Minimum points '98	Title (NOT to be entered on Application Form)
LC017	370	Construction Economics & Management (Quantity Surveying)
LC018	340	Property Valuation & Management (Valuation Surveying)
LC019	325	Construction Engineering & Management (Construction/Civil)
LC024	360	Software Development

DIPLOMAS/CERTIFICATES

Code	Minimum points '98	Title (NOT to be entered on Application Form)	
LC002	300	Business Studies (Accounting/Finance)	CT + DP
LC003	300	Applied Computing	CT + DP + DG
LC004	205	Construction Studies	CT + DP
LC005	205	Engineering (Civil)	CT + DP
LC006	270	Engineering (Electronics)	CT + DP
LC007	210	Engineering (Electro-Mechanical Systems)	CT + DP
LC008	200	Science (Applied Chemistry)	CT + DP + DG
LC009	215	Business Studies (Marketing)	CT + DP
LC011	200	Science (Environmental & Analytical)	CT + DP + DG
LC012	270	Engineering (Electronics & Communication Systems)	CT + DP
LC013	215	Engineering (Electronics & Marine Communications)	CT + DP
LC016	270	Engineering (Electronics and Computer Engineering)	CT + DP
LC020	205	Science (Applied Biology)	CT + DP
LC021	180	Technology (Automobile))	CT
LC022	180	Engineering (Manufacturing)	CT
LC023	305	Business Studies with Computer Applications	CT + DP + DG
LC001	580	Art and Design (Restricted - see page 2)	DP + DG
LC010	350	Architectural Technology	DP + DG

MARY IMMACULATE COLLEGE, LIMERICK

DEGREES

Code	Minimum points '98	Title (NOT to be entered on Application Form)
MI005	465*	B. Ed.
MI006	420	B. Ed.- Gaeltacht Applicants - Liberal Arts (Apply for LM047)

DEGREES

Code	Minimum points '98	Title (NOT to be entered on Application Form)
LM020	485	Law and Accounting
LM021	455	Languages with Computing
LM040	370	European Studies (including approved combinations of: Languages, Modern History, Political Studies, Economics, Law and Sociology)
LM041	375	Public Administration(including Government, Public Law, Economics, Sociology and Organisational Analysis)
LM042	465	Law and European Studies
LM043	405	International Insurance and European Studies
LM044	475	Applied Languages (applicants may take either two or three languages to degree level. Approved combinations of French, Gaeilge, German, Japanese and Spanish are offered.)
LM045	400	Language and Cultural Studies (including specialisms in English Studies/French/Gaeilge/German/Spanish)
LM046	400	History, Politics and Social Studies
LM047	390*	Arts - offered at Mary Immaculate College, Limerick
LM048		An Léann Éireannach/Irish Studies
LM050	415	Business Studies (including major options in Accounting/Finance, Economics/Finance, Marketing, Personnel Management, Risk Management & Insurance)
LM051	385	Computer Systems
LM052	445	Business Studies and a Modern Language (French)
LM053	435	Business Studies and a Modern Language (German)
LM054	400	Business Studies and a Modern Language (Spanish)

PONTIFICAL UNIVERSITY

St. Patrick's College Maynooth

Further details from:

The Theology Office,
St. Patrick's College,
Maynooth,
Co. Kildare

Tel: 01-7083600
     01-7083892
Fax: 01-7083441
E-Mail:
Theology.office@may.ie

DEGREE PROGRAMMES

Baccalaureate in Theology & Arts (B.A. Th.) Code MU001 (C.A.O. Application – Large choice of Arts subjects)

Baccalaureate in Theology (B.Th.) Apply direct to College B.A.Th. and B.Th. qualify for Fee Remission Schemes.

POSTGRADUATE PROGRAMMES

Master's in Theology (M.Th.)

Doctorate in Theology (Ph.D.)

Higher Diploma in Pastoral Studies

Master's Degree in Pastoral Studies (M.P.S.)

TRDBI

**TIPPERARY RURAL AND
BUSINESS DEVELOPMENT
INSTITUTE**

**FORAS FORBARTHA TUAITHE
AGUS GNÓ THIOBRAID
ÁRANN**

AN INNOVATIVE DEVELOPMENT INSTITUTE FOR THE 21st Century!

WHY TRBDI?
- ❖ Intensive, computer based learning
- ❖ An emphasis on learning while doing
- ❖ Work placement directed towards career choice
- ❖ Social and work skills to achieve your maximum potential

TRBDI – CÉN FÁTH?
- ❖ Tréan-fhoghlaim a bhaineann feidhm as an ríomhaire
- ❖ Béim ar an bhfoghlaim phraiticiúil
- ❖ Cur i bpost dírithe ar shlí bheata a roghnú
- ❖ Scileanna sóisialta agus oibre chun mianach iomlán an mhic léinn a bhaint amach

WHAT COURSES?
- ❖ National Diploma in Business Studies (SME Development)
- ❖ National Diploma in Sustainable Rural Development (SRD)
- ❖ National Diploma in Information & Communications Technology

CAD IAD NA CÚRSAÍ
- ❖ Dioplóma Náisiúnta i Staidéar Gnó (Forbairt SME)
- ❖ Dioplóma Náisiúnta i bhForbairt Inmharthanach Tuaithe (SRD)
- ❖ Dioplóma Náisiúnta i dTeicneolaíochtaí an Eolais agus na Cumarsáide.

**For further information
Tel: 1850-778-779
email: info@trbdi.ie**

**Chun tuilleadh eolais a fháil:
Fón: 1850-778-779
ríomh-phost: info@trbdi.ie**

LM055	405	Business Studies and a Modern Language (Japanese)
LM059		Computer Systems with French
LM060	370	Mathematical Sciences and Computing (with major options in Mathematics, Statistics, Computing and Financial Mathematics)
LM061	435	Industrial Chemistry (with specialisms in Analytical Chemistry, Catalysis, Organic Pharmaceuticals and Sensor Technology)
LM062	315	Materials Science (with specialisms in Biomaterials and Optical Fibres, Semi-conductor Fabrication and Physics of Materials)
LM063	345	Production Management
LM064	430	Industrial Biochemistry (with specialisms in Molecular Immunology, Enzyme Processing, Recombinant DNA Technology)
LM065	430	Applied Physics
LM066	380	Environmental Science (including Environmental Protection, Clean Technology, Environmental Impact Assessment)
LM067	340	Wood Science and Technology
LM068	365	Food Technology (including Food Chemistry, Quality and Safety, Novel Preservation Techniques and Ingredients Technology)
LM069	455	Computer Engineering (including Computer Architecture, Communications Networks and Software Engineering)
LM070	455	Electronic Engineering (including specialisms in Telecommunications and Integrated Circuit Design)
LM072	††	Industrial Design (Restricted)
LM073	450	Mechanical Engineering (also including major options in Materials & Design and Biomedical Engineering)
LM077	440	Aeronautical Engineering
LM078	440	Mechanical Engineering with a Language (German)
LM079		Manufacturing Engineering
LM080	345	Electronic Systems (including Semi-conductor Technology, Control & Instrumentation, Quality and Reliability for Electronic Industries)
LM081	325	Manufacturing Technology (including Productivity Methods, Manufacturing Processes and Industrial Automation)
LM083	375	Information Technology and Telecommunications
LM089	480	Sport & Exercise Sciences
LM090	490*†	Physical Education with concurrent Teacher Education
LM092	430	Science with concurrent Teacher Education (Biological Sciences with Physics or Chemistry)
LM093	380	Equine Science
LM094	430	Materials and Construction Technology with concurrent Teacher Education
LM095	400	Materials and Engineering Technology with concurrent Teacher Education
LM096		Science with concurrent Teacher Education (Physics and Chemistry)

DIPLOMAS/CERTIFICATES

Code	Minimum points '98	Title (NOT to be entered on Application Form)	
LM180	380	Equine Science	CT + DP + DG

NATIONAL UNIVERSITY OF IRELAND, MAYNOOTH

DEGREES

Code	Minimum points '98	Title (NOT to be entered on Application Form)
MH101	360*	Arts, Philosophy, Celtic Studies

MH101 360* Arts, Philosophy, Celtic Studies
First year subjects are divided into eight groups as follows (students choose three subjects with not more than one subject being taken from the same group):
Group 1: Minority Languages (Celtic & Basque), Philosophy, Welsh.
Group 2: Greek, History, History incl. History through Spanish
Group 3: Geography, German.
Group 4: English, Mathematics, Mathematical Studies.

Group 5: Nua-Ghaeilge.
Group 6: Biology, Economics, Greek and Roman Civilization.
Group 7: Anthropology, Music, Sociology.
Group 8: French, Introduction to Irish Studies, Latin, Mathematical Physics.
Students who wish to pursue the three-year degree B.A. in Mathematical
Science take two double subjects - Honours Mathematics and Honours
Mathematical Physics - in first year.

MH102	360*	Finance

Two Degree options are available:
Route 1)   Joint Honours – Economics and Finance.
Route 2)   Major/Minor – Major (Economics and Finance), Minor (Another sub-
ject from: English, French, Geography, German, History, Latin, Mathematics or
Mathematical Physics).

MH103	†	Music (Restricted)
MH104		French and Historical Studies
MH105		German and Historical Studies
MH106		Psychology
MH201	310	Science

First Year Science students take Mathematics and three other subjects from
Biology, Chemistry, Computer Science, Experimental Physics or Mathematical
Physics.
Students who wish to pursue the three-year degree B.Sc. in Mathematical
Science take two double subjects - Honours Mathematics and Honours
Mathematical Physics - in first year.

MH202	380	Biotechnology
MH203	370*	Computer Science & Software Engineering
MH301		Computer Engineering
MH302		Electronic Engineering
MH303		Communications Engineering

ST PATRICK'S COLLEGE
(Pontifical University), Maynooth

DEGREES

Code	Minimum points '98	Title (NOT to be entered on Application Form)
MU001	355	Theology and Arts.

First year students take Theology and choose two Arts subjects from the following groups (with not more than one subject being taken from the same group):
1. Philosophy,
2. Modern History, Greek, Greek for Beginners
3. English, Mathematical Studies
4. Nua-Ghaeilge
5. Biology, Economics, Greek & Roman Civilisation
6. Sociology, Music, Anthropology
7. French, Latin, Mathematical Physics, Introduction to Irish Studies.

SHANNON COLLEGE OF HOTEL MANAGEMENT

DEGREES

Code	Minimum points '98	Title (NOT to be entered on Application Form)
SN001		Commerce Degree

(plus Shannon Diploma in International Hotel Management - (Restricted)

DIPLOMAS/CERTIFICATES

Code	Minimum points '98	Title (NOT to be entered on Application Form)	
SN101		Business Studies (plus Shannon Diploma in International Hotel Management) (Restricted)	DP

INSTITUTE OF TECHNOLOGY, SLIGO

DEGREES

Code	Minimum points '98	Title (NOT to be entered on Application Form)
SG341		Bachelor of Science in Quality Management
SG441	335	Environmental Science and Technology
SG442	335	European Environmental Engineering Science

DIPLOMAS/CERTIFICATES

Code	Minimum points '98	Title (NOT to be entered on Application Form)	
SG101	235	Business Studies	CT + DP + DG
SG102	170	Business Studies in Marketing and French	CT + DP + DG
SG103	AQA	Business Studies in Marketing and German	CT + DP + DG
SG104	AQA	Business Studies in Marketing and Spanish	CT + DP + DG
SG105	230*	Business Studies in Office Information Systems	CT + DP

SG107	230*	Computing	CT + DP + DG
SG108	205	Business Studies in Accounting and Computing	CT + DP + DG
SG131	170	Business Studies in European Business with French	DP + DG
SG132	100	Business Studies in European Business with German	DP + DG
SG133	145	Business Studies in European Business with Spanish	DP + DG
SG134	310	Business Studies in Recreation and Leisure	DP + DG
SG135	260*	Business Studies in Applied Tourism	DP
SG201	345	Applied Social Studies in Social Care	CT + DP + DG
SG231	355	Art (Restricted)	DP
SG232	AQA	Design in Industrial Design	DP
SG301	AQA	Engineering in Civil Engineering	CT + DP + DG
SG302	AQA	Construction Studies	CT + DP
SG303	AQA	Engineering in Mechanical Engineering	CT + DP + DG
SG304	120	Engineering in Computer-Aided Precision Engineering	CT + DP + DG
SG305	AQA	Engineering in Electronics Engineering	CT + DP + DG
SG306		Engineering in Automation	CT + DP + DG
SG336	340	Design in Interior Architecture	DP
SG401	AQA	Science	CT + DP + DG
SG431	AQA	Science in Analytical Chemistry	DP + DG
SG432	230	Science in Pollution Assessment and Control	DP + DG
SG433	200	Science in Safety, Health and Industrial Hygiene	DP + DG
SG434	215	Science in Pharmaceutical Science	DP

ST ANGELA'S COLLEGE

Lough Gill, Sligo

DEGREES

Code	Minimum points '98	Title (NOT to be entered on Application Form)
AS001	450*	B. Ed. (Home Economics and Biology).
AS002	430	B. Ed. (Home Economics and Catechetics).
		- Arts (Economic and Social Studies) Apply for GY102

TIPPERARY RURAL and BUSINESS DEVELOPMENT INSTITUTE

At THURLES

DIPLOMAS/CERTIFICATES

Code	Minimum points '98	Title (NOT to be entered on Application Form)	
TN001		Business Studies (SME Development)	DP
TN002		Sustainable Rural Development	DP
TN003		Information and Communication Technologies	DP

At CLONMEL

Code	Minimum points '98	Title (NOT to be entered on Application Form)	
TN101		Business Studies (SME Development)	DP
TN103		Information and Communication Technologies	DP

INSTITUTE OF TECHNOLOGY, TRALEE

DEGREES

Code	Minimum points '98	Title (NOT to be entered on Application Form)
TL320		Computing with Enterprise Studies

DIPLOMAS/CERTIFICATES

Code	Minimum points '98	Title (NOT to be entered on Application Form)	
TL210	415	Advanced Business Studies	CT + DP + DG
TL220	220	Business Studies	CT + DP + DG
TL260	255	Business Studies (Languages & Business - French)	CT + DP + DG
TL270	265	Business Studies (Languages & Business - German)	CT + DP + DG
TL310	295	Computing	CT + DP + DG
TL350	265	Business Studies (Office Information Systems)	CT + DP + DG
TL410		Science (Aquaculture)	CT
TL420	175	Science (Applied Biology)	CT + DP + DG
TL440	250	Science (Applied Chemistry)	CT + DP + DG
TL460	190	Science (Photonics)	CT + DP
TL480	310	Science (Health & Leisure Studies)	CT + DP + DG
TL620	150	Engineering (Civil)	CT + DP + DG
TL630	160	Construction Studies	CT + DP + DG
TL640	185	Engineering (Agricultural - Forestry)	CT + DP
TL650	185	Engineering (Agricultural)	CT + DP
TL670	120	Engineering (Mechanical)	CT + DP
TL700		Engineering (Manufacturing)	CT + DP
TL101	†	Humanities (Folk Theatre Studies)	DP + DG
TL120		Business Studies (Tourism)	DP + DG
TL140		Business Studies (Tourism & Languages)	DP + DG
TL160		Business Studies (International Hospitality Management)	DP + DG
TL690	165	Engineering (Mechanical & Electronic)	DP

WATERFORD INSTITUTE OF TECHNOLOGY

DEGREES

Code	Minimum points '98	Title (NOT to be entered on Application Form)
WD025	310	Construction Management
WD026	300	Electronics
WD027	†††	Music (Restricted)
WD028	330	Applied Computing
WD048	340	Business Studies
WD049	340	Business Studies with French
WD071	340	Business Studies with Marketing

WD079	310	Administration
WD080	340	Business Studies with German
WD084		Accounting
WD085		Manufacturing Systems Engineering
WD086		Electronic Engineering

DIPLOMAS/CERTIFICATES

Code	Minimum points '98	Title (NOT to be entered on Application Form)	
WD003	310	Business Studies	CT + DP + DG
WD005	265	Construction Studies (Construction Economics)	CT + DP + DG
WD006	310	Construction Studies (Architectural Technology)	CT + DP + DG
WD007	240*	Engineering (Civil Engineering)	CT + DP
WD008	265	Science	CT + DP + DG
WD009	350	Agricultural Science.	CT
WD010	240	Engineering (Electronics Engineering)	CT + DP + DG
WD011	240	Engineering (Mechanical Engineering)	CT + DP + DG
WD012	265	Engineering (Production Engineering)	CT + DP + DG
WD013	300	Legal Studies	CT + DP + DG
WD014	315	Commercial Computing	CT + DP + DG
WD015	270	Industrial Computing	CT + DG
WD039	230	Business Studies (Hotel and Catering Supervision)	CT + DP
WD040	245	Engineering (Environmental Engineering)	CT + DP
WD066	330	Computer Applications	CT + DP
WD067	340	Multimedia Applications Development	CT + DP
WD018	345	Applied Social Studies in Social Care (Restricted)	DP + DG
WD019	330	Business Studies (Recreation and Leisure)	DP + DG
WD020	270	Business Studies (French and Marketing)	DP + DG
WD021	270	Business Studies (German and Marketing)	DP + DG
WD022	350	Art	DP
WD023	350	Design (Communications)	DP
WD076	280	Forestry	DP

A view of Cork Institute of Technology's new Information Technology Centre.

COLLEGES AND RELATED INSTITUTES NOT IN CAO

Honourable Society of Kings Inns, Henrietta St., Dublin 1. Tel: (01) 8744840

Inc. Law Society of Ireland, Blackhall Place, Dublin 7. Tel: (01) 6710711/6710448

National Distance Education Centre, D.C.U. Dublin 9. Tel: (01) 7045481

National Centre for Continuing Education, Plassey, Limerick. Tel: (061) 333644

Open University, P.O. Box 200, Milton Keynes, MK76YZ, U.K./Holbrook House, Holles St., Dublin 2. Tel: (01) 6785399

Royal Irish Academy of Music, 36-38 Westland Row, Dublin 2. Tel: (01) 6764412/3

EDUCATION AUTHORITIES AND RELATED BODIES

Aontas (Adult Education Assoc.), 22 Earlsfort Tce., Dublin 2. Tel: (01) 4754121

Department of Education & Science, Marlborough St., Dublin 1. Tel: (01) 8734700

Higher Education Authority, 21 Fitzwilliam Sq., Dublin 2 Tel: (01) 6612748

National Centre for Guidance in Education, 189 Parnell Street, Dublin 1. Tel: (01)-8731411

National Council for Curriculum and Assessment, 24 Merrion Sq., Dublin 2. Tel (01) 6617177

National Council for Educational Awards, 26 Mountjoy Sq., Dublin 1. Tel: (01) 8556526

National University of Ireland, 49 Merrion Sq., Dublin 2. Tel: (01) 6767246

National Council for Vocational Awards, Marino Institute of Education, Griffith Avenue, Dublin 9. Tel: (01) 8531910

NORTHERN IRELAND THIRD LEVEL COLLEGES

St. Mary's College of Education, Falls Road, Belfast BT12 6FE. Tel: 08-01232-327678

Stranmillis College, Belfast BT9 5DY Tel: 08-01232-381271

The University of Ulster (with four campuses at Coleraine, Londonderry, Jordanstown and Belfast Coleraine, Co. Derry. (Tel. 0801265-44141)

Queens University of Belfast, Belfast BT7 1NN. Tel: 08-0232-245133

Applications for Northern Ireland Colleges to:
Universities and Colleges Admissions Service (UCAS),
P.O. Box 67, Cheltenham,
Gloucestershire, GL5O 3SH.

CAO PARTICIPATING INSTITUTIONS

LOCATION	INSTITUTION/ADDRESS	TELEPHONE	FAX
ATHLONE	Athlone Institute of Technology, Dublin Road, Athlone.	(0902)24400	(0902)24417
BALLVAUGHAN	Burren College of Art, Ballyvaughan, Co. Clare	(065)77200	(065)77201
CARLOW	Carlow College, College Street, Carlow.	(0503)31114	(0503)40258
	Institute of Technology, Carlow, Kilkenny Road, Carlow.	(0503)70400	(0503)70500
CORK	Cork Institute of Technology, Bishopstown, Cork.	(021)326100	(021)545343
	Cork School of Music, Union Quay, Cork.	(021)270076	(021)276595
	Crawford College of Art & Design, Sharman Crawford St, Cork.	(021)966777	(021)962267
	University College Cork (NUI), Western Road, Cork.	(021)276871	(021)903233
DUBLIN	All Hallows College, Gracepark Road, Dublin 9.	(01)837 3745	(01)837 7642
	American College Dublin, 2 Merrion Square, Dublin 2.	(01)676 8939	(01)676 8941
	Church of Ireland College of Education, Upper Rathmines Road, Dublin 6.	(01)497 0033	(01)497 0878
	Coláiste Mhuire, Marino, Griffith Avenue, Dublin 9.	(01)833 5111	(01)833 5290
	Dublin Business School, 13/14 Aungier St, Dublin 2.	(01)475 1024	(01)475 1043
	Dublin City University, Dublin 9.	(01)704 5338	(01)704 5504

CAO PARTICIPATING INSTITUTIONS - Contd.

	Dublin Institute of Technology, Admissions Office, 30 Upr Pembroke St, Dublin 2.	(01)402 3445	(01)402 3392
	Dun Laoghaire Institute of Art, Design & Technology, Kill Avenue, Dun Laoghaire, Co. Dublin.	(01)214 4600	(01)214 4700
	Froebel College of Education, Sion Hill, Blackrock, Co. Dublin.	(01)288 8520	(01)288 0618
	Griffith College Dublin, South Circular Road, Dublin 8.	(01)454 5640	(01)454 9265
	Institute of Technology, Blanchardstown, Dublin 15	(01)885 1000	(01)885 1001
	Institute of Technology, Tallaght, Tallaght, Dublin 24.	(01)404 2000	(01)404 2700
	L S B College, Balfe House, Balfe Street, Dublin 2.	(01)679 4844	(01)679 4205
	Mater Dei Institute of Education,Clonliffe Road, Dublin 3.	(01)837 6027	(01)837 0776
	Milltown Institute of Theology & Philosophy, Milltown Park, Dublin 6.	(01)269 8388	(01)269 2528
	National College of Art and Design, 100 Thomas St, Dublin 8.	(01)636 4200	(01)636 4207
	National College of Ireland (NCI), Sandford Road, Ranelagh, Dublin 6.	(01)406 0500	(01)497 2200
	Portobello College, South Richmond Street, Dublin 2.	(01)475 5811	(01)475 5817
	Royal College of Surgeons in Ireland, 123 St. Stephen's Green, Dublin 2.	(01)402 2228	(01)402 2451
	St Catherine's College of Education, Sion Hill, Blackrock, Co. Dublin.	(01)288 4989	(01)283 4858
	St. Patrick's College of Education, Drumcondra, Dublin 9.	(01)837 6191	(01)837 6197
	Trinity College Dublin, College Green, Dublin 2.	(01)677 2941	(01)872 2853
	University College Dublin (NUI), Belfield, Dublin 4.	(01)706 7777	(01)706 1070
DUNDALK	Dundalk Institute of Technology, Dublin Road, Dundalk.	(042)70200	(042)33505
GALWAY	Galway-Mayo Institute of Technology, Administrative Headquarters, Dublin Road, Galway.	(091)753161	(091)751107
	National University of Ireland, Galway, Newcastle, Galway.	(091)524411	(091)525700
LETTERKENNY	Letterkenny Institute of Technology, Port Road, Letterkenny.	(074)64100	(074)64111
LIMERICK	Limerick Institute of Technology, Moylish Park, Limerick.	(061)208208	(061)208209
	Mary Immaculate College, Limerick.	(061)314588	(061)313632
	University of Limerick, National Technological Park, Limerick.	(061)202700	(061)330316
MAYNOOTH	National University of Ireland, Maynooth, Co. Kildare.	(01)708 3822	(01)708 3935
	St. Patrick's College (Pontifical University), Maynooth, Co. Kildare.	(01)708 3600	(01)708 3441
SHANNON	Shannon College of Hotel Management, Shannon Airport, Co. Clare	(061)475075	(061)475160
SLIGO	Institute of Technology, Sligo, Ballinode, Sligo.	(071)55222	(071)60475
	St. Angela's College, Lough Gill, Sligo.	(071)43580	(071)44585
THURLES	Tipperary Rural and Business Development Institute, 3, Slievenamon Road, Thurles, Co. Tipperary.	(0504)24488	(0504)24671
TRALEE	Institute of Technology, Tralee, Co. Kerry.	(066)7145600	(066)7125711
WATERFORD	Waterford Institute of Technology, Waterford.	(051)302000	(051)378292

STUDYING ABROAD

Every year some 2000 Irish students study in Europe for a period from 3 months to a year. Most of them do so with the aid of an EU mobility grant. A language taken as a major or minor optiion is usually necessary for this. Undertaking a full course of third level study abroad is a more difficult and expensive option.

UNITED KINGDOM

Despite the fact that eligible Irish students can carry their local authority grants to the UK for 'approved courses' the number of students applying to UK colleges has fallen. This may be partly due to the introduction of a Stg£1,000 fee for UK third level courses. (UK local authorities offer help with this fee on a means tested basis – see below). There are also some certificate holders progressing to degree level in the UK.

The introduction of the Further and Higher Education Act 1992, saw the end of the traditional division between universities and polytechnics. Prior to this, universities in the U.K. ranged from ancient collegiate foundations such as Oxford and Cambridge to newer technological universities dating from the sixties such as Aston and Bath. In 1993 a new breed of university was introduced – former polytechnics which now have power to award their own degrees.

With the exception of the Open University, applications for 1999 entry to First Degree, Diploma of Higher Education, Higher National Diploma and some University DIploma courses offered by British Universities including most Scottish colleges, are processed through **UCAS – Universities and Colleges Admissions Service** – a clearing house offering a service similar to the CAO. Their selection system however, differs considerably from that in Ireland, with personal statements and academic references/ records being taken into consideration. With the exception of applications to Oxford and Cambridge, which must be received before 15 October, applications will be accepted between 1 September and 15 December. Applications sent between December and the end of June 1999 may be considered, at the discretion of the individual university. After June 1999 any applications received will be held until 'clearing' in late August. For heavily subscribed courses such as Medicine or Veterinary Science students should ensure that applications are in before15 December, but in courses with more places available colleges will continue to look at applications after the olooing dato. Howovor, oarly application is advisable as admissions tutors start making their decisions even before the final closing date.

For an application fee of **stg £14** students may make up to 6 choices, though unlike the CAO they are listed alphabetically, not in order of preference. A reduced fee of **stg£4** applies to those who apply for consideration by one institution for a single course.

Offers, which will be "**conditional**" if you are sitting the Leaving Certificate for the first time, are usually made by March of the year of entry and you can hold two, one "**firm**" which means that you will take this place if you meet the requirements and one insurance. Conditional means that a place is reserved for you provided you achieve specified grades in your exams. The provisional acceptance is for insurance purposes and should of course have lower conditions than for your firm acceptance. Unconditional offers are generally made only to those who already have the results of their exams; there are no more conditions to be met – a place is reserved. Some colleges may of course reject your application. You do not have to make a decision on any offer until you have heard from all your chosen colleges.

The Art and Design Admissions Registry - ADAR has merged with UCAS and applications for admissions to degrees and HNDs in art and design are now made through UCAS. Applications can be made through two routes:

Route A - Simultaneous Application: Applicants may enter up to six choices in the order in which they appear in the UCAS Handbook but may reserve four for later application through Route B. The closing date is December 15, 1999 but applicants are strongly advised to apply before mid-November.

Route B - Sequential Application: Applicants may enter up to four choices in the order in which they appear in the Handbook, but will indicate on a separate form the order in which they wish to be interviewed or to have their portfolios considered by the institutions. The closing date will be towards the end of March 2000.

Some specialist courses such as drama, agriculture and music require direct applications to the colleges concerned.

PARAMEDICAL COURSES

Application for undergraduate courses in **Physiotherapy**, **Radiography** and **Occupational Therapy** are now processed through UCAS. Applicants for such courses in England and Wales should contact the colleges for information on funding for Irish students.

HIGHER EDUCATION IN SCOTLAND

There are 23 higher education institutions in Scotland - 13 universities and 10 colleges. Between them they offer a complete range of courses at all levels, both undergraduate and post-graduate. Most of the colleges and universities are members of UCAS and applications will be pro-

cessed by them. Application for admission to most Scottish-based degree level courses in Art and Design is made on one application form which is common to Duncan or Jordanstone College, Edinburgh College of Art, Glasgow School of Art and The Robert Gordon University (Gray's School of Art) and available from the art institutions in October/November. Intending students can apply to two centres, listing them in order of preference.

THE BRITISH COUNCIL

The British Council office in Dublin welcomes enquiries from prospective students regarding opportunities for higher education in the U.K. Their offices are open to the public from **2.30p.m. to 5.00p.m. Monday to Friday.** They operate a postal enquiry service in addition to a comprehensive reference library which carries copies of prospectuses from all U.K. institutions offering higher education. In addition they provide a computerised information service – **ECCTIS**, offering quick and easy access to details of over 80,000 courses in the U.K. including **Business and Technology Education Council (BTEC), City & Guilds** and **Royal Society of Arts (RSA.)** (Send an A4 S.A.E. – 40p for booklet, 72p if a printout of courses is required.)

GRANTS/FEES

The Irish Government have extended the provision of grants to means tested Irish students going to study in the UK or N. Ireland. Beware however of the exclusion of grant provision to certain courses such as Medicine, Dentistry, Veterinary, Teacher Training (consult your local grant awarding authority). With the introduction of a £1,000 fee for third level courses in the U.K. an Irish student will only be eligible for free tuition if the combined income of student and parents is below the equivalent of about **stg £23,000** per annum. As in previous years students will apply to the local authority in which the college is situated but this year the student will be required to give financial information backed by relevant documents. Further details will be found in the Department for Education and Employment's booklet: *Help with Tuition Fees for EU Students* – available from the British Council.

> **The majority of the British colleges require the submission of an academic reference. Please give plenty of notice to your referee as they may have several to complete.**

FURTHER INFORMATION

The British Council, Newmount House, Lower Mount St., Dublin 2. Tel: (01) 6764088/6766943.

UCAS – *The UCAS Handbook* – free from UCAS, P.O. Box 67, Cheltenham, Glos., GL50 3SH. TEL: 0044- 242-222444.

The UCAS website gives details on courses, colleges, applications etc. http://www.ucas.ac.uk; Non-academic information on UK colleges is available on the national student web service, student UK at http://www.studentuk.com

The Students Guide to Higher Education - free of charge from The Standing Conference of Principals, Edge Hill University College, Ormskirk, Lancashire, L39 4QP. Tel: 0044-1695-584211.

Entrance Guide to Higher Education in Scotland - cost Stg£8.50 (including p&p) from John Smith & Son Ltd, 57 St. Vincent St., Glasgow G2 5TB.

The College of Occupational Therapists, 6-8 Marshalsea Road, London SE1 1HL. Tel: 0044-171-3576480.

The Chartered Society of Physiotherapy, 14 Bedford Row, London WC1 RED. Tel: 0044-171-2421941.

Society & College of Radiographers, 183 Eversholt Street, London NW1 1BW. Tel: 0044 171 3914500.

Open University, 40 University Road, Belfast BT7 1SU. Tel: 08 01232 245025 , or Holbrook House, Holles Street, Dublin 2. Tel: 01-6785399.

Study UK – Published regularly throughout the year by Hobsons Press it is available for reference at the British Council's office and may be available from your guidance office.

NORTHERN IRELAND

Irish maintenance grants can be brought to colleges in Northern Ireland even for courses like medicine and teaching which are not 'approved courses' in England, Scotland or Wales.

Queens University (Belfast)

The College offers a wide range of degree courses in several faculties: Arts, Law, Economics and Social Sciences, Engineering, Medicine, Agriculture and Food Science and Theology. Applications are submitted through UCAS.

Contact the Admissions Office, QUB, University Rd., Belfast BT7 INN, Tel: 08-01232-245133, for a copy of their undergraduate prospectus.

University of Ulster

The University of Ulster, with its four campuses - Coleraine, Jordanstown, Belfast and Londonderry, offers degree courses in the Faculties of Art and Design, Business and Management, Science and Technology, Education, Humanities, Informatics, Social and Health Sciences.

Applications are made through UCAS for degrees and Higher National Diplomas, while those for certificate and diploma courses are made directly to the Admissions Office, University of Ulster, Coleraine, BT52 ISA. Tel: 08-01265-44141.

The North also has some colleges offering courses similar to those in our PLC's and ITs; here are some examples:

The Belfast Institute of Further and Higher Education, Information Services, Park House, 87/91, Gt. Victoria Street, Belfast. Tel:08-01232 265265.

Northern Ireland Hotel and Catering College, Ballywilliam Road, Portrush BT56 8JL. Tel: 08 01265-823768.

North West Institute of Further and Higher Education, Strand Road, Derry, BT48 7BY. Tel: 08-01504-266711.

EUROPE

With the advent of the Single European Market, there is an increased need for young people to acquire a sound experience of education and training with a European dimension. For the first time, there is now a general system for the recognition of higher education degrees awarded after a minimum of 3 years of study.

This European dimension to third level education is reflected in two E.U. programmes SOCRATES and LEONARDO. SOCRATES programme includes ERASMUS which permits third level students to spend a period - usually one year - of their studies in another Member State through such measures as a mobility grant. The LEONARDO programme provides bursaries for persons in vocational education and training e.g. PLC, IT Certificate and Diploma, enabling them to undertake part of their training in another Member State for periods from 3 weeks up to one year. In addition Leonardo provides support for graduates wishing to have a placement in industry in another Member State.

Like to study, train or work in Europe?

Information from:

National Centre for Guidance In Education,
189 Parnell St., Dublin 1.
Phone: 01-8731411.

Provides information on Vocational, Technical and Higher Education opportunities in the EU.

FÁS,
27–33 Upper Baggot St., Dublin 4.
Phone: 01-6070500.

Provides information on Vocational Training and Labour Market opportunities in the EU.

The European Handbook for Guidance Counsellors published by the Commission is available through schools and Youth Information Centres. In addition, all guidance counsellors should have a copy of the Institute of Guidance Counsellor's (IGC) "Higher Education Training & Work in Europe" which should prove essential reading for all contemplating study or employment in the E.U. The video "No Frontiers", dwelling on the experiences of young Irish people in Europe may be viewed courtesy of your school's guidance counsellor.

As members of an E.U. country, Irish students can compete for places in universities and institutes of higher education on the same basis as residents of member states and this includes payment of fees or their non-payment as the case may be. Generally application must be made to the individual college as there is no central clearing system like UCAS or CAO. You need to plan a year in advance as there are quotas for foreign students. Getting recognition for Leaving Cert grades may be difficult and fluency in the relevant language is essential. There are, however some European countries where you can study through English e.g. Finland and the Netherlands.

The best guide for anyone contemplating study in Europe is the "Directory of Higher Education Institutions in the European Community". Published by the Commission of the European Communities, it is available from shops and libraries or may be purchased from the Government Publication Sales Office, Sun Alliance House, Molesworth St., Dublin 2. A very useful leaflet entitled "Guide to Work and Study in the European Community" is available by contacting: Mary Bannotti, EURO PARLIAMENT OFFICE, 43 Molesworth St., Dublin 2. Tel: (01) 671 0328.

U.S.A.

With over 500 fields of study available in almost 2,000 institutions throughout the United States, investigating the possibilities of studying there appears at first to be an enormous and daunting task. However, you will find the staff at the U.S. Embassy only too willing to assist you. Contact the U.S. Embassy, Ballsbridge, Dublin 4, Tel: (01) 6688777 for full details of the services they offer.

CANADA

Despite an enormous amount of interest in Canada as a place to study, in reality the number of students who eventually make the trip is extremely small as there is limited funding for international students at undergraduate level. The Canadian Embassy, at 65, St. Stephen's Green, Tel: (01) 01-4781988 have a number of booklets/leaflets relating to studying in Canada which they will send you out or if you are based in Dublin you can call in to use their reference library.

GRANTS, SCHOLARSHIPS/AWARDS

Grants for PLC

PLCs are now covered by the Higher Education Grants Scheme. The same means test applies to both and application is made on the same form, available in early summer.

TAX RELIEF FOR PRIVATE COLLEGE FEES
The 'free' fees scheme does not apply to private colleges. However, tax relief at the standard rate is available for full time and part time fees in colleges approved by the Department of Education (a list of such colleges is available).

HIGHER EDUCATION GRANTS
Each year your local authority produces a detailed explanatory booklet and application form explaining the provision of grants to students going to college. These are advertised in the national press and are usually available in early summer.

STUDENTS FROM AREAS OF HIGH UNEMPLOYMENT
In recent years there have been a number of initiatives to encourage students from areas of high unemployment to participate in third level education. Some merely offer easier access to courses, others give financial assistance in addition to the local authority grant. For example, the North Dublin Access project offers both easier access and financial assistance to a number of students from certain designated schools in North Dublin for courses in Dublin City University. Check with your guidance counsellor, your local area-based partnership or local college to find out if such schemes operate in your area. Some area-based partnerships throughout the country assist third level students from low income families in a variety of ways, e.g. bus passes, money for books etc.

TABLE A	HIGHER EDUCATION GRANTS SCHEME 1999 Reckonable Income Limits +			
Number of Dependent Children	Full Maintenance and full fees	Part Maintenance (50%) & full fees	Full Fees Only	Part Fees (50%) Only
Less than 4	£19,200	£20,400	£23,000	£24,300
4 - 7	£21,100	£22,300	£24,900	£26,200
8 or more	£23,000	£24,300	£26,800	£28,100

Table A shows the reckonable income limits for those applying for maintenance grants in July 1999 (one could assume an increase in line with the consumer price index for subsequent years).

MAINTENANCE GRANT RATES		
	Non-Adjacent Rate	Adjacent Rate
Full Maintenance	£1,690	£676
Part Maintenance (50%)	£845	£338

+ In the 1999/2000 academic year where 2 or more children (or the candidate's parent) are pursuing a course of study listed below the reckonable income limits may be increased by £2,160 where there are 2 such children, £4,320 where there are 3 such children and so on, by increments of £2,160:
(i) attending full-time third level education
(ii) attending a recognised PLC course, student nurse training or student garda training.
(iii) participating in a CERT course of at least one years duration.
(iv) attending a full time Teagasc course in an agricultural college.

STUDENTS WITH DISABILITIES
The Department of Education has set up a special fund for students with disabilities at third level. Students make application in September/October each year through the appropriate person in their third level college e.g. Access Officer, College Counsellor or Student Services Officer.

SPORTS SCHOLARSHIPS

Outstanding achievements are required if you are to have any chance of being selected for a sports scholarship. These are available for study both here and abroad, particularly in the U.S. but colleges generally have their own contacts who propose exceptional individuals. Your local clubs should have details or contact BLE - Bord Luthcleas na hEireann, 11, Prospect Road, Glasnevin, Dublin, Tel: (01) 830 8925. Ask your guidance counsellor for NCGE Fact Sheet 2.

A variety of Sports Scholarships/Bursaries are awarded annually by many third level colleges. These are awarded to outstanding athletes who must also meet the requirements laid down for entry to their chosen course.

ENTRANCE SCHOLARSHIPS

Quite a number of third level colleges including those in the private sector, encourage academic excellence by offering a number of entrance scholarships. These are usually based on the results of the Leaving Certificate Examination but special application may be required and scholarships may be confined to students from particular schools or localities. Check with the Admissions Office of the relevant colleges for full details.

Private colleges sometimes act as guarantors for students taking out loans to cover the cost of fees. Check with any college that interests you and they will be only too pleased to send you up to date details

SIPTU

If your parents are members of SIPTU, you may benefit from some of their EDUCATIONAL SCHOLARSHIPS AWARDS which include 5 Third Level Scholarships of up to £2,500 for approved courses, fifty Senior Cycle Post-Primary scholarships valued at up to £250 each and one hundred and fifty Gaeltacht Scholarships covering full board and stay for a three week period at specified Gael Linn Colleges. Forms are available from local SIPTU branches.

COLLEGES OF AMENITY HORTICULTURE BOTANIC GARDENS, DUBLIN 9.

Tuition is free but the value of the ESF aided maintenance grant is based on the distance of the student's home from the college. Application forms are available in May and selection is based on written aptitude test and interview, held immediately after the Leaving Certificate.

Full details from: Dr. Paul Cusack, Principal, Teagasc College of Amenity Horticulture, National Botanic Gardens, Dublin 9. Tel: (01) 837 4388.

SCHOLARSHIPS TO AGRICULTURAL AND HORTICULTURAL COLLEGES

Co-funded by the European Social Fund, Teagasc grants are available to applicants over the age of 17 who are considered suitable at a pre-entry assessment. Contact your nearest Teagasc Office, Agricultural College or Teagasc Education Section, 19, Sandymount Avenue, Dublin 4, Tel: 01-668 8188 for the latest information. Maintenance grants for agricultural and horticultural colleges are *not* means tested.

DEPARTMENT OF EDUCATION AND SCIENCE SCHOLARSHIPS

Irish Scholarships

For students who have studied and taken at least three subjects through Irish in their Leaving Certificate (excluding Irish) twenty scholarships (TriGhaeilge: Teoranta) are available to pursue certain degrees through Irish in UCG, St. Mary's, Marino (Teacher Training) and DCU's Airgeadas, Riomhaireacht & Fiontraiocht, in addition to 15 unrestricted scholarships (Neamh - Theoranta) for other approved courses.

An additional 15 scholarships are available to students from the Gaeltacht. Application forms and full details are available in mid May and must be submitted by the end of June/early July each year.

Easter Week Commemorative Scholarships

A total of seven of these scholarships are awarded annually by the Department of Education, based on performance in the Leaving Certificate and it is not necessary to submit an application form. Information on eligibility requirements for any of the above can be obtained by contacting: Higher Education Grants Section, Department of Education, Portlaoise Road, Tullamore, Co. Offaly. Tel: (01-873 4700 or 0506 21363).

ROYAL COLLEGE OF SURGEONS IN IRELAND

Application to this college is now made through CAO but a college examination is held for the award of 5 scholarships (only certain subjects are included in this exam). Another 5 scholarships are awarded to applicants with the highest Leaving Cert results.

FÁS

Over one hundred and sixty different training courses for the over 16's are provided by FAS through its nationwide training centres. Participants are paid an allowance and accommodation costs are subsidised for those who must live away from home during the course. Transport costs are also subsidised for those who travel more than three miles to the centre. Contact your local FÁS Employment Service Office or FÁS training centre for full information or see the relevant section in this directory.

STUDYING ABROAD

U.K. - Irish students, like other E.U. citizens attending most colleges in the U.K. are now required to pay Stg£1,000 although local authorities can provide assistance on a means-tested basis. The Education Officer at The British Council, Ms. Angela Crean, can answer any of your questions. She can be contacted at their offices at Newmount House, 22/24 Lower Mount Street, Dublin 2, Tel: (01) 676 4088.

Maintenance Grants are now allowed for most UK courses.

U.S.A. - There is very limited funding at undergraduate level for study in the U.S. However, at Postgraduate level the Ireland - United States Commission for Educational Exchange administers the Fulbright Scholarship program, offering a number of grants to assist study or research at an accredited academic institution. Contact the Commission at 79 St. Stephen's Green, Dublin 2. Tel: (01) 4768 0822 for full details.

EUROPEAN UNION PROGRAMMES

Substantial funds have also been allocated by the EU to increase youth mobility as part of two E.U. programmes which came on stream in 1995 with a life span to 1999. The SOCRATES programme includes ERASMUS which permits third level students to spend a period - usually one year of their studies in another member state through such measures as a mobility grant. The LEONARDO programme provides bursaries for persons in vocational education and training e.g. PLC, IT Certificate and Diploma, enabling them to undertake part of their training in another member state.

Details from: Leargas, Avoca House, 189 Parnell Street, Dublin 1. Tel: (01-873 1411).

AIB (FINANCIAL SERVICES) SCHOLARSHIPS

AIB Capital Markets is headquartered at the International Financial Services Centre, and wishes to provide an opportunity for young people from within the local area of the IFSC to equip themselves for a career in financial services, by pursuing an appropriate degree programme in Dublin City University.

AIB Capital Markets is offered a maximum of three Third Level Scholarships for attendance at Dublin City University. The Scholarships are of £1,300 p.a. for the duration of the course, and are available to students from Dublin North Inner City only.

The scholarships also includes an offer of summer employment with AIB Capital Markets for each year of the duration of the course.

For further information contact: Carole Frost, Communications & Marketing, AIB Capital Markets, AIB International Centre, IFSC, Dublin 1. Tel: 874 0222.

OTHER OPTIONS TO CONSIDER

Private companies and local interested bodies sometimes offer awards to deserving students. Check with your own school and colleges you are interested in.

Insurance Schemes - details of such schemes can be obtained from any insurance broker, but most require long term commitment to a policy in order to gain maximum benefit when it matures.

Competitions - why not try to win some cash prizes in some of the many competitions listed in this directory.

Paid Training Schemes - Organisations such as the Defence Forces, accountancy and computing companies and banks may train you, give you study leave, pay your fees, pay you a training allowance or some combination of the above. Check first with your guidance counsellor who may have details.

Bank/Credit Union Loans
Part-time Work

If you do have financial difficulties while at college, tell your tutor or counsellor or have a chat with the admissions officer as many colleges set aside funds for those in difficulty either long or short term and in some cases fees may be partially or fully waived.

USEFUL BOOKLETS

Third Level Support, published by the Department of Education.

A Guide to Grants, Scholarships and Disability Benefits for Third Level Students with Disabilities in Ireland, published by AHEAD Education Press, 86 St. Stephen's Green, Dublin 2. Tel: 01-475 2386. Fax: 01-475 2387. email: ahead@iol.ie

Do your Sums

Going to college is expensive. To give yourself and your family a rough idea of the cost use the table below. Do not forget to multiply the figure by the number of years in your proposed courses. It is also helpful to remember that there are approximately thirty-five weeks in an academic year.

Application Fee
(CAO, etc) . . . .   £ . . . .

College Fees . . . .   £ . . . .

Books/Equipment . . . .   £ . . . .

Accommodation . . . .   £ . . . .

Travel . . . .   £ . . . .

Food/Drink . . . .   £ . . . .

Clothes/Leisure . . . .   £ . . . .

Miscellaneous . . . .   £ . . . .

                        Total   £ . . . .

GRANTS INFORMATION

(For information on Higher Education Grants, Community Projects and Employment in Local Government and Services) – Contact your local authority listed below.

Carlow County Council,
County Offices,
Carlow.
(Tel. 0503-31126)

Cavan County Council,
Courthouse,
Cavan.
(Tel. 049-31799)

Clare County Council,
Courthouse
Ennis, Co. Clare.
(Tel. 065-21616).

Cork Corporation,
City Hall,
Cork.
(Tel. 021-966222)

Cork County Council,
County Hall,
Carrigrohane Road,
Cork.
(Tel. 021-276891)

Donegal County
Council
County House,
Lifford, Co. Donegal.
(Tel. 074-72222)

Dublin Corporation,
Civic Offices, Wood
Quay,
Dublin 8.
(Tel. 01-6796111).

Dun Laoghaire/Rathdown,
4 Marine Road,
Dun Laoghaire, Co.
Dublin.
(Tel. 01-2054700)

Fingal County Council,
46/49 Upr. O'Connell St.,
Dublin 1.
(Tel. 01-8727777).

Galway County
Council,
County Buildings,
Prospect Hill, Galway.
(Tel. 091-563151)

Kerry County Council,
Thomas Ashe
Memorial Hall,
Tralee, Co. Kerry.
(Tel. 066-21111)

Kildare County Council,
Naas,
Co. Kildare.
(Tel. 045-873800).

Kilkenny County
Council,
St. John's Green,
Kilkenny.
(Tel. 056-52699)

Laois County Council,
County Buildings,
Portlaoise, Co. Laois.
(Tel. 0502-22044)

Leitrim County Council,
Courthouse,
Carrick-on-Shannon,
Co. Leitrim.
(Tel. 078-20005).

Limerick Corporation,
City Hall,
Limerick.
(Tel. 061-415799)

Limerick County
Council,
79–84 O'Connell
Street,
Limerick.
(Tel. 061-318477)

Longford County
Council,
Great Water Street,
Longford.
(Tel. 043-46231)

Louth County Council,
County Offices,
Dundalk, Co. Louth.
(Tel. 042-35457).

Mayo County Council,
Courthouse,
Castlebar, Co. Mayo.
(Tel. 094-24444)

Meath County Council,
County Hall,
Navan, Co. Meath.
(Tel. 046-21581)

Monaghan County
Council,
County Offices,
Monaghan.
(Tel. 047-82211).

Offaly County Council,
Courthouse,
Tullamore, Co. Offaly.
(Tel. 0506-46800)

Roscommon County
Council,
Courthouse,
Roscommon.
(Tel. 0903-26100)

Sligo County Council,
Riverside,
Sligo.
(Tel. 071-43221).

South Dublin County
Council
Town Centre, Tallaght,
Dublin 24.
Tel: 4149000

Tipperary County
Council, S.R.,
Emmet Street,
Clonmel, Co.
Tipperary.
(Tel. 052-25399)

Tipperary County
Council, N.R.,
Courthouse,
Nenagh, Co. Tipperary.
(Tel. 067-31771)

Waterford Corporation,
City Hall,
Waterford.
(Tel. 051-783501).

Waterford County
Council,
Davitt's Quay,
Dungarvan,
Co. Waterford.
(Tel. 058-42822).

Westmeath County
Council,
Mullingar,
Co. Westmeath.
(Tel. 044-40861)

Wexford County
Council,
Spawell Road,
Wexford.
(Tel. 053-42211)

Wicklow County
Council,
Council Buildings,
Wicklow.
(Tel. 0404-20100).

VOCATIONAL EDUCATION COMMITTEES

For information on V.E.C. Scholarships, Post Leaving Cert.
courses and European Social Fund (E.S.F.) Allowances.

Co. Carlow VEC,
Athy Road, Carlow,
Co. Carlow.
(Tel.0503-31813)

Co. Cavan VEC,
Keadue., Cavan,
Co. Cavan.
(Tel. 049-31044)

Co. Clare VEC,
Station Road, Ennis,
Co . Clare.
(Tel. 065-28107)

City of Cork VEC,
Emmet Place, Cork,
Co. Cork.
(Tel. 021-273377)

Co. Cork VEC,
County Hall,
Cork.
(Tel. 021-285343)

Co. Donegal VEC,
Ard O'Donnell, Letterkenny
Co. Donegal.
(Tel. 074-21100)

City of Dublin VEC,
Town Hall, Ballsbridge,
Dublin 4.
(Tel.01-6680614)

Co. Dublin VEC,
Main Road, Tallaght,
Dublin 24.
(Tel. 01-4515666)

Dun Laoghaire VEC,
Pearse St., Sallynoggin,
Co. Dublin.
(Tel. 01-285 2997)

City of Galway VEC,
Island Hse, Cathedral Square,
Galway.
(Tel. 091-562292),

Co. Galway VEC,
Hynes Buildings,
Galway.
(Tel. 091-562138)

Co. Kerry VEC,
24 Denny St., Tralee,
Co. Kerry.
(Tel. 066-21248)

Co. Kildare VEC,
Limerick Road, Naas,
Co. Kildare.
(Tel. 045-897358)

Co. Kilkenny VEC,
Butler Court, Patrick Street,
Kilkenny.
(Tel. 056-70966)

Co. Laois VEC,
Ridge Road, Portlaoise,
Co. Laois.
(Tel. 0502-21352)

Co. Leitrim VEC,
Main St., Carrick-on-Shannon,
Co. Leitrim.
(Tel. 078-20024)

City of Limerick VEC,
30 Upper Cecil St.,
Limerick.
(Tel. 061-417476)

Co. Limerick VEC,
58 O'Connell St.,
Limerick.
(Tel. 061-412692)

Co. Longford VEC,
Vocational School,
Longford.
(Tel. 043-46493)

Co. Louth VEC,
Chapel St., Dundalk,
Co. Louth.
(Tel. 042-34047)

Co. Mayo VEC,
Newtown,
Castlebar.
(Tel. 094-24188)

Co. Meath VEC,
Vocational School, Abbey Rd.,
Navan, Co. Meath.
(Tel. 046-21447)

Co. Monaghan VEC,
Beech Hill,
Monaghan.
(Tel. 047-81833)

Co. Offaly VEC,
O'Connor Sq., Tullamore,
Co. Offaly.
(Tel. 0506-21406)

Co. Roscommon VEC,
Lanesboro St., Roscommon,
Co. Roscommon.
(Tel. 0903-26151)

Co. Sligo VEC,
Riverside, Sligo,
Co. Sligo.
(Tel. 071-61511)

Co. Tipperary VEC (N.R.),
Church Road, Nenagh,
Co. Tipperary.
(Tel. 067-31250)

Co. Tipperary VEC (S.R.),
Vocational School,
Co. Tipperary.
(Tel. 052-21067)

City of Waterford VEC,
30 The Mall,
Waterford
(Tel.051-74007)

Co. Waterford VEC,
Wolfe Tone Road, Dungarvan,
Co. Waterford.
(Tel. 058-41780)

Co. Westmeath VEC,
Bridge House,
Belvue Road,
Mullingar,
Co. Westmeath.
(Tel. 044-48389)

Co. Wexford VEC,
Iberius House, Wexford,
Co. Wexford.
(Tel. 053-23799)

Co. Wicklow VEC,
A C C House,
Co. Wicklow.
(Tel. 0404-67338)

AN ROINN OIDEACHAIS AGUS EOLAÍOCHTA
DEPARTMENT OF EDUCATON AND SCIENCE

Are you interested in a career in Teleservices? – (dealing with customers, making hotel/airline reservations etc. using a phone and a PC).

Do you have a minimum of a grade B in pass level English and one continental language in the Leaving Certificate or equivalent?

Are you interested in participating on a two year full-time training programme which includes an extensive work experience placement overseas?

If so, a Post Leaving Certificate course in International Teleservices in one of the following locations is for YOU.

International Teleservices PLC Courses 1998/99		Phone	Places	Languages
Co. Cavan	Cavan College of Further Studies	049-32633	24	French/German
Co. Carlow	Carlow Vocational School, Kilkenny Road, Carlow	0503-31187	20	French/German
Co. Clare	Ennis Community College, Ennis	065-29432	40	French/German
City of Cork	College of Commerce, Cork City	021-270777	60	French/German/ Italian/Spanish/ English (1 year)
Co. Donegal	Letterkenny Vocational School	074-21047	20	German
City of Dublin	Colaiste Ide, Cardiffsbridge, Road, Finglas, Dublin 11	01-8342333	40	French/German
City of Dublin	Senior College, Ballyfermot, Dame Street Branch	01-6269421	50	French/German/ Italian/Spanish/ English (1 year)
City of Dublin	Whitehall House Senior College	01-8376011	40	French/German
City of Dublin	Ballsbridge College of Business Studies	01-6684806	24	French/German
City of Dublin	Colaiste Dhulaigh, Clonshaugh Road, Coolock	01-8474399	24	French/German

Contd. on next page

City of Dublin	Ringsend Technical Institute, Cambridge Rd, Ringsend	01-6684498	20	English (1 year)
City of Dublin	Rathmines Senior College, Town Hall, Dublin 6	01-4975334	20	French
City of Dublin	Crumlin College of Business and Technical Studies, Dublin 12	01-4540662	20	French/German
Co. Dublin	Stillorgan Senior College	01-2880704	20	French/German
Co. Dublin	Greenhills College, Limekiln Ave., Walkinstown	01-4507138	24	German
Co. Dublin	Grange Community College, Donaghmede	01-8471222	20	French/German
Co. Dublin	Riversdale Community College, Blanchardstown	01-8201028	20	English (1 year)
Borough of Dun Laoghaire	Community College, 17 Cumberland Street,	01-2809676	40	French/German
City of Galway	Galway Technical Institute, Galway City	091-581342	40	French/German/Spanish
Co. Kerry	Killorglin Community College	066-61168	40	French/German/Spanish
Co. Kerry	Listowel Community College	068-21023	15	French
Co. Kildare	St. Conleth's Vocational, Newbridge	045-431417	24	French/German
Co. Kilkenny	Ormonde College, City Vocational School, Kilkenny	056-22108	40	French/German
Co. Laois	Vocational School, Portlaoise	0502-21352	20	French
City of Limerick	Limerick Senior College	061-414344	40	French/German
Co. Louth	Drogheda College of Further Studies	041-37105	40	French/German
Co. Mayo	College of Further Education, Newtown, Co. Mayo	094-24188	20	French
Co. Monaghan	Monaghan Institute of Further Education & Training	047-84900	40	French/German
Co. Sligo	Municipal Technical Institute, Ballinode, Sligo	071-61511	20	French
City of W/ford	Central Technical Institute, Waterford City	051-874053	24	French/German
Co. Westmeath	Moate Business College, Moate, Co. Westmeath	044-48389	20	French/German
Co. Wexford	Vocational School, Enniscorthy,	053-23896	20	French/German
Co. Wicklow	Bray Senior College, Bray	01-2829668	20	French/German/Italian

This programme is aimed at school leavers, people preparing to return to work and returned emigrants. Tuition is free, and a student support scheme will provide substantial assistance (of up to £2000 per person) towards the cost of the overseas placement. For further information contact the Department of Education and Science Further Education Section. Telephone 01-8734700. International Teleservices Support Structure Telephone 01-4535487 or one of the centres listed.

PLC Courses are funded by the Department of Education and Science with assistance from the European Social Fund

LOOK, LISTEN, READ

PUBLICATIONS

- *Administration Yearbook* – I.P.A.
- *Applying to College* – Undergraduate Publications
- *CAO/CAS College Guide* – Careers & Educational
- *Career Choice (Annual)* – Level 3
- *Careers & Courses* – Celtic Press
- *Careers for Graduates* – Gill and Macmillan
- *Gairmeachale Gaeilge (Careers with Irish)* – Bord na Gaeilge
- *Guide to Evening Classes in Dublin* – Wolfhound Press
- *Guide to Evening Classes in Your Area* – Oisin
- *Guide to Nursing in Britain* – Irish Chaplaincy
- *Health Care Careers* – Best Guides
- *Make the Right Choice* – Folens
- *Maximum Points – Minimum Panic* – Marino
- *Media Careers* – Best Guides
- *Money for College* – Best Guides
- *NCEA Directory of Approved Courses* – N.C.E.A.
- *Private Colleges* – Best Guides
- *Student Guide of Ireland* – Madison

- *Student Yearbook & Career Directory Parts 1 and 2* – Student Yearbook Ltd.
- *Telling it As it is* – Emigrant Advice
- *The Work Experience Handbook* – Educational Co.
- *What Will I Be?* – Marino

COMPUTER SOFTWARE

- *Careers World* – Woodgrange
- *Chap* – Brian Lennon
- *Ecctis +*
- *Gairm* – FÁS
- *Jobscan* – Brian Lennon
- Pathfinder
- *My Future* – Seamus McDermott
- N.C.E.A. DIRECTORY of approved courses
- *Qualifax*
- *The Worlds of Engineering* – NCGE/Forfas

The Internet – You will find useful information on the following sites:

ASTI – http://www.asti.ie
CAO – http://indigo.ie~cao
CERT
http://www.cert.ie
Doras Directory –
http://doras.tinet.ie
Ednet –
http://www.ireland.iol.ie/ednet
FAS – http://www.fas.ie
GAIRM – http://www.fas.ie/
IDA Ireland –
http://www.idaireland.com
INTO – http://www.into.ie
Irish Jobs Page –
http://www.exp.ie
Irish Times –
http://www.irish-times.com
Irish Independent –
http://www.independent.ie/

Leaving Certificate Applied Programme –
http://www2.shanncdc.ie/lca/
Leaving Certificate Vocational Programme –
http://www.indigo.ie/lvcp
National Centre for Technology in Education –
http://www.ncte.ie
National Centre for Guidance in Education –
http://www.iol.ie/ncge/
National Council for Vocational Awards –
http://www.ncva.ie
Youth Information –
www.youthinformation.ie
RTE – http://www.rte.ie/
SCOILNET –
http://www.scoilnet.ie
TheTransition Year –
http://ireland.iol.ie/~sjbosco/
TUI – http://www.tui.ie
Youthreach –
http://www.youthreach.org/publi.html

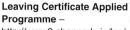

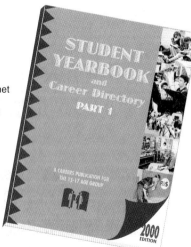

INTERNET • PUBLICATIONS • SOFTWARE • VIDEOS

INTERNATIONAL SITES

B.B.C. –
http://www.bbc.co.uk/education/home/

European Information –
http://www.estia.educ.goteborg.se/

Homework Central(USA) –
http://homeworkcentral.com/

Life Work(Canada) –
http://www.realgame.ca/

VIDEOS

- *A Career in Marketing* – Marketing Institute
- *Accountancy* – Chartered
- *CAO Video* – CAO
- *Defence Forces* – Dept. of Defence
- *Going For Gold* – FÁS
- *Its the Business (Catering)* – CERT
- *Making Experience Work* – Transition Year Support Team
- *Software* – IDA
- *PLCs* – Dublin CDU/VEC
- *Software* – IDA
- *Standards Based Apprenticeship* – FÁS
- *The Real Thing* – FÁS
- *The Real World/Guide to Interview Techniques* – An Post
- *Training for Careers in Fishing* – Bord Iascaigh Mhara
- *Training to Succeed* – FÁS

SERIES FOR STUDENTS IN THE IRISH TIMES

- *May 1999-June 2000: Careers World*
- *June 9-25, 1999, Exam Times column*
- *August 1999: College Places supplement*
- *Mid-August to Mid-September 1999: College Places column*
- *September 22, 23, 24 1999: Higher Options Conference, RDS*
- *September 1999 - June 2000: Business 2000 and Media Scope*
- *January 2000: College Choice supplement*
- *January 3-31, 2000: College Choice column*

The Irish Times
10–16 D'Olier Street,
Dublin 2
Tel: (01) 679 2022
E&L Fax: (01) 679 2789
Newspaper Sales: 1 800 798884

NEWSPAPERS AND PERIODICALS

If you are concerned about any issue you should write to the letters column of a newspaper, or if you fancy yourself as a journalist or writer, submit a sample of your work — some of the newspapers and magazines will be helpful. For job seekers pay special attention to Friday and Sunday editions.

You should also read your local paper, but pay particular attention to specialised magazines as these will contain information of relevance to careers.

Guidance Counsellor's Handbook
The Handbook contains comprehensive listings of literature, software and publishers. It is published by the National Centre for Guidance in Education and is available in all schools from the guidance counsellor.

STUDENT YEARBOOK DIRECTORY OF USEFUL ADDRESSES

REPRESENTATIVES ORGANISATIONS AND SELECTED GOVERNMENT SERVICES

Government Services

Civil Service Commission, 1 Lower Grand Canal Street, Dublin 2 (01-6615611).

Defence, Department of, Infirmary Road, Dublin 8. (01-8042000).

Education and Science, Department of, Marlborough St., Dublin 1 (01-8734700).

Enterprise, Employment and Trade, Department of, Kildare St., Dublin 2 (01-6614444).

Finance, Department of, Upper Mount Street, Dublin 2 (01-6767571).

Health and Children, Department of, Hawkins House, Dublin 2 (01-6714711).

Justice, Equality and Law Reform, Department of, Garda Síochána HQ, Phoenix Park, Dublin 8 (01-6771156).

Social Community and Family Affairs, Department of, Áras Mhic Dhiarmada, Dublin 1 (01-8748444).

Tourism, Sport and Recreation, Department of Kildare St. Dublin 2. (01-6621444)

Many of the organisations listed below will supply you with careers information.

An Bord Altranais, 31 Fitzwilliam Sq., Dublin 2 (01-6760226)

An Taisce, Taylor's Hall, Dublin 8 (01-4541786).

Association of Advertisers in Ireland, 44 Lower Leeson St., Dublin 2 (01-6761016).

Association of Chartered Certified Accountants, 9 Leeson Park, Dublin 6 (01-4963144).

Association of Chambers of Commerce, 22 Merrion Square, Dublin 2 (01-6612888).

Association of Consulting Engineers of Ireland, 51 Northumberland Road, Dublin 4 (01-6600374).

Association of Garda Sergeants and Inspectors, 6th Floor, Phibsboro Tower, Dublin 7 (01-8303166).

Association of Irish Nurserymen, 54 Merrion Sq., Dublin 2.

Association of Opthalmic Opticians of Ireland, 10 Merrion Sq., Dublin 2 (01-6616933).

Association of Secondary Teachers of Ireland, Winetavern St., Dublin 8. (01-6719144).

Bord na Gaeilge, 7 Cearnog Muirfeann, Átha Cliath (01-6763222).

CERT Ltd, CERT House, Amiens Street, Dublin 1. (01-8556555).

Chartered Institute of Management Accountants, 44 Upper Mount St., Dublin 2 (01-6761721).

Chartered Institute of Transport in Ireland, 1 Fitzwilliam Place, Dublin 2 (01-6763188).

Chartered Society of Physiotherapists, c/o Physiotherapy Department, St. James's Hospital, Dublin 8.

Chartered Society of Physiotherapists, College of Surgeons. (4780200, ask to be put through to ISCP Office).

City and Guilds of London Institute, 76 Portland Place, London W1N 4AA.

Civil Service Commission 1 Lr. Grand Canal St., Dublin 2 (01-6615611).

CLÉ (Bookpublishers Association), 43 Temple Bar, Dublin 2 (01-6707393).

Comhaltas Ceoltóirí Éireann, Cearnog Belgrave, Baile na Managh, Co. Bhaile Átha Cliath (01-2800295).

Commission of the European Communities, 39 Molesworth St., Dublin 2 (01-6712244).

Computer Education Society of Ireland,
c/o Colaiste an Spioraid Naoimh, Bishopstown, Cork.
Construction Industry Federation,
Canal Road, Dublin 6 (01-4977487).
Corporation of Insurance Brokers,
58 Merrion Sq., Dublin 2.
Council for the Status of Women,
64 Lr. Mount St., Dublin 2 (01-6615268).
Crafts Council of Ireland, Powerscourt Townhouse,
Sth. William Street, Dublin 2 (01-8778467).
Director of Vocations, Kimmage Manor, Dublin 12
(01-4554994).
Dublin Institute of Adult Education,
1–3 Mountjoy Sq., Dublin 1 (01-8787266).
Economic and Social Research Institute,
4 Burlington Road, Dublin 4 (01-6671525).
Educational Research Centre, St. Patrick's College,
Drumcondra, Dublin 9 (01-8373789).
Electrical Industries Federation of Ireland,
Sth Brown St., Dublin 6.
Employment Equality Agency,
36 Upr Mount St., Dublin 2 (01-6624577).
Farm Apprenticeship Board, Irish Farm Centre,
Bluebell, Dublin 12 (01-4501022).
FÁS, P.O. Box 456, 27–33 Upper Baggot St., Dublin 4
(01-6685777).
Federated Union of Irish Chemical Industries,
13 Fitzwilliam Sq., Dublin 2 (01-765116).
Football Association of Ireland,
80 Merrion Sq., Dublin 2 (01-6766864).
Forbairt, Ballymun Road, Dublin (01-8370101).
Free Legal Advice Centres, 49 Sth. William Street,
Dublin 2 (6794239).
G.A.A., Croke Park, Dublin 3 (01-8363222).
Gael-Linn, Príomhfheidhmeannach,
Herman Ó Briain, 26 Cearnóg Mhuirfean,
Baile Átha Cliath 2. (Guthán: 01-6767283)
Gorta, 12 Herbert St., Dublin 2 (01-6615522).
Honourable Society of King's Inns,
Henrietta St., Dublin 1 (01-8744840) (Barristers).
I.R.F.U., 62 Lansdowne Road, Dublin 4 (01-6684601).
Incorporated Law Society, Blackhall Place, Dublin 7
(01-6710711) (Solicitors).
Industrial Development Authority, Wilton Place,
Dublin 4 (01-6602244).
Institute of Accounting Technicians in Ireland,
87/89 Pembroke Road, Dublin 4 (01-6602899).
Institute of Advertising Practitioners in Ireland,
8 Upr Fitzwilliam St., Dublin 2 (01-6765991).
Institute of Bankers, Nassau House, Nassau St.,
Dublin 2 (01-6793311).
Institute of Biology of Ireland,
R.D.S., Ballsbridge, Dublin 4 (01-680645).
Institute of Certified Public Accountants in Ireland,
9 Ely Place, Dublin 2 (01-6767353).
Institute of Chartered Accountants in Ireland,
87-89 Pembroke Road, Dublin 4 (6680400),
11 Donegal Sq., South, Belfast (321600)
Institute of Chemical Engineers,
c/o Chemical Engineers Dept., U.C.D.,
Upper Merrion St., Dublin 2.
Institute of Chemistry, R.D.S., Ballsbridge, Dublin.
Institute of Food, Science and Technology,
Agricultural Institute, Castleknock, Co. Dublin
(01-8383222).

Institute of Guidance Counsellors,
17 Herbert Street, Dublin 2. (01-6761975)
Institute of Horology, Blanchardstown, Co. Dublin (01-
8213352) (Watchmaking).
Institute of Industrial Engineers,
35 Shelbourne Road, Dublin 4 (01-6602216).
Institute of Personnel and Development,
7 Upper Mount Street, Dublin 2 (01-6766655).
Institute of Physics, c/o Dr. J.A. Scott, Physics Dept.,
U.C.D., Dublin 4 (01-2693244, ext. 2231).
**Institute of Professional Auctioneers, Valuers and
Livestock Salesmen,** 39 Upr. William St., Dublin 2 (01-
6785685).
Institute of Public Administration,
49 Lansdowne Road, Dublin 4 (01-6059530).
Institute of Structural Engineers,
Thomas Prior House, R.D.S., Dublin 4.
Institution of Electrical Engineers,
6Tivoli Close, Dun Laoghaire.
Institution of Engineers of Ireland, 22 Clyde Road,
Dublin 4 (01-6684341).
Insurance Institute of Dublin, 32 Nassau St.,
Dublin 2 (01-6797765).
Irish Amateur Boxing Association, National Boxing
Stadium, S.C.R., Dublin 8 (01-4543525).
Irish Association for Gifted Children, 63 Hazel Ave.,
Kilmacud, Dublin 14 (01-886614).
Irish Association of Master Mariners, 22 Kildare St.,
Dublin 2.
Irish Association of Social Workers, 114 Pearse St.,
Dublin 2 (01-6774838).
Irish Association of Speech Therapists,
PO Box 1344, Tel. 01-803142.
Irish Auctioneers and Valuers Institute,
38 Merrion Square East, Dublin 2 (01-6611794).
Irish Business and Employers Confederation,
84-86 Lr. Baggot Street, Dublin 2 (6601011).
Irish Business Equipment Trade Association Ltd.
(IBETA), 59 Merrion Sq., Dublin 2 (01-682052).
Irish Computer Society, 22 Clyde Road, Dublin 4
(6670599)
Irish Congress of Trade Unions, 19 Raglan Road,
Ballsbridge, Dublin 4 (01-6680641).
Irish Country Woman's Association,
58 Merrion Road, Dublin 4 (01-6680453).
Irish Dental Association, Richview Office Park,
Clonskeagh Road, Dublin 4. (01-2830499).
Irish Farmers Association, Irish Farm Centre,
Bluebell, Dublin 12 (01-4501166).
Irish Federation of Musicians, 63 Lr. Gardiner St.,
Dublin 2 (01-8744645).
Irish Ferries, 2 Merrion Row, Dublin 2 (01-6610511).
Irish Fisherman's Organisation Ltd., Cumberland
House, Fenian St., Dublin 2 (01-6612400).
Irish Hairdressers Federation, 19 Broadford Avenue,
Dublin 16 (01-4946907).
Irish Institute of Landscape Architects,
8 Merrion Sq., Dublin 2.
**Irish Institute of Purchasing and Materials
Management,** John Player House,
South Circular Road. (01-4546544).
Irish Institute of Secretaries and Administrators,
Deloitte & Touche House, Earlsfort Tce., Dulbin 2
(01-4754433).

Irish Institute of Training Managers Ltd.,
c/o 16 Merrion Row, Dublin 2 (01-4977487).
Irish Insurance Association,
50 Northumberland Road, Dublin 4 (01-681962).
Irish League of Credit Unions,
Castleside Drive, Dublin 14 (01-4908911).
Irish Master Printers Association, 33 Parkgate St.,
Dublin 8 (01-6793679).
Irish Medical Organisation, 10 Fitzwilliam Place,
Dublin 2 (01-6618299).
Irish National Teachers Organisation,
35 Parnell Sq., Dublin 1 (01-8722533).
Irish Nurses Organisation, 11 Fitzwilliam Place,
Dublin 2 (01-6760137).
Irish Nutrition and Dietetic Institute,
Dundrum Business Centre, Frankfort, Dundrum, Dublin
14. (01-2987466).
Irish Pharmaceutical Union, Butterfield Hse.,
Butterfield Ave., D. 14 (01-4936401).
Irish Print Union, 35 Lower Gardiner St., Dublin 1 (01-8743662).
Irish Productivity Centre, Mgmt. Conslts.,
42 Lr. Mount Street, Dublin 2 (01-6623233).
Irish Professional Photographers Association,
5 Knocklyon Road, Dublin 16 (01-4939488).
Irish Quality Control Association, Merrion Hall,
Strand Road, Dublin 4 (01-2695255).
Irish Society of Chartered Physiotherapists,
Profession Body, Royal College of Surgeons,
St. Stephens Green, Dublin 2 (4022148).
Irish Taxi Hackney Owners Association,
9 Hanover St., Dublin 2 (01-6766666).
Irish Trade Board, Merrion Hall, Strand Road,
Dublin 4 (01-2066000)
Irish Water Safety Association, 4 Northbrook Road,
Ranelagh, D. 6 (4963422).
Leargas, 189 Parnell St., Dublin 1 (01-8731411).
Marketing Institute, South County Business Park,
Leopardstown, Dublin 18 (01-2952355).
National Parents Council, Marino Institute of
Education, Griffith Avenue, Dublin 9. (01-8570522).
National Union of Journalists, Liberty Hall, Dublin 1
(01-8741207).
National Union of Journalists, Liberty Hall, Dublin 1
(01-8741207).
Office of the Ombudsman, 52 St. Stephen's Green,
Dublin 2. (01-6785222).
Olympic Council of Ireland, 27 Mespil Road,
Dublin 4. (01-6680444).

Opticians Board, 18 Fitzwilliam Sq., Dublin 2
(01-6767416).
Pharmaceutical Society of Ireland,
37 Northumberland Road, Dublin 4 (01-6600699).
Photographic Society of Ireland, 38 Parnell Square,
Dublin 1 (01-8721397).
Plastics Industry Association, Confederation House,
Kildare St., Dublin 2 (01-6779801).
Prison Officers Association, 18 Merrion Sq, Dublin 2
(01-6625495).
Professional Golfers Association, 34 Hampton Court,
Vernon Ave., Clontarf, Dublin 3 (01-9321193)
Psychological Society of Ireland, 13 Adelaide Road,
Dublin 2 (01-4783916).
Public Relations Institute of Ireland, 78 Merrion Sq.,
Dublin 2 (01-6618004).
R.A.C.E., Curragh House, Kildare, Co. Kildare
(045-441205).
Royal Dublin Society, Ballsbridge, Dublin 4
(01-6680866).
Royal Institute of Architects of Ireland,
8 Merrion Sq., Dublin 2 (01-6761703).
Royal Institution of Chartered Surveyors,
5 Wilton Place, Dublin 7 (01-6765500).
Royal Town Planning Institute, 5 Wilton Place, D. 2.
School of Radiography, St. Vincent's Hospital,
Elm Park, Dublin 4 (01-2694533).
Society of Designers in Ireland, 67A Upr. Georges
St.,
Dun Laoire (01-2841477)
Society of St. Vincent de Paul, 8 Cabra Road, Dublin
(01-8384164).
Teachers Union of Ireland, 73 Orwell Road, Rathgar,
Dublin 6 (01-4922855).
Teagasc, 19 Sandymount Ave, Dublin 4 (01-6688188).
The Dental Council, 57 Merrion Sq., Dublin 2
(01-6762226).
Trócaire, 169 Booterstown Ave., Co. Dublin (01-2885385).
Údarás na Gaeltachta, Na Forbacha, Gaillimh
(091-92011).
Union of Students in Ireland, 2 Aston Place, Dublin 2
(01-8786366).
USIT, Aston Quay, Dublin 2 (01-6798833).
Zoological Society of Ireland, Phoenix Park, Dublin 8
(01-6771425).

EAGRAÍOCHTAÍ GAEILGE

Bord na Gaeilge,
7 Cearnóg Mhuirfean,
Baile Átha Cliath 2.
(Guthán: 01-6763222).

An Fáinne,
46 Sráid Chill Dara,
Baile Átha Cliath 2.
(Guthán: 01-6794780)

Comhdháil Náisiúnta na Gaeilge,
46 Sráid Chill Dara,
Baile Átha Cliath 2.
(Guthán: 01-6794780)

Comhar na Múinteorí Gaeilge,
7 Cearnóg Mhuirfean,
Baile Átha Cliath 2.
(Guthán: 01-6763222)

Comhchoiste Náisiúnta na gColáistí
Samhraidh,
46 Sráid Chill Dara,
Baile Átha Cliath 2.
(Guthán: 01-6790213)

Conradh na Gaeilge,
6 Sráid Fhearchair,
Baile Átha Cliath 2.
(Guthán: 01-4757401/2)

ADDRESSES/NOTES

John O'Shaughnessy
15 Retreat Park
Athlone
Co. Westmeath (0902) 75337

Ronan Tighe - 24867

Michael Maloney
Rinanney Rd.
Foxford
CO. MAYO
087 2326915
094 56158

Cormac Donoghue
8 Caeragh Dr,
Knocknacarra Rd,
Salthill,
Galway.
086 - 8795997

My Eircell mobile number is
Name: Vinnie
087- 6326606
eircell Ready to Go

Well Johnny
I can't spell + were in
borring Honors English 16/2/00
Blackburn are muck
Galway are sh?te
Mayo are class
well done opera 98, 99, +Jan'00
als rem. L.F.C. Rule

Cathal Carty
Carramore Mee.
Knock
Co. Mayo
094-88119.

Irish Quote:
"I put it in Ms. Laheen's Box" => MM
Full version:
Cammi = Did Ya do it?
Mal = Well, I gave it to Ms. Laheen.
Cammi = Did ya put it in Ms.
        Laheen's box then?
(Class goes wild)
Cammi = There's one for touch!

Cammi = I cleaned out my
        bag last night.
        Jasus, that didn't sound
        to good!

Vinny Browne
Drumraney
Athlone
Co. Westmeath
087-6326606
vinnyb @ hotmail.com.

Mocks in 2weeks
I'm dead meat
row Vinny o Lough 11/2

Johnny,
Murf here. I can't believe
it took me this long to sign
your homework journal (today
is April 7th 2000). Look shan
the best & luck in everything
you put your hand to (or on !!)

Ciarán Murphy, Kilclooney,
Milltown, Co. Galway (093) 51373.
~~ciaran~~ ciaran 53 @ hotmail.com
murphy @ esatclear.ie.

www.er.uqam.ca/merlin/

fg 591543/gm/

65
'55
70
70
80
80
420

INDEX